ART

CANADA, ART, AND THE GREAT WAR

AT THE SERVICE OF WAR

The Canadian War Memorials Exhibition opened in the galleries of the Royal Academy in Burlington House in January 1919. Featuring four hundred paintings and sculptures depicting the Canadian Expeditionary Force in the First World War, the exhibition became the gala event of the London art season.

Art at the Service of War is the story of how artists as diverse as modernist Paul Nash, the revolutionary Vorticist Wyndham Lewis, and young Canadians such as A.Y. Jackson came to paint Canada's war. Bringing together the artists, critics, and art gallery owners with patrons, military leaders, and politicians, the experience exposed Canadians to modern art at a time when the artists themselves were just beginning to explore this area.

First published in 1984, *Art at the Service of War* remains a major contribution to Canadian cultural history. With the approaching hundredth anniversary of the outbreak of the Great War, this book provides a timely reminder of the impact of this conflict even beyond the military and political spheres.

MARIA TIPPETT is an emerita senior research fellow in the Faculty of History at Cambridge University. She has won numerous awards for her writing, including the Governor General's Award for Non-Fiction and the John A. Macdonald Prize of the Canadian Historical Association.

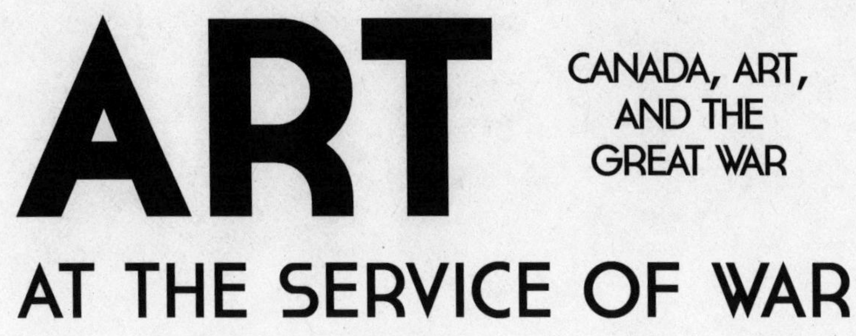

ART AT THE SERVICE OF WAR

MARIA TIPPETT

WITH A NEW INTRODUCTION

UNIVERSITY OF TORONTO PRESS

TORONTO   BUFFALO   LONDON

First printed 1984

ISBN 978-1-4426-4792-3 (cloth)
ISBN 978-1-4426-1604-2 (paper)

Publication cataloguing informaton is available from Library and Archives Canada.

University of Toronto Press acknowledges the financial assistance to its publishing program of the Canada Council for the Arts and the Ontario Arts Council.

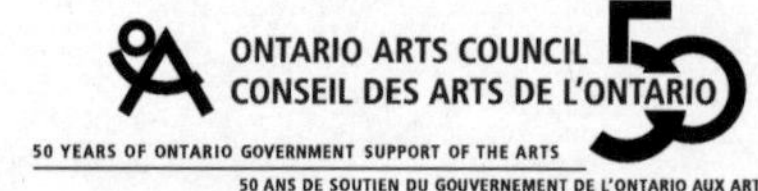

University of Toronto Press acknowledges the financial support of the Government of Canada through the Canada Book Fund for its publishing activities.

The location of the works of art as of 1984 is given in the captions. NGC: reproduced by the National Gallery of Canada, Ottawa. CWM: permission to reproduce granted by the Canadian War Museum, National Museum of Man, National Museums of Canada. The paintings in the Senate are owned by the Canadian War Museum.

Quotation on page 1 from Evelyn Waugh, *Brideshead Revisited* (London 1967; first published 1945) 302: Reprinted by permission of A.D. Peters & Company Limited.

This book has been published with the help of a generous gift to the University of Toronto Press from the Herbert Laurence Rous Estate, a grant from the Canadian Federation for the Humanities, using funds provided by the Social Sciences and Humanities Research Council of Canada.

For Judy and John Kendle

Contents

Illustrations

Introduction

It is generally agreed that the 1914-1918 World War played a crucial role in forging Canadian identity. It began one hundred years ago; its memory, however, continues to be a salient feature in the Canadian imagination. For while English-speaking Canadian soldiers may have entered the Great War fighting for the "Old Country," by the conflict's end the Canadian Expeditionary Force had become a potent symbol of a "New Country." Many of Canada's artists underwent a similar transformation. They entered the war in the shadow of their British and European counterparts; when they emerged from it they were artists in their own right.

On the face of it, war and art seem incompatible: soldiers destroy and artists create. However, the Canadian-born newspaper baron Max Aitken, who became Lord Beaverbrook in 1917, thought otherwise. Operating with his assistants at the London-based Canadian War Records Office, Beaverbrook became convinced that only the artist was capable of reconstructing unrecorded events, of producing long-lasting memorials when film had a lifespan of twenty-five years, and of adequately giving an emotional response to the conditions of modern warfare. The Canadian War Memorials Fund (CWMF), which Beaverbrook established in 1916, accordingly hired artists to record every aspect of Canada's participation in the war with a view to giving the country a national war memorial at the end of it. Moreover Beaverbrook, along with his colleague and fellow newspaper proprietor Lord Rothermere and their art advisor Paul Konody, wanted to demonstrate that Canada was committed to the arts precisely as the Germans were seen to be committed to destroying western civilization.

The CWMF commissioned not only Canadians but Britons, Australians, Serbians, and Belgians. Over one hundred artists were sent to the front line, into war-producing factories, training camps, and field hospitals, and onto the sea and into the air. By the end of the hostilities the CWMF had amassed over two thousand paintings, drawings, sculptures, and prints. No other war art program in the twentieth century would provide such a comprehensive record of a major conflict.

The Canadian project was unique mainly because no other program of its kind had such an energetic and foresighted man at its helm. Never one to miss an opportunity, Beaverbrook not only commissioned artists, he promoted the work that was produced, putting the paintings, drawings, and watercolours of eighty artists on show at the Royal Academy's prestigious Burlington House in London just two months after the 11 November Armistice in 1918. Attended by the Canadian prime minister, Sir Robert Borden, and visited by hundreds of civilians and ex-servicemen, the Canadian War Memorials Fund Exhibition was arguably the first blockbuster exhibition of the century. There was a lavish souvenir catalogue; maquettes and prints of the exhibited work were available for purchase; marching bands performed; and, in the Academy's forecourt, there was an impressive display of weaponry. No wonder the art critic for Britain's *Colour Magazine* called the CWMF exhibition 'the most important art exhibition ever held in London.'[1]

The work had been created, of course, at a crucial point in world history. Moreover, the second decade of the twentieth century was a pivotal moment in the history of western art. The collection thus covered a wide ambit of artistic styles: late-nineteenth-century Romantic-Realism was juxtaposed with paintings created in an Impressionist idiom, and examples of art nouveau with experiments in Vorticism. There were traditional battle paintings – some reaching gigantic proportions of ten or twenty feet – reconstructing the Second Battle of Ypres, Cavalry charges, and hand-to-hand combat. There were portraits of solemn-faced high-ranking political and military figures. There were modernist works depicting the horrors of a gas attack, or capturing the boredom and disorientation of the ordinary soldier who had no influence over the course of events into which he had been thrown. And some artists, rather than directly recording what they had seen at the front, opted for renderings of bombed-out buildings, roadside crucifixes, and endless rows of war graves.

The works on show offered more than a contrast between old and new ways of depicting the first modern war of the century: they established the characteristic images that would come to define the Great War. The soldiers themselves remained largely invisible, camouflaged in their drab khaki-coloured uniforms, hidden in their trenches, or going over the top shrouded in fog or darkness – or sometimes in yellow clouds of mustard gas.

The land over which the troops fought, however, was always in view. Bruised by aerial bombardment, by machine guns, by tanks and artillery, 'no man's land' stretched between the hostile trenches from Belgium's north coast to the Swiss border. It contained all the refuse of modern warfare: headless trees, water-filled craters, twisted fragments of metal, splintered duckboards – and thousands of sun-bleached bones. Arching above this horror was an enormous sky that was illuminated at night by gun flashes and searchlights or by the glow of a soldier's cigarette (at once a source of human comfort and a potential target for enemy snipers). Previously nothing more than a background for the spectacle of warfare, in the hands of many war artists the landscape itself became a visual metaphor for death and destruction, for the contrast between the young and old, the Home and War Fronts, and the claret-swigging generals and the men who had been driven like cattle to the slaughter.

For some artists like Irish-born William Orpen and Canada's F. H. Varley the landscape stood for more. Varley depicted a Canadian Scottish Regiment gravedigger in the process of dumping a cartload of his comrades' bodies into a mass grave. Varley thus not only defied instructions to avoid painting Canada's war dead, he specifically challenged the Imperial War Graves Commission's claim that every soldier got his own grave. Even more dramatically, by calling his painting *For What?* Fred Varley asked: why had the war been fought and for what purpose had so many men and women sacrificed their lives?

After the London exhibition closed, the work was shown in New York, Toronto, and Montreal before reaching the National Gallery of Canada in Ottawa. In order to remind future generations what Canada had accomplished in the war and also serve as a warning, Lord Beaverbrook wanted the CWMF collection to be put on permanent display in the nation's capital. He offered to pay for a building to house the collection, and even hired an architect to design it. But government officials in Ottawa did not take up Beaverbrook's offer, perhaps responding to public opinion.

There is evidence that many people wanted a more tangible and specific way of honouring the sixty thousand men and women who did not make it back to Canada at the end of the Great War. During the interwar years hundreds of cenotaphs and monuments inscribed with the names of the fallen were erected in cities, towns, and villages across the country. On the salient of Vimy Ridge, overlooking the Douai Plain in northwestern France, an impressive memorial commemorating all of Canada's war dead was unveiled in 1936. The Vimy Memorial and Ottawa's National War Memorial, along with less ostentatious sites of memory erected across Canada, re-shaped the memory of the Great War. They gave meaning, significance, and order to the conflict, testifying that the sacrifices – of civilians and soldiers alike – had not been in vain. This was a very different message from the chaos and hopelessness conveyed in the paintings of war artists like Orpen and Varley.

The project that Beaverbrook had fostered, however, was not forgotten. At the outbreak of the Second World War in September 1939, many Canadian artists of a new generation were quick to demonstrate that they had a role to play in the war. Some painted in war-producing shipyards and shell-producing factories. Others made prints of well-known Canadian paintings to decorate mess halls. Acknowledging that art was a therapeutic activity, many taught drawing and painting to weary service personnel. Prompted by the fact that Britain now had war artists in the field, as did the United States after its entry into the war in December 1941, artists along with organizations like the Royal Canadian Academy of Art and individuals like Canada's High Commissioner in London, Vincent Massey, lobbied the federal government to establish another war artists' program.

Their arguments were founded on the belief that artists could boost public morale and, as in the First World War, produce paintings, drawings, and sculptures for posterity. It was not until February 1943, however, that fifteen artists were attached to the Army, Navy, and Air Force under the direction of Major C. P. Stacey and Colonel A. Fortescue Duguid in London and the Director of the National Gallery of Canada, H. O. McCurry, in Ottawa.

But these men did not possess the energy or audacity of Beaverbrook – or indeed the private means that had enabled him to hire artists months before receiving official approval by paying them out of his own pocket. This time, the more bureaucratically minded organizers told Canada's official war artists what to paint: action episodes, transportation and training scenes, and personalities – in that order. They designated the size and the number of works to be produced. They warned against painting portraits. They instructed artists to study the CWMF collection, but not to produce large works re-creating events or landscape paintings without providing explicit evidence of Canada's soldiers.

In spite of these restrictions, the Canadian War Artists Program succeeded in breaking some new ground. More women artists than before were invited to paint the home front in Canada, and one of them, Molly Lamb Bobak, was sent to Europe to record the women's services. And although some artists did paint portraits, these were not just of the commanders but also of ordinary service personnel. Moreover, like the artists of the Great War, Canada's Second World War artists were not restricted to one war zone. They followed the Canadian Forces to the North Atlantic and the Pacific, to the Alaskan coast at Kiska, and to North Africa as well as to Europe.

Artists did not wait until the end of the war to show their work. As early as 1943, with the Italian campaign under way, an exhibition was held in Campobasso in southern Italy, which saw three thousand troops lining up in a former fascist gymnasium to view the work of Charles Comfort and Will Ogilvie. The two-day exhibition was such a success that the flamboyant General Montgomery, commanding the Eighth Army to which the Canadians were attached, had the entire exhibition pinned to the wall of the officers' mess at his headquarters in the nearby village of Vasto. In 1944, after the D-Day landings and the Canadian advance along the north coast of mainland Europe, three official war artists exhibited their European field sketches in Brussels' Palais des Beaux-Arts.

Following the hostilities, two major exhibitions organized by the National Gallery of Canada toured the country in 1945 and 1946. It was clear to anyone who saw these shows that few artists had reconstructed events or spent much time producing studio portraits of high-ranking military officials. No official Canadian war artist had asked why the war had been fought. And the landscape motif, which had dominated the canvases of First World War artists, was subsumed by the figure and, to a lesser extent, by the tank and aircraft. Second World War artists had, of course, been instructed to portray the spirit of Canada's troops. But they had not been told to make an explicit attempt to portray the troops' fear and panic before an attack or to give a frank treatment of the dead and half-dead whom they encountered in the extermination camps.

Today it might seem pointless to send artists into combat zones when international camera crews can get pictures of any conflict onto our television screens before an artist has had a chance to set up his or her easel in the field. However, two schemes, the Canadian Armed Forces Civilian Artists Program (1968–95) and later the Canadian Forces Artists Program (2001–), have deployed artists in a war zone. Canada's artists have thus recorded peacekeeping and humanitarian missions as well as explicitly military conflicts in, among other places, Somalia, Croatia, the Arabian Gulf, Mogadishu, and Afghanistan.

Much of their work is stylistically little different from the paintings and drawings produced by First and Second World War artists. Working outside of official war art programs and basing their work on eyewitness reports, newspaper photographs, and documentary films, some post-Second World War artists have reconstructed such unsavoury themes as torture by Canadian soldiers and the international community's failure to protect the killing of UN workers. While these not-for-art's-sake "war paintings" are unlikely to find their way into the permanent collection of the Canadian War Museum, curators at that institution have demonstrated that they are sympathetic to all ways of representing war.

In 2009 the Canadian War Museum mounted a retrospective exhibition, *A Brush with War*. It spanned painting from the Great War to the first decade of this century, as a testimony of the Canadian military's involvement in wartime and peacekeeping activities. This, along with the Museum's earlier exhibition *Canvas of War: Masterpieces from the Canadian War Museum* (2000) and the writings of Jonathan Vance and Ross King, have similarly woven the story of Canadian artists' participation in the Great War into their cultural and art histories respectively.

When I first viewed the CWMF collection in 1979, most of it was housed on the top floor of a building in downtown Ottawa, occupied below by Ogilvy's department store. Convinced that most of the work resulting from the First and Second World Wars were memorials, not works of art, the National Gallery of Canada had transferred the majority of the collections to the Canadian War Museum in 1971. It was not, however, until 2005 that the Canadian War Museum was to have a purpose-built facility east of downtown Ottawa; meanwhile the collection for which it was responsible had been put in the custody of Hugh Halliday and another former member of the military, Fred Azar, in this makeshift accommodation. Their own best efforts, however, could not compensate for the lack of sufficient resources to maintain the collection properly. The premises were hardly conducive for viewing, let alone preserving, the collection. There were few display racks; many of the paintings were stacked against the cold bare walls; there were virtually no temperature controls. The frequent eruption of a temperamental pot-bellied stove veiled some of the paintings in a thin film of soot, and I had to clean some of the works with a cloth before viewing them.

True, Joan Murray had mounted a successful exhibition at the Robert McLaughlin Gallery in Oshawa in 1977, *A Terrible Beauty: The Art of Canada at War*, based on Heather Robertson's book of the same name. But it was clear to me, as I began my own work a couple of years later, that war art had a low priority in Canada's museum and art gallery world. Yet despite the unpromising circumstances, as I studied the works themselves, whether housed above Ogilvy's department store, in the Canadian senate, in the National Gallery of Canada, or in a government art warehouse on the outskirts of Ottawa, I was overwhelmed by the significance of what I saw. It did not take me long to appreciate the extent to which Canada's First World War artists had built on their new connections with art critics, private patrons, and established figures in the Canadian gallery world when they returned to Canada. Nor how they and their fellow artists had transferred the iconography of the limbless and tortured trees of the bruised landscape in France and Flanders to northern Ontario, the Rockies, and the Canadian Arctic. Nor the extent to which all of this had been a crucial factor in elevating the newly formed Ontario-based Group of Seven and their followers to national status, thereby giving Canadians a national art.

In 1987 I had an opportunity to reflect upon the significance of war art when Nancy Poole, the director of the London Regional Art and Historical Museums, invited me to organize an exhibition of Canada's First and Second World War artists. *Lest We Forget* opened in 1989, to commemorate the fiftieth anniversary of the outbreak of the Second World War. Even Derwent Wood's much-contested *Canada's Golgotha*, a bronze sculpture re-creating the alleged crucifixion of a Canadian soldier during the Second Battle of Ypres, was now exhibited for the first time since being excluded from exhibition after 1920.

It was instructive to compare the work of both collections and to select the best of it for exhibition. I was struck by the Second World War artists' attempts to express the psychology of warfare. They had captured this in various ways: servicemen and -women dozing or staring blankly into space during their journey on the London tube; a dead German soldier lying in a tranquil landscape, with only shattered farm buildings and the hulking figure of a restless cow to remind the viewer that something terrible had happened – or was about to.

I was not alone in my response to the exhibition. It was during one session, when I was instructing the gallery's docents, that I saw the impact of the work in a unique way. At the end of the session one of them, now in her mature years, guided me to a charcoal drawing by the then-eighteen-year-old Canadian war artist Abe Bayefksy. He and Alex Colville had accompanied the Canadian contingent that had liberated Bergen-Belsen Concentration Camp. 'I was there,' the woman said as she pointed to Bayefksy's drawing of a malnourished victim. 'And that,' she said, 'is what it was like.' Seeing the modest charcoal sketch of a man who would die the next day had prompted the woman to share her experience at Bergen-Belsen. I was left in no doubt that all wars are a collective cultural practice. I saw for myself that these paintings and drawings still spoke, still moved, and still played a part in the public consciousness of Canadians. In this sense they were not just memorials – they were artworks of extraordinary power.

M.W.T.
2013

n.a. *Colour Magazine* (Feburary 1919) xiv

Preface

This book is a study in cultural history. It is concerned with the institutional framework of an organization, the Canadian War Memorials Fund, which, from its creation in November 1916 until shortly after the Great War ended, commissioned, created, and exhibited over eight hundred paintings, sculptures, and prints. The book's sub-themes are not confined to artists' biographies or to the analysis of works of art but include considerations of private and public patronage during the war; changing artistic, curatorial, and public attitudes towards war art; the effectiveness of private and professional entrepreneurial involvement in war-related activities; the war's contribution to the maturation of an indigenous school of painting in Canada; and many other themes. It is, then, as much about how a work of art gets done as about what is actually produced.

My work has been completed with the assistance of libraries, archives, and art galleries in Canada, the United States, and Great Britain. Material relating to the organization and operation of the Canadian War Memorials Fund was found in the Beaverbrook Papers in the House of Lords' Record Office and in the Paul Konody Papers in the Imperial War Museum in London; in the Sir Edmund Walker Papers in the Thomas Fisher Rare Book Library at the University of Toronto; in the Sir Edward Kemp and Sir George Perley Papers as well as in the records of the Canadian Expeditionary Force in the Public Archives of Canada and in the curatorial files of the National Gallery of Canada in Ottawa. To the staff of all of these institutions, and in particular to Joseph Darracott of the Imperial War Museum, Barbara Wilson and Peter Robertson of the Public Archives of Canada, I am most grateful.

The paintings and sculptures commissioned by the Canadian War Memorials Fund, some of which are reproduced in this volume, are located in the Canadian War Museum, in the National Gallery of Canada, and in the Senate, all in Ottawa. To the curators of the Canadian War Museum, L.F. Murray, Hugh Halliday, and Fred Azar, I wish to express my gratitude for their kind assistance in helping me to view and to photograph the collection.

Information on the artists who worked for the Fund came, in Britain, from the artists' files and manuscript collections in the Imperial War Museum, the Tate Gallery, the Victoria and Albert Museum Library, the Royal Academy of Art Library, the Bodleian Library, Oxford, and the Fitzwilliam Museum Library, Cambridge; in Canada it was found in the National Gallery, the Art Gallery of Ontario, the Public Archives of Canada, the Public Archives of Ontario, the McMichael Canadian Collection in Kleinburg, Ontario, the Montreal Museum of Fine Arts, and the McCord Museum in Montreal.

Hunter Bishop, archivist of the Arts and Letters Club of Toronto, Joan Murray of the Robert McLaughlin Gallery in Oshawa, Mary MacCausland of the Woodstock Public Library and Art Gallery, Elise Stoesser of the Dunlop Art Gallery in Regina, and Andrew J. Oko of the Art Gallery of Hamilton, were also helpful. Lilian Bomberg gave permission to use the David Bomberg Papers in London; James Byam Shaw generously shared John Byam Lister Shaw's manuscripts as well as his own memories of Paul Konody; and John P. Crabb, Mary Viscountess Rothermere, C.S. Williams, Bill Young, Peter N. Moogk, Sue Malvern, Myles Gleeson-White, and Peter Larisey, sj, also gave valuable assistance. J.M. Winter's lectures on the First World War at the History Faculty, Cambridge University, were stimulating. To Peter Clarke, now of St John's College, Cambridge, and formerly of the University of London where my dissertation on this subject was completed, I owe special thanks for allowing me to wander into the relatively untrodden field of cultural history and for supporting a study that is a long way from Hobhouse, the New Liberalism, and voting patterns in Lancashire.

Rachel Bendall typed the manuscript and, along with Trilby Smith, offered helpful editorial suggestions. Gerald Hallowell of the University of Toronto Press gave superb advice. Douglas Cole and Helen Gray of Simon Fraser University, John Kendle of the University of Manitoba, and Judy Kendle of Winnipeg gave valuable suggestions on the thesis. Allan Smith of the University of British Columbia helped to make the thesis into a book. And the Department of History of the same institution provided a room in which to do it. Any errors that follow may be attributed to the splendid view of the Gulf Islands from my Buchanan Tower office.

M.W.T.
University of British Columbia
Vancouver, January 1984

ART
AT THE SERVICE OF WAR

'Oh, but you should be an artist. I had one with my squadron during the last war, for weeks – until we went up to the line.'

Evelyn Waugh, *Brideshead Revisited*

1   Artists and the war

On 4 January 1919 the Canadian War Memorials Exhibition opened in the galleries of the Royal Academy of Art at Burlington House in London. It was a fine sunny day and about two thousand people came to see how the Canadians had memorialized, on canvas and in bronze, their participation in the Great War. The crowd passed through a cobble-stoned courtyard, where the 17th Canadian Reserve Battalion Band was playing the old, familiar marching tunes, then climbed two sets of stairs to the central gallery. There they waited until the dignitaries seated on the platform had spoken. At precisely 12 o'clock Sir Edward Kemp, the minister for the Overseas Military Forces of Canada, rose. He introduced the gathering's most prestigious guest, the Canadian prime minister Sir Robert Borden, who had taken a short respite from his preparations for the Paris Peace Conference to attend the ceremony. Borden would later tell his wife that he had neither understood nor appreciated the modern works on display. But the exhibition had attracted a great deal of attention in the London press: the sheer number of exhibits, totalling some four hundred, was impressive.[1]

The man who had done so much to bring the exhibition about was now to be thanked. Lord Beaverbrook took obvious pleasure in hearing the prime minister praise the enormous energy which had enabled him to bring the unrivalled collection of pictures and sculptures of the war to fruition in just over two years. He was also pleased by the recognition of his foresight in commissioning over one hundred of Canada's and Britain's most important artists during the course of the war and of the administrative genius which had permitted him to co-opt Canada's art officials so that activities on the home front might be recorded too. Following Beaverbrook's gracious response to Sir Robert Borden's speech, the exhibition was declared open.

The crowd streamed into the galleries where they found a wide range of artists, styles, and recorded events. Almost every prominent British artist, from the traditional landscape painter David Cameron to the revolutionary Vorticist Percy Wyndham Lewis, had been hired to paint the Canadian

Expeditionary Force at Vimy Ridge, at the training camps in the south of England, and as occupational forces in the Rhineland. The Canadian artists, who were fewer in number and less well known, might have been overlooked if not for A.Y. Jackson's thirty-five oil panels, which comprised the largest contribution of any artist, and the stirring canvases of his friend F.H. Varley.

It was not just the variety of artists and styles, the breadth of subject matter, that made the Canadian exhibition the most exciting event of the London season. Beaverbrook had wanted spontaneous, eyewitness records of the war; the artists had been allowed to roam the front-lines and sketch whatever they wanted. As a result, only a few reconstructed paintings, largely of unwitnessed events, were among the exhibited works. For the most part finished canvases had been produced from on-the-spot sketches. The eyewitness nature of the work appealed to those who had not been in the theatre of war as well as to those who had: the first were given an opportunity of seeing what it had really been like, the latter a chance of reliving their experiences.

The Beaverbrook scheme did not of course create artists of the trenches and the home front. Long before the Canadian War Memorials Fund was established, artists from every fighting nation had put their art to work for the war: they drew on the backs of envelopes during long periods of inactivity at the front; they made field reconnaissance sketches; they designed honour rolls and war posters; and they donated their pictures to patriotic fund-raising exhibitions. Nor was the CWMF solely responsible for awakening the general public to what the artists were doing. By 1917 exhibitions sponsored by Britain's Department of Information as well as by private galleries had introduced a small portion of the Allied and neutral public to the munition-production and front-line drawings of Muirhead Bone, Joseph Pennell, and others. What the CWMF did do was to give an unprecedented and wide-ranging number of artists an opportunity to express their war experiences in bronze, watercolour, and oil at a time when it might have been considered frivolous to do so. It also enabled many unknown artists to be recognized by gallery officials and art critics, and to have their work exhibited, then deposited, in a major collection. At the same time, the Fund gave Canadians a permanent memorial of their involvement in the Great War – at almost no cost to the government. And, even more important, it brought Canada's critics, artists, and art gallery officials together for the first time; after the war Canada had an infrastructure of artists, patrons, and critics, which enabled a national school of art to flourish.

The conditions that prompted Canadian and British artists, along with those of other nationalities, to join the scheme arose from the vicissitudes of war that had not only put artists behind desks, in factories, or in khaki but had also altered their relationship to patrons, private and public galleries, art critics, and the public in general. In the first summer of the war the British painter Augustus John predicted that the war was 'going to be bad for art.' The grave consequences he foresaw affected British artists gradually and at different times. During most of 1915 William Roberts was able to pay 'more attention to matters of art and picture-making than to the war taking place in France.' Other artists, however, were affected earlier: another modernist, Percy Wyndham Lewis, noted by the summer of 1915 that the war had 'stopped Art dead'; while David Cameron, the Scottish landscape painter, found that these were 'difficult days.' Others observed 'a lack of opportunity for artists and an increasing feeling of despair as the war progressed,' until for some, like pacifist Mark Gertler, the atmosphere became so 'hateful' that it was 'difficult to create.' Even the more geographically remote Canadian artists could not escape the feeling of despair that set in after the Second Battle of Ypres. Painting in the rural community of Emileville in Quebec, in the late spring of 1915, A.Y. Jackson was too disturbed by the war 'to make any great progress.' The president of the Royal Canadian Academy of Art, William Brymner, was saddened not so much by the news of Canada's first weeks in combat as by the declining art market and the people who seemed to be 'thriving on munitions.'[2]

Yet it was more than the gloomy war news and the paucity of sales that made work difficult. The very act of sketching out of doors put artists under suspicion, especially in Britain where 'amateur spy catchers abounded.' Prohibited sketching areas were not just restricted to military compounds. No sooner had the Canadian artist James Wilson Morrice taken out his sketch pad and pencil in London when a policeman tapped him on the shoulder and escorted him to Scotland Yard. Alfred Munnings, who did practically all of his painting *en plein air*, recalled that there 'came a time when an artist dared not be seen sketching out of doors in the country. He might have been reported as a spy! – and out-of-door painting without a permit was practically forbidden.' 'Spy catchers' were also evident in Canada. It was 'absolutely impossible' for Arthur Lismer to draw in the vicinity of Halifax harbour after a munition ship explosion devastated the city in December 1917.[3]

The suspicion, even hostility, shown towards artists by a nervous, war-weary public manifested itself differently in the columns and pages of art journals and literary magazines. There, writers and critics debated whether artists had a right to exist at all. 'Germany sinks the *Lusitania*,' declared one writer for the American journal *Arts and Decoration*, quoted in *Current Opinion*, 'a thousand people are destroyed, and one of our bright young painters, moved by the great sensitive soul of the artist, goes forth into the country to paint a placid hillside, a stupid pool, a winding road, a blue sky. And the pity is that he does not sally forth in search of a reaction from horror and paint these things with the breadth and force and liberty of a soul on fire.' Not every critic agreed. In a lecture at the University of Manchester in 1916, the director of the Manchester Art Gallery, Lawrence Haward, argued that the artist need not concern himself with the war because he dealt in 'aesthetic and not in moral values'; if the artist had any mission at all, it was 'to counteract the influence of war by emphasizing what he values to be the real values in life.' The early wartime issues of the London-based *Art Journal, Colour Magazine*, and *Connoisseur* reflected Haward's belief that art could remain in sublime isolation from contemporary events. Yet as the war progressed many writers came to believe that artists could straddle both sides of the fence. Duncan Phillips, writing in the *American Magazine of Art*, said: 'We need the pleasure which the beauty of art can bring to refresh us when we are tired and cheer us when we are dispirited and discouraged.' He added: 'We need art in our business of winning the war. We need Art to clarify our understanding of the ever-changing situations of the conflict. We need art to help us create a single mind out of the many minds which confuse our country.'[4]

For most artists it was not so much a question of whether art had a right to exist during the war, for they would continue to paint in spite of 'spy catchers' and art critics who labelled their occupation unpatriotic. It was more a question of whether the galleries would exhibit their work, the critics write about it, the public buy it, and the government subsidize it. For the modernists – those artists ranging from Canada's Impressionist, Symbolist, and Art Nouveau inspired Group of Seven to Britain's abstract Vorticists and Italian-inspired Futurists – the problem became more acute as the war gained momentum.

Only months before the outbreak of hostilities the English Vorticists and Futurists had invited the public to join with them in celebrating the machine, the gun, and warfare.[5] After the war began many art critics, patrons, and advisers on both sides of the Atlantic equated modernism with 'the same spirit of unrest which [had] brought about the great clash of arms.'[6] They linked modern painting to German *Kultur*, then, after the October Revolution, to Bolshevism. But whatever malady modern art was accused of possessing, most predicted that the war would purge it of its unhealthy elements and eliminate the 'hangers-on' and those who 'thought too little of the public who after all must be their customers.'[7] One official at the British Department of Information felt the war would 'be the making' of Augustus John; the bohemian artist would be 'brought into contact with reality and the hard facts of warfare, instead of doing things entirely out of his own head.' Others believed that when hostilities had ceased, art would be practised 'only by real artists.' It would reflect 'a world which will have turned from the dread realities of war to understand and appreciate the real blessings and the true pleasures of peace, those of the hearth and the home, to the beautifying of which art, itself chastened, will come with its message from the heart of nature and the soul of man.'[8]

By 1915 some of these prophecies were being fulfilled. On Varnishing Day at the Royal Academy that spring, one writer delighted in observing a 'complete absence of the young painter with flowing hair, eccentric necktie, and velvet jacket. In his place came men bronzed of face, alert in bearing, and wearing khaki uniform, who had turned aside for an hour from military duties to give final touches to pictures.' The following year Estelle M. Kerr declared in the *Canadian Magazine* that 'ultra-modern art which had its birth in Germany had been killed by the war.'[9]

The critics were not far from wrong. The Vorticists and the emerging Group of Seven – not to mention Germany's *Blaue Reiter* and Italy's Futurists – were dispersed by the war. Among the English Vorticists the French-born sculptor of Polish origin Henri Gaudier-Brzeska and the critic T.E. Hulme were killed in 1915; by 1916 most of the group's members were in uniform. Launched in 1914, Britain's first modernist movement was unable to do more than hold one exhibition and bring out two issues of their organ, *Blast*. Canada's nationalist group of landscape painters were not much better off. With A.Y. Jackson and F.H. Varley sketching in France, Arthur Lismer and Frank Johnston painting the home front in Canada, J.E.H. MacDonald illuminating honour rolls, and Tom Thomson drowning on Canoe Lake in 1917, the group, in its formative stages before the war, ceased to exist during it.

Yet many modernists were convinced that their art had a place in the future. The war, according to C.R.W. Nevinson, was 'a violent incentive' to the Futurist movement of which he was a part. For Jackson the war would enable Canadian art to 'emerge from all its tribulations. Its worst foe materialism is being walloped, and will never be quite so formidable again. And all the academic bunch are dying off, gradually very gradually ... the future will take care of us.' The only modernist to have doubts about the future was Wyndham Lewis. 'After the war,' he wrote, 'England will [not] change her skin so much that she will become a wise and kind protector of the Arts.'[10]

The many-sided discussion regarding art's relation to the war, modern art's purported association with German and Russian excesses, and the claim that the war had sounded the death knell for traditional and modern painting alike, broadened the cleft between those on the inside of the artistic establishment and those on the outside. People who had never thought of making a choice between modern and traditional art now did so. Patrons became careful about whose work they purchased. The Canadian banker and philanthropist Sir Edmund Walker, who had been buying Japanese prints largely outside Canada before the war, now made a point of spending money on Canadian art inside the country. Others were not concerned where but on whom they spent their money. When Frederick March joined Britain's Department of Information he and the pacifist artist Mark Gertler parted company. 'I had come to the conclusion,' Gertler wrote, 'that we two are too fundamentally different to continue to be friends.' Art patron Walter Cohen told Vorticist David Bomberg that he 'was not buying any more pictures while the war went on and advised the artist to seek some more "essential work" where he would be replacing a man who had "joined up." '[11] (Bomberg in fact enlisted in the Royal Engineers in November 1915, but Gertler remained a pacifist throughout the war.)

The more established artists, who were generally beyond conscription age, rarely encountered these problems. In fact their clientele mushroomed. Solomon J. Solomon, filling commissions for posthumous portraits, had never been so busy; Ambrose McEvoy and Charles Shannon continued to receive portrait commissions from members of the British establishment; William Nicholson's Eaton Square studio 'became a social centre, people turned up for sittings, or simply because they enjoyed good company.'[12] Most artists, however, were dependent upon commercial galleries and public institutions for the sale of their work.

When the war began commercial gallery owners wondered what it would do to their business. They feared the market might not tolerate art, particularly controversial modern art, in time of war; they feared they might be accused of indulging in luxuries. But as the war progressed they discovered that patriotism and profit went hand in hand. Feeding the public's insatiable appetite to see anything and everything connected with the war, they exhibited war photographs, cartoons, posters, and the work of exiled Belgian and Serbian artists, often to the disadvantage of their regular stock of painters. The Ackermann Gallery, the Corporation Art Gallery, the Doré Gallery, the Goupil Gallery, the Fine Arts Society, the Grafton Galleries, the Leicester Galleries, and other London showrooms burgeoned with a new clientele. Though many never bought, those who did enabled most galleries to increase their profits. Only months after the outbreak of the war, business was better than usual.

While cartoonists, photographers, and exiled artists were taking up exhibition space in private galleries in all the Allied countries, public art institutions and art societies were simply closing their doors. Some lost government sponsorship and had no other choice; others, such as the Chicago Art Institute, lost the patronage of its alumni members when the United States entered the war; still others, such as London's National Gallery and the South Kensington Museums, turned over their galleries to government departments more closely associated with the war effort. The situation was much the same in France. Major exhibitions, through which artists sold works, received commissions, and gained recognition, were cancelled.

The National Gallery of Canada had its operating costs reduced by three-quarters in 1916. The same year the Ontario Society of Artists lost its best patron, the Department of Education of the provincial government. The federal government reduced the Royal Canadian Academy to half its pre-war budget in 1917, though it continued to give it an annual $1,000 travelling scholarship. Such drastic reductions placed these organizations in a perilous financial position, and some institutions felt compelled to make voluntary concessions as well. Elderly art club and art society executives cancelled annual exhibitions and invested what funds they had in Victory Loans, all to the detriment of their young, unestablished members.

These cutbacks led some artists to think that it might be wise to try to attract public support for their activity by demonstrating it could indeed be relevant. The most ostentatious display of support for the war by Canadian artists was the Canadian Artists' Patriotic Fund Exhibition of 1914-15. After condemning 'the wanton destruction of historic buildings, public monuments, libraries, works of sculpture and pictorial art,' the executive committee of the Ontario Society of Artists approached the Royal Canadian Academy with the idea of organizing an exhibition to raise money for the dependants of soldiers and sailors active in the war. A large number of artists, residing chiefly in Toronto and Montreal, donated work. The collection was assembled in Toronto in December 1914, then travelled from there to Winnipeg, Halifax, Saint John, Quebec City, Montreal, Ottawa, and Hamilton. The exhibition was a success: the work of eighty-two artists became better known in eight Canadian cities, and by donating their paintings the society members had publicly expressed their 'patriotic aspirations.' And, as Montreal art critic H. Mortimer Lamb pointed out, the money collected from the sale of pictures and catalogues along with entrance fees, totalling $10,514.28, was 'a necessary preliminary to successful recruiting,' for soldiers knew their families would be cared for if they were killed.[13]

While the Patriotic Fund Exhibition was touring Canada, artists in England were engaged in similar fund-raising activities. Members of the Royal Society of Painters in Watercolour auctioned their pictures through Christie's for the benefit of the St John's Ambulance Society and the British Red Cross. A year later, in 1916, British artists raised money for the Red Cross by donating frames which they undertook to fill in for their purchasers. This sale raised a considerable sum and brought Muirhead Bone to the attention of Department of Information director C.F.G. Masterman: weeks later the technically superb, though traditional, printmaker from Glasgow was hired as Britain's first war artist.[14] The Chelsea Art Union sponsored an artists' draw from which subscriptions totalling over £14,000 were given to 'Our Blinded Sailors at St. Dunstan's.' The Royal Academy of Art cancelled its 1915 winter exhibition of old masters and held in its place an exhibition of contemporary works; the pictures were sold and the profits divided among the Red Cross, the Artists' General Benevolent Institution, and St John's Ambulance. The following year the academy simply gave its galleries to the Red Cross until the commencement of its May exhibition.

Artists from neutral countries were also eager to support the Allied forces. In appreciation of the teachers who had trained them in France, a committee of one hundred American artists raised funds in 1914 for the families of French artists at the front.

By the end of 1915 many artists had been affected by private patrons who stopped spending money on art; by commercial galleries that changed their policy to accommodate public sentiment and boost their earnings; by governments that slashed or discontinued financial assistance to galleries and art organizations; by art societies that cancelled their annual exhibitions and held fund-raising drives in their place; and, finally, by art historians and critics who devoted their columns to poster art, photographs, and cartoons and questioned the artist's usefulness during the war. All of these things, radically altering the infrastructure of art patronage in both Canada and Britain, undermined the well-being of many artists. Most, as a result, had little choice but to seek their livelihood through the force that had disrupted it: the war.

While some people felt Canadian artists were 'given over to idleness and depression' during the Great War, in reality they 'became soldiers as readily as any other man.'[15] In fact, artists from all the nations at war were engaged in the fighting from its beginning. German Expressionists Karl Schmidt-Rottluff and Max Beckmann served on the Russian front; Erich Heckel became a medical orderly, Otto Dix a machine-gunner, László Moholy-Nagy an artillery officer, Paul Klee and George Grosz infantrymen – all for the Deutsche Reichswehr or the Kaiserliche und Königliche Armee.

Outraged by the German occupation of Belgium and by the destruction of art treasures, Allied artists joined just as eagerly. Cubists Fernand Léger and André Derain enlisted in the French army within the first year of the war. Paul and John Nash, Edward Handley-Read, David Bomberg, and Stanley Spencer joined the British Expeditionary Force in the second. Some were spurred on by their friends, others by military regiments such as the Artists' Rifles, which had been founded in 1859 as a volunteer corps by Lord Leighton of the Royal Academy. Still others claimed they possessed 'no patriotism' but were 'pursued by the urge to do something.'[16]

In Canada, Ernest Fosbery, Arthur Nantel, Randolph Hewton, Louis

Keene, and J.L. Graham, among others, joined up in the first year of the war. A.Y. Jackson was not 'in any desperate hurry' to get in the fight until he heard the devastating news of the Germans' second gas attack upon the Canadians at the Battle of St Julien in April 1915 and saw the poster that read: 'You said you would go when you are needed. You are needed now.' David Milne, who had lived in the United States for over a decade before the war, returned to Canada for military training early in 1918.[17]

Artists who were physically unfit, disabled through war injuries, or simply too old for active service also contributed. In Germany many artists supported the war by lending their names to a manifesto asserting 'that German culture was a civilizing force in the world and that there was no German wrong-doing in this war.'[18] Artists Max Liebermann and Ernst Barlach made posters supporting Germany's war effort. In Britain, Frank Brangwyn, George Clausen, Alfred Munnings, and Gerald Spencer-Pryse designed posters for the London Electric Railway Company, the Red Cross, and the Parliamentary Recruiting Committee. John Byam Lister Shaw produced war cartoons for the *Evening Standard* and the *Sunday Times*.

Those who found themselves in exile in 1914 also contributed to the war. The Canadian Florence Carlyle, who had settled in England in 1912, sold her finest paintings to aid the Red Cross, then joined the staff of London's Queen Mary's Hospital. The Serbian nationalist Ivan Meštrović organized an exhibition of Serbian work at the Grafton Galleries, the profits of which went to the Serbian Relief Fund.[19] The Montreal artist J.W. Morrice, who spent the early years of the war travelling between his Paris base and the south of France, contributed to an exhibition aiding French artists, widows, and orphans.

Some artists found war-related jobs, though few were employed full-time. In New York, the Canadian artist Arthur Crisp joined American artists in painting a huge mural advertising the Liberty Loan; and in Toronto artists painted murals for Victory Loans at the Canadian National Exhibition and designed 'original jig-saw toys' with war motifs. F.H. Varley illustrated the imperial Royal Flying Corps' publication and contributed war-related sketches to the *Canadian Courier*. In Britain, Augustus John designed a poster for the War Office's Topical Film Company. Canadian artist J.E.H. MacDonald was so busy illuminating addresses and honour rolls that he had 'no chance … to indulge in the luxury of painting.' MacDonald's activity, although interrupted by a nervous breakdown, was exceptional; if artists wanted to do more for the war, they usually had to put on a uniform.[20]

In April 1917 Norman Wilkinson, a paymaster in the Royal Navy, proposed that the British War Office 'paint a ship with large patches of strong colour in a carefully thought out pattern and colour scheme, which will so distort the form of the vessel that the chances of successful aim by attacking submarines will be greatly decreased.' Within a month the Admiralty had accepted his proposal and ships were camouflaged in what became known as 'dazzle painting.' Wilkinson headed the camouflage operation, which established itself at the Royal Academy in Burlington House. Military leaders were not, however, always so prompt to take up an artist's suggestion. The distinguished portrait painter Solomon J. Solomon, 'entirely out of his element in the military world' as a reserve member of the Artists' Rifles, invented screens to conceal the trenches from German bombers. Set up at the Woolwich Dockyard the screens were found upon inspection to be unsuitable. Solomon persisted, inventing a 'sham tree' observation post and camouflage patch-work painting for tanks and guns, and these were accepted. Sculptor Derwent Wood, like Solomon, was too old for active military service, but he joined the Royal Army Medical Corps in 1915. There he organized a unit that made metallic masks for the facial deformations of the wounded. Louis Weirter designed the 'Whirter Retractor,' a sketching kit to help soldiers draw field reconnaissance sketches.[21]

Few artists were so fortunate as to be able to ply their art full-time while in uniform. Yet as a trained observer every artist could be of some use. Jackson made diagrams and enlargements from maps of the sector of the line in which he served while a private. So did David Bomberg. Edward Handley-Read devised large colour diagrams to teach the men he was instructing to use machine-guns. Lawren Harris painted cityscape targets for marksmanship practice while a musketry officer at Camp Borden. William Topham made a number of large panoramic observation sketches for battery work, as did gunner William Roberts. Stanley Spencer was given the job of painting the letters indicating men's and sergeants' latrines while serving as a Red Cross orderly in Salonika. Artists Alan Beddoe and Arthur Nantel, who were taken prisoner during the Second Battle of Ypres and sent to Giessen Camp in Hessen, painted watercolours of prison life; after almost three years' imprisonment Beddoe painted a full-length portrait of his German guard, who then forged his papers to give him a medical release.[22]

The matter of producing work of a more sophisticated nature while in uniform proved to be more difficult. Early in the war, during long periods of inactivity, artists like Beddoe and Cyril Barraud filled sketch-books and made watercolour drawings. During a lull on the front in 1915 Topham erected a studio in part of a reserve dugout on the Albert-Bray roadside. In November of the same year the Artists' Rifles held an exhibition, just behind the British lines, of the work of amateur and professional artists serving in the trenches.[23]

Even when given the opportunity to sketch many demurred. Ernest Fosbery 'hadn't felt it right to think about doing anything in the way of painting.' German Expressionist Franz Marc simply put art aside, declaring 'das kann erst nach dem Kriege wiederkommen; jetzt hat man anderes zu tun' ('this can wait until after the war; now we've got other things to do.') Wyndham Lewis had time for painting while stationed in an artillery camp in England, but found it diffcult because there was 'only the old stuff to go over' and he had 'no objective to work at.' David Milne felt much the same. 'Once in a while I have a fleeting longing to sit down or stand up and paint,' he wrote from Kinmel Park Camp in England, 'but the life here swamps pretty much everything else including the war.' John Nash made a few sketches in letters home but recalled that 'drawing wouldn't have been encouraged by a commanding officer in the line; I might have been taken for a spy.'[24]

Convalescence from war wounds and other disabilities provided many artists with an opportunity to create. Paul Nash was able to complete work only after he had fallen down a fire-step and broken a rib. Similarly, A.Y. Jackson's opportunity to paint came after receiving a 'blighty' at Maple Copse in June 1916. Wyndham Lewis was able to do some coloured pen-and-ink sketches a year later while recovering from trench fever in a hospital in Etaples and later in a convalescent home in Dieppe. C.R.W. Nevinson produced work while convalescing in London; his activities as a Red Cross ambulance driver and motor mechanic in Flanders had resulted in a nervous breakdown. Eric Kennington and Edward Handley-Read also found serious painting possible only during convalescence.

From 1915 the work of artists who had seen active service began to appear in London's commercial galleries. It was soon apparent that a new kind of artist, one who challenged the war-illustrator, the sketch-artist, the cartoonist, the photographer, had emerged. As one critic noted after viewing an exhibition of war photographs in July 1917: 'The whole collection of them really tells less of what war actually really is than a single painting by Nevinson or a single watercolour by [Paul] Nash.' Gone were the nineteenth-century battle-art conventions of hand-to-hand fighting, colourful banners, uniforms. Action, visibility, and colour had, as A.Y. Jackson put it, 'gone underground. There was little to see. The old heroics, the death and glory stuff, were obsolete.'[25] But even the few artists fortunate enough to obtain one or even two solo exhibitions were, after convalescence and once conscription had been enforced, subject to re-enlistment. Their work thus came, all too frequently, to an abrupt end.

Set up in November 1916, the Canadian War Memorials Fund offered artists a full-time opportunity to paint, officer's rank and pay, current acclaim by art critics and public institutions, and the chance for recognition by posterity. They applied in large numbers. It attracted, too, those who feared being conscripted and those who were unhappy with their changed relationship to art patrons, galleries, art societies, and critics.

The artists came to the Fund in a variety of ways. William Roberts was a gunner in the trenches when he heard early in 1918 through his friend Wyndham Lewis that artists were being hired by the Canadians. He was able 'to slip away at odd times to a small unoccupied army hut that formed part of the camp.' There, on a sheet of paper, he made a drawing which he submitted to the CWMF for approval. The British artist Colin Gill wrote to the adviser of the Canadian art program the same year: 'I joined up in 1914 and have been in the line in France for nearly 3 years. I am now invalided home and marked down for home service and want tremendously to have an opportunity to record my ideas of war on the Western Front.' David Bomberg began his work for the Canadians while on leave and before his transfer to the CWMF had been ratified. Augustus John was exempted from active service in the British army because of a knee injury: his employment by the Canadians ended 'a year in limbo, with the constant threat of being compelled to do office work – a prospect more alarming than trench warfare'; becoming a Canadian major 'appeared to offer him a new life, a fresh stimulus for his painting.' Eric Kennington was also 'afraid of being called up again ... and being set to some completely inappropriate work.' Mentally shattered by his experiences as an ambulance driver, C.R.W. Nevinson too lived in 'terror of being called up again'; his journalist father, Henry Nevinson, made several unsuccessful attempts to obtain a visa for his son's emigration to Spain or the United States, and he also urged the Department of Information and the CWMF to employ his son as an artist. A.Y. Jackson was in a reserve battalion at Shoreham Camp in the south of England when fellow Canadian artist Ernest Fosbery told him about the CWMF and then arranged for an interview with Lord Beaverbrook. Camp life had been anything but pleasant: there was 'not enough food and too many military police'; the soldiers, mostly casualties, were 'drilled and disciplined by men who had not been in France.' Jackson left Shoreham and joined the CWMF just before a small mutiny broke out among the men.[26]

The CWMF offered more than an escape from the threat of active service. British painter Laura Knight accepted the commission to paint the Canadians training at Witley Camp because 'the money was too good to miss.' Canadian David Milne wanted recognition from the man who was in charge of hiring the artists, Paul Konody. 'He is quite enthusiastic about the pictures,' Milne told his friend and patron James Clarke, 'and spoke of an exhibition here' (this was important because the artist planned to settle in London after the war).[27] Recognition was also critical to Byam Shaw: the commission would give his anachronistic Pre-Raphaelite style a new impetus and a new audience.

The sweeping dimensions of the canvases commissioned by the Fund were another attraction for artists. 'Opportunities to take big subjects and make big pictures of them' were, Eric Brown of Canada's National Gallery wrote, 'priceless.' 'If we paint large important works – even if good,' Robert Gagen told the gallery director, 'we cannot sell them and in these days when the price of canvas & paint is awful we cannot afford to do so on spec.' Few British artists, as John Rothenstein later observed, would ever again have an opportunity to work on such a scale. Augustus John, for example, relishing the idea of producing a forty-foot mural into which he could throw all the elements of the war, finished the cartoon sketch for it in next to no time.[28]

There were other reasons, too, why artists joined the CWMF. The opportunity to paint ships under construction at the Vickers plant in Montreal ended Albert Robinson's three-year employment in a munitions factory. The chance of obtaining a permit to paint Halifax harbour after the devastating explosion was 'too great an opportunity' for Arthur Lismer to miss; he also believed the scheme would have 'a great deal to do with the development of our art in Canada.' Maurice Cullen, on the other hand, was anxious to accompany Varley, J.W. Beatty, and C.W. Simpson to the front because his four stepsons had already enlisted. Lawren Harris refused to join the CWMF (as did Marc Aurèle de Foy Suzor-Côté), but it did not dampen his enthusiasm for those who did participate. After meeting several artists who 'were busy or about to be busy on memorial work' during a luncheon at the Arts and Letters Club in Toronto, Harris told Eric Brown: 'It means so much to them – has benefited them in in [sic] every way and the enthusiasm the idea has engendered will, I am certain, be productive of the best work they have ever done. It is very gratifying in every way and a great pleasure to me to see them all so content and busy (young and old, particularly the old).'[29]

So great was the enthusiasm that many artists lowered their prices. As Arthur Crisp told Brown in reference to one of his own paintings: 'If it were for a private party I would charge five hundred more but I feel very pleased & honoured to have been asked to do this picture & if that price is out of scale with what is being done I am perfectly willing to have you & Sir Edmund Walker change it to any figure you & he may think is what you can afford.' The society portraitist Ambrose McEvoy felt it would have been wrong to refuse the commission even though accepting it meant a dramatic reduction in his income. John Lavery, even better established, wanted 2,000 guineas for his work, but according to his agent was prepared 'to reduce the price to 1,500 ... as he fully realizes it will be included in a fine collection of works.' Alfred Munnings, who would ask exorbitant prices for his pictures after the war, recalled of his forty-five works purchased by the CWMF: 'The amount was small, but I would have been prepared, had they so wished, to present them to the Canadian Government, for no artist had been given a better chance to paint in such unforeseen circumstances.'[30]

Some artists, such as William Orpen, E.M.E. Pratt, R.G. Matthews, Patrick Adam, and Frank Armington, did give their pictures to the Fund. As Orpen told the art critic Robert Ross, 'the last thing I want is to make money out of the sights I have seen out here.' Herbert Palmer and Robert Gagen, on the other hand, asked for *more* than the CWMF offered. And Nevinson, who had begun to receive a substantial income through private exhibitions in 1916, was 'a little frightened' when requested to give up all of his work to the British Ministry of Information in 1918. 'It may prove a bad business proposition for me,' he told Masterman, 'and above all I might lose that sense of freedom, which is necessary for the creative faculty and without which I cannot experiment.'[31]

But few haggled for higher prices, and most lowered them. Even the requirement that no work done for the scheme be exhibited while hostilities continued was accepted cheerfully. Most artists in fact displayed the 'flood of patriotism' which the Fund's organizers hoped would not only inspire 'the highest efforts' but enable them to amass a prestigious collection of paintings and sculptures at little cost.[32]

2   Canada's impresario of art

In the spring of 1916 Arthur Doughty, the Dominion archivist, sailed to England. Before leaving Canada he visited the civic-minded president of the Canadian Bank of Commerce, Sir Edmund Walker, whose taste as much as his community standing had brought him to the chairmanship of the National Gallery of Canada's board of trustees. During the course of the evening, Doughty told Walker that the purpose of his journey was to 'save the material from which a true account of the share of Canada in the war could be written ... so that we shall not depend on such men as Sir Max Aitken, whose book, *Canada in Flanders*, has just appeared.'

It was not, of course, merely the publication of Aitken's popular account of the Canadian Contingent's first months at war that took Doughty across the Atlantic. Nor was he moved solely by a desire to collect war trophies and souvenirs. Far more was at issue, for the recent establishment of the Canadian War Records Office in London by Sir Max Aitken threatened to do nothing less than eclipse the archivist's role – *his* role – as historian of the war and collector of war documents and memorabilia.

Upon arriving in London in May of 1916, Doughty donned a 'brand-new' uniform, complete with a CMG ribbon, and looking 'like a weather-beaten war-worn army veteran' strode manfully into the CWRO in St James. He announced to Aitken and his assistant, Lieutenant Henry Beckles Willson, 'that, as Dominion Archivist, all Canadian records – civil, naval, and military were by statute under *his* control.' Then he disappeared. The two men stared at one another in amazement. 'I forget who burst into laughter first,' Beckles Willson later recalled.

If Doughty intended commandeering Aitken's four-month-old empire, as Beckles Willson has suggested, he soon dropped the idea. After a few days observing Aitken's operation he realized that the Canadian War Records Officer was 'in earnest.' 'The office was conducted in a careful manner [with] no unnecessary expense.' And, as he told the Canadian prime minister, Sir Robert Borden, Aitken seemed 'determined' to make the CWRO 'a success'

and 'at practically no cost to the Government.' Within a week of his arrival
in England, the archivist was convinced that Sir Max Aitken was 'the right
man in the right place.'[1]

The thirty-nine-year-old Canadian from Newcastle, New Brunswick, who
had so easily won over the proud archivist, was an old hand at bringing
dissonant elements together. At the age of twenty-eight Max Aitken had
made his first million, then gone on to make several more by merging
the cast-iron trade, the manufacture of freight cars, grain elevators, hydro-
electric stations, and finally cement companies. During the six years spanning
his arrival in Britain to the day Arthur Doughty walked into his 'extensive
office in an expensive section of the city,' he had obtained a seat in the British
Parliament – as a Unionist for Ashton-under-Lyne – received a knighthood,
acquired among other business interests shares in the *Daily Express*, and
befriended Andrew Bonar Law, Rudyard Kipling, and Lord Rothermere.[2]

Despite this heavy involvement in the life of the mother country, he had
not forgotten his native land. Shortly after the outbreak of the war he had
returned to Canada where his small, quick-moving figure was frequently
seen on recruiting platforms. He had long talks with Borden and the minister
of militia, Sir Sam Hughes, about the ways in which he might help 'maintain
their soldiers as a distinctive force' while asserting 'Imperialist solidarity,'
and he convinced both men that he 'was the right man to become the voice
of Canada in Great Britain.' For all his interest in the war effort, Aitken –
who was medically exempt from military service – did not become actively
involved in it until 6 January 1915 when an order-in-council appointed him
to undertake work 'connected with records generally appertaining to the
c.o.e.f., and particularly the reporting of all casualties occurring therein
from the time of the arrival of the said forces in England.'[3]

Aitken's position, which enabled him to roam freely about the Canadian
lines, was unique. Canada had no war correspondents at the front, nor did
Britain (Canadians relied on the American Associated Press until the Department of Public Information was set up under Major M.E. Nicholls in
the autumn of 1917). Consequently the reports Aitken sent to England and
Canada were unrivalled; they gave both countries a largely uncensored account of the performance of Canada's troops. As well as providing information to government officials and to the presses of Canada and Britain,
Aitken dispatched news to the troops. From December 1915 a daily news
bulletin kept 'the men in the Field in touch with events at home.'[4] By then,
however, accredited British correspondents had arrived at the front. Aitken
left it shortly thereafter, his eyewitness reports ceased, and he devoted more
time to his position as Canadian War Records Officer.

From the moment he had landed in France, Aitken recalled that 'a continual
flood of detailed information was passing into my keeping.' 'These records

were snatched from the firing line and from men still red hot from the fiery ordeal of action,' and deposited in the vault of Aitken's new Lombard Street office in the City. This material, which included the official daily reports of commanders of brigades, divisions, and army corps, as well as maps, photographs, and war diaries, was by late 1915 in a state of chaos. With the intention of systematizing and collating the material, Aitken applied to Borden in January 1916 for a civil grant of $25,000.[5] At the same time, he staffed his eight-room office with half the London-based Dominion Archives force and with men obtained through the Director of Recruiting and Organization and the Canadian Casualty Assembly centre. The appropriation came from Ottawa in mid-February and the CWRO was officially established in March, though it had been functioning at Aitken's own expense since the first of January.

When Beckles Willson joined the CWRO in early February, he recalled, it 'might almost have been a corps headquarters in the field.' Three months later Doughty counted seventeen men and eleven officers – including the three attached to headquarters in France where they were collecting and forwarding news, reports, and photographs from the front.

Photographs, indeed, were considered by Aitken to be a central element in the CWRO's work. He believed it was necessary to '*see* our men climbing out of the trenches to the assault before we can realize the patience, the exhaustion, and the courage which are the assets and trials of the modern fighting man.' The immediate publication of front-line activities in Canada would 'do much to maintain patriotism and enthusiasm and eager interest in our Army in France.' The preservation of photographs in the archives would 'form a source of information of the utmost value to Canadian historians' and provide 'records of enduring interest to Canadians of the present and future generations.' As for cinematography, its value, according to Aitken, could 'hardly be overstated': the presentation of films in neutral countries would 'enormously enhance the knowledge and renown of Canada,' while in the Dominion itself recruiting campaigns would be assisted.[6]

In April 1916 the CWRO made Captain H.E. Knobel Canada's first war photographer (he was replaced in August by Lieutenant Ivor Castle); in July, Lieutenant F.O. Boville became Canada's first war cinematographer. The CWRO was also considering the acquisition of 'original paintings and drawings, depicting actions in which the Canadians have participated.' The paucity of official photographs had already prompted Aitken to secure illustrations for the 1915 volume of *Canada in Flanders* and to consider purchasing reconstructed battle scenes.[7] The matter of commissioning specific works of art was not, however, discussed.

Doughty's arrival at the CWRO in May 1916 did not threaten the organization Aitken had set into motion. Aitken merely took the step that had always proved successful in resolving matters of conflict: co-operation. He proposed that all material assembled by the CWRO be handed over to the Dominion Archives of Canada at the end of the war and he offered Doughty a position on his staff. In return Doughty seconded the remaining half of his London-based Dominion Archives staff to the CWRO and offered his professional advice on how to maintain and organize the material being acquired. The functions of the archivist were thus combined with those of the Canadian War Records Officer, though there was no doubt as to who was in charge. 'My work in England is under the direction of Colonel Sir Max Aitken,' Doughty told one official in August 1916.[8]

Doughty could never ascertain whether Aitken was motivated by 'politics or pure patriotism,' and Aitken himself gave various reasons for establishing the CWRO. In his first official report to Sir Robert Borden in May 1916 he stressed that it was 'of imperative importance that honor should be given where honor is due.' In order to accomplish this he set out 'to increase Canadian prestige and correct still prevalent misconceptions as to Canadian affairs' by making 'every effort … to keep the British press informed, by means of communiqués and special articles, as to the doings of Canadian troops in the Field.' The promotion of voluntary recruitment was, he argued, another reason for publicizing Canada's achievements in the war. By the spring of 1916 recruitment figures had begun to fall drastically. With conscription apparently still a long way off (the Military Service Act did not come into effect until after the December 1917 election), the Canadian situation, as Aitken told Borden, was 'a special one for over here [in Britain] the necessary men can be got by compulsion and publicity in consequence is not essential to keep up the supply.' There was also a question of timing: if the business of collecting and analysing war records was left until after the war, Aitken believed it would be both more difficult and more expensive to acquire them. Nor did he overlook the historical value of the material he was collecting. 'The aim of this office,' he wrote early in 1917, 'has not been to supply an essay for the moment, but a possession for all times.' Publications like *Canada in Flanders* were immediate – their 'sole aim … [being] to increase the repute of Canada and her soldiers.' But the real history of the war could not be written until long after the hostilities had ceased. And to that end, Aitken continued, the CWRO had neglected nothing that could 'prove to be of the slightest use to the future historian.'[9]

The functions of the CWRO were, therefore, fourfold: to disseminate information in Allied and neutral countries with the intention of publicizing Canada's achievements in the war; to promote recruitment in Canada; to compile as complete a record as possible to enable future historians to write the history of the war; and to provide the British and Canadian presses as well as government officials with news of the Canadian troops.

Aitken was not alone in viewing the war as both a conflict between the 'physical bodies of men,' and the 'ideas which animate their minds.'[10] He stood by himself, however, in the skill with which he gave force to his ideas and in the energy with which he exploited every possible means to disseminate the information he acquired. Not surprisingly his accomplishments, and the brash methods he often used to bring them about, brought the CWRO under attack. In Canada, members of Parliament were suspicious of the merits of propaganda; in Britain, military officials questioned Aitken's violation of censorship laws, for his eyewitness reports to the press not only named regiments and men but also criticized the High Command's strategy.[11] But if the criticism made establishing each branch of the CWRO no easy task, Aitken continued to regard the operation as 'the fountain-head of reliable information concerning Canadian affairs and the Canadian troops in the Field.' The information it circulated, there can be no doubt, had an impact. Cabling from the United States where he was setting up the British War Mission, Lord Northcliffe complained that 'the boosting of the Canadians' was not only affecting American opinion but discouraging recruitment in Canada; the Canadians, he claimed, felt 'their young men are being sacrificed and the British troops are being spared.' John Buchan, who followed C.F.G. Masterman as the director of Britain's Department of Information, wrote that the distribution of CWRO photographs in Britain and America might well lead one to believe 'that Canada is running the war.' The CWRO's publicity of Canada's involvement in the war was, in fact, so successful that a reporter for the *Manchester Guardian* wrote in 1919 that it was 'long open to doubt whether there was anybody but Canadians fighting in France.'[12]

The shortage of photographs that had prompted Aitken to employ artists to illustrate the first volume of *Canada in Flanders* did not become acute until early in 1915. Mobilization at Valcartier, along with the departure from England and the arrival in France of the First Canadian Contingent, had been well documented by officers and men who were permitted to carry cameras. In March 1915, however, Routine Order Number 189 asked for the withdrawal of all cameras. With neither professional nor amateur photographers at the front, Canada's participation in the Second Battle of Ypres and in the battles of St Julien, Festubert, St Eloi, and Givenchy went largely unrecorded.[13] While these battles were far from decisive, characterized as they were by poor equipment and by the tactical blunders of the High Command, the Canadian troops had 'proved themselves equal to any in the world' at Ypres.[14] The fact that they had escaped visual recording therefore seemed especially unfortunate to those anxious that the Canadian contribution be recognized.

W.B. Wollen, R. Caton Woodville, and other artist-illustrators attempted to fill the photographic void of Canada's stand at Ypres by reconstructing the events of April and May 1915. But their reconstructions were flawed by their limited knowledge of the battles along with their more general ignorance of conditions on the Western Front. As one critic noted, their pictures lacked 'conviction, the scenes have not been witnessed and they have not been resolved in the artistic consciousness of the painters. Most of the war-pictures have little to do with art. They are worked up from collected material. They neither inspire nor console.'[15]

The absence of photographers not only resulted in imperfect reconstructions of battles; it also produced faked photographs and films. One Canadian official grumbled in January 1915 that 'numbers of sensational war pictures of the "fake" variety' were being exhibited all over Canada. Photographers' technicians used dark-room techniques to make their photographs more convincing. They introduced 'the convention of pictorialism, or the deliberate infusion of art standards of composition, design, and technique into the photographic image' by suppressing inartistic detail with the soft focus lens, by outlining, and by foreshortening the viewpoint.[16] France's agency for war propaganda, the Maison de la Presse, had a large photography section especially designed for this purpose. A number of Ivor Castle's CWRO photographs depicting the CEF at the Battle of Courcelette in September 1916 'were "made," or rather pieced together, from [photographs of] shell bursts taken at a British trench-mortar school outside St. Pol.' This was not always accomplished with subtlety: Castle's famous 'Over the Top' photographs (still used to illustrate the CEF at the front) showed Canadian soldiers going into battle at Courcelette with heavy packs on their backs and canvas breeches over their rifles. When these photographs were exhibited at the Grafton Galleries in 1916, they drew large crowds. However, not everyone was deceived. When Castle returned to the trenches to take more photographs he encountered a good deal of ridicule from the men who had seen or heard about the extraordinary photographs. By 1918 the publication and exhibition of faked or touched-up photographs had become so prevalent that journals like the CWRO's *Canadian War Pictorial* were moved to state that no 'specimen of "faked" pictures' would be found among its pages.[17]

Not only did photographs begin to lose their credibility; as the war progressed it became apparent that the camera could not seize the full effect of the moment – even with the aid of some heavy-handed touching-up. Nor, as J.E. Crawford noted in the preface of an exhibition catalogue devoted to the war paintings of C.R.W. Nevinson, could photographs 'speak the language of the spirit.' 'What we all want revealed,' wrote another reviewer who was seeking a significant visual record of the war in 1916, 'is the humanity, the simple and astounding truth. For of that living actuality the camera can give us little at all.'[18]

It had been the Germans who had first realized, as the American art critic Robert Cortes Holliday wrote in 1918, that only the painter could interpret 'the visible scene in the light of the spirit in which it is lived.' They sent several artists to the front shortly after the war began. By 1915 paintings of German and Austrian home and war front activities had made their way into American publications, and a year later into galleries in Vienna, Berlin, and Weimar. The French, for their part, by 1916 had two artists in the field under the Mission des Beaux-Arts. The Australians had also seen the point of this activity, sending artists to sketch the Gallipoli Campaign in 1915 (the resulting work was exhibited at the Fine Arts Society Gallery in London and used to illustrate *The Anzac Book*.[19])

The British, however, lagged far behind. Aitken's British counterpart, C.F.G. Masterman, believed that 'accurate information about the war [could be conveyed] through the eye of the artist,' but he did not establish a department of pictorial propaganda at London's Wellington House until February 1916. His hiring of the Scottish artist Muirhead Bone 'to make appropriate war scenes at the Front and in this country for the purpose both of propaganda at the present time and of historical record in the future' did not take place until July 1916. And Bone was not at the front until August.[20]

Sir Max Aitken remained convinced throughout the war that photographs and films were the supreme instruments of propaganda. Yet over the summer of 1916 he continued to regret that Canada's great achievement in holding the line at the Second Battle of Ypres had gone unrecorded; he became aware as well that the photographs now being taken by his CWRO photographers had a lifespan of only twenty-five years. The growing realization that works of art bore the virtues of permanency and prestige made him realize that, whatever the advantages of photography might continue to be, only paintings could provide 'the most permanent and vital form in which the great deeds and sacrifices of the Canadian Nation in the war could be enshrined for posterity.'[21]

In the late summer of 1916, therefore, Aitken asked Sir Sam Hughes, for whom he had been general representative for Canada at the front since September 1915, to authorize the employment of an artist to be attached to the CWRO. He raised the matter as well at the CWRO's committee meetings in September, where it was suggested that the distinguished, fifty-year-old, British portrait painter Richard Jack be employed by the CWRO for the purpose of producing one picture. While Hughes gave verbal consent to Aitken's request to 'send [an] artist to the front to do sketches,' he put nothing into writing. By late October Aitken was still waiting for authorization from the War Office, and he cabled Hughes, now back in Canada: 'An English artist has been in France for some time our man is held up.'[22]

The Minister of Militia and Defence was in no position to be of assistance. His reputation had suffered as a consequence of his having issued defective equipment (now replaced) to the First Canadian Division; it was tarnished further when he embarrassed the Canadian government by openly attacking the ineptitude of the British High Command. By 1916, Sir Robert Borden, who had been Hughes' most tolerant supporter, began to lose patience. Hughes' creation of a Sub Militia Council to administer his department's affairs in London and France conflicted with the prime minister's newly established Ministry of the Overseas Military Forces of Canada, set up under the Acting Canadian High Commissioner, Sir George Perley. Tired of Hughes' continual interference, Borden dismissed him in early November, and A.E. Kemp, chairman of the War Purchasing Committee, took his place.

The Ministry of the Overseas Military Forces of Canada did not solve all the problems that had arisen from the rivalry between Hughes and Perley, but it did centre all Canadian military activity in Britain under a single authority. Through Major-General R.E.W. Turner, Kemp's chief military adviser, direct contact was also established with British General Headquarters in France.[23] Aitken's direct and official access to the War Office now terminated. Requests for appointments, such as those relating to artists, would be channelled through the OMFC before going to the War Office for authorization.

Aitken's request for an artist was received by the chief of British Military Intelligence, General John Charteris. Seemingly unaware that Muirhead Bone had been in the field since August, Charteris claimed that he was considering a 'new scheme to give a few selected artists a chance of getting impressions of the war.' 'Sooner or later,' he wrote, 'someone will have to paint the big picture of the war.' His preference, however, was that the British should do the job. The Canadians, he thought, had already had their share of coverage by the available instruments of propaganda. Aitken, in consequence, met with 'opposition' from the 'quick-witted, observant, humorous, [and] methodical' chief of British Intelligence.[24]

To what extent Charteris' unhelpful response made Aitken seek the assistance of his friend, Harold Harmsworth, Lord Rothermere, is not known. That estimable figure, none the less, was asked by him in the autumn of 1916 for suggestions as to how a war art program might be established for Canada.

This was not the first time Lord Rothermere, 'whose interest in all things Canadian' was great, had helped the CWRO.[25] Bertram Lima, chairman of the directors of Rothermere's *Daily Mirror* and *Sunday Pictorial* newspapers, had been associated with the CWRO's publications and photographs since the summer of 1916. So too had *Daily Mirror* photographer Ivor Castle, who, on Rothermere's suggestion, replaced the ailing Captain Knobel. Considered 'number 2 man' in the Harmsworth family – second to his brother, Lord Northcliffe, an even more powerful press baron – Rothermere brought 'his financial abilities and sound business judgement' to the CWRO, sharing his time between it and the director-generalship of the Royal Army Clothing Department and, from November 1917, the Air Ministry.[26] The scheme he now proposed for organizing and financing a record of war pictures for Canada was ingenious. It avoided the government's authority – implicit even in Aitken's CWRO and the hierarchy that mushroomed above it – by giving the directors of the organization full control, personal credit for, and ownership of the collection.

Rothermere suggested that the contemplated war pictures scheme be registered as a charity fund under the recently established War Charities Act.[27] The fund's directors would receive no financial compensation and administrative costs would be assumed by the CWRO. Artists would receive honorary commissions in the Canadian Expeditionary Force and be paid, according to their rank, by the Canadian government. Additional expenses such as travelling, materials, and studio rental would be met through the CWRO's sale of photographs, films, and publications. At the end of hostilities, the pictures would be presented to the Canadian people as a gift from the fund's directors.

Rothermere's proposal seemed sound because, as Aitken had told Lord Northcliffe a month earlier, the 'only justification for securing publicity for Canada through this office is that it pays.' The various departments of the CWRO were organized, he claimed, 'to make sufficient money to meet the expenditure involved.' While profits had been negligible up to the autumn of 1916 (indeed Aitken had liquidated the CWRO's deficits, as he told Northcliffe, 'out of my own pocket'), earnings were expected. The first two volumes of *Canada in Flanders*, published in Britain, Canada, and the United States, had done well, and a third volume was imminent. The *Canadian War Pictorial*, issued by the CWRO in September 1916, achieved 'great success.' Simultaneously, the CWRO's first film, *The Battle for Courcelette*, was being shown to 'crowded houses' in Canada, and within a few months it would earn profits of $20,000.[28] And in November 1916 Lord Rothermere bought the copyright of the CWRO photographs, had them made into postcards, and guaranteed a minimum profit of £500 from their sale. More revenue was expected from *Canada in Khaki*, a lavish CWRO magazine scheduled for publication in January 1917. But the largest income would come from the sale, and particularly the viewing fees collected from exhibitions, of CWRO photographs. Rothermere's scheme, finally, would direct these profits to the new charity: money earned by the CWRO would be spent by the semi-private fund.

Sir George Perley approved of Rothermere's proposal, as did Sir Robert Borden.[29] And there is no evidence to suggest that the War Office balked at the idea either. Application to register the charity was made at the London County Council on 7 November. On 17 November 1916 the Canadian War Memorials Fund was officially established for the purpose of providing 'suitable Memorials in the form of Tablets, Oil-Paintings etc., to the Canadian Heroes and Heroines in the war.'[30] Rothermere became the Fund's chairman; Aitken and Lima were committee members; and Mrs S. Melville was secretary until Lieutenant J. Harold Watkins replaced her at the end of the month.

Thirteen days after the Fund was incorporated, the OMFC, by permission of the War Office, granted Royal Academy associate Richard Jack a six-month honorary commission as major for the purpose of producing one picture depicting the Canadians at the front. The Canadian government agreed to pay Jack's salary according to his military rank; materials and a bonus of £250 would come from CWRO's profits.

It is not surprising that the Fund's committee asked Richard Jack to portray the Canadians at the Second Battle of Ypres. The event, as mentioned earlier, had not been photographed by the Canadians, nor had it been reconstructed by any artist to the satisfaction of Aitken. Yet it had been the site of a splendid performance by the CEF during its first major encounter. The retention of the salient left Belgian territory still untrodden by the German heel and Channel ports in Allied hands. The battle had been the only German offensive on the Western Front since the beginning of 1915, and it had come within a hair's breadth of success. Even more memorable, it had introduced the Canadians to the new and terrifying weapon, chlorine gas.

The scale of Jack's picture, some twelve by twenty feet, was as heroic as the saving of the salient itself. But the approach was unimaginative in the extreme. In order to glorify the Canadian troops Jack employed every hackneyed nineteenth-century battle art convention: a wounded officer waving his men on into battle; a soldier dying in the arms of his comrade; puffs of smoke indicating distant artillery action (or was this the ominous, yellow-green cloud of chlorine gas?); the villainous faces of the enemy in contrast to the smiling faces of the Canadians; and a silhouetted figure of a Canadian soldier bayoneting a German.

As depicted by Jack, *The Second Battle of Ypres, 22 April to 25 May, 1915* (Fig. 1), could have been any late-nineteenth-century skirmish. Even Elizabeth Butler, an earlier and once much-admired English battle painter, had achieved more truth in her battlefield scenes by putting her men through wholly simulated manoeuvres. Not so Major Jack. While he had visited the ground where the fighting took place, interviewed several survivors (some were models for his painting), and studied 'all manner of military accoutrements,'[31] it was clear he had not witnessed the event. His soldiers fought behind a parapet of sandbags instead of in trenches. They wore heavy packs on their backs. Their commanding officer stood in full view of the enemy. Only one note of truth rang through Jack's picture: its entirely realistic depiction of the dead.

Aitken might, ironically, have resented this last note, for his one instruction to photographers had been to cover up Canadian corpses before taking pictures. Yet he was not displeased with Jack's painting. Ten months after the artist had commenced the work, Aitken visited his studio to find that he had 'almost completed a most wonderful battle scene.'[32] For all its deficiencies, then, the picture became what Aitken seems so clearly to have thought of it as being: a kind of monument as the first of what would be hundreds of works of art commissioned by the new 'charity,' the Canadian War Memorials Fund.

By the summer of 1917 the anticipated CWRO profits had begun to accumulate, leaving Lord Beaverbrook – Aitken had been elevated to the peerage in January – free to build the CWMF in any direction he so desired. Besides money from publications, there were enormous earnings from exhibitions of CWRO photographs. Over eighty thousand people had queued to see the 'monster attraction' – a photograph measuring some twenty-two by eleven feet depicting the Canadians at Vimy Ridge – at the Official Canadian War Photographs Exhibition in the Grafton Galleries in July. Money was also promised by Sir Edward Kemp, who offered the Fund 25 per cent of the proceeds from the sale of CWRO films in Canada and the United States (this was particularly gratifying to Beaverbrook because it indicated that the Fund was receiving 'official recognition in Canada').[33]

Beaverbrook now began to devote even more of his considerable energies to the CWMF. He had, after all, 'placed the argument [for the CWRO] on its legs.' There was, moreover, less for him to do in other areas. The meeting of the first Imperial War Cabinet in March 1917 had opened the door for direct consultation, at least in theory, between the Imperial and Dominion governments. Sir Robert Borden's Military Service Act of June 1917 heralded the implementation of conscription the following year. And, the same month, the Canadian Corps had come under the command of the Canadian-born Major-General Sir Arthur Currie. Canadian pride was never higher than in April 1917, when the corps' four divisions, working together for the first time, took and held Vimy Ridge. With a major and successful fighting force in the field, with less urgency for propaganda, and with the task of establishing the CWRO accomplished, Beaverbrook was, quite simply, becoming bored. Nor could his other activities – chairmanship of the Colonial Bank, ownership of the *Daily Express*, member of the Advisory Committee in Britain's Department of Propaganda among them – assuage his appetite for work. Had he been called to the British cabinet or even been used as a go-between, as during the cabinet crisis of December 1916, he would have left the CWRO. But, with nowhere else to go, the 'frustrated and disappointed seeker after employment' remained.[34]

It was good that he did, for while the CWRO might not have needed his attention its undernourished step-child, the CWMF, plainly did. Facing rivals at home and abroad, having to contend with problems in Canada, it presented just the sort of challenge Beaverbrook relished. One rival, in fact, was very close indeed. The painting activity of Britain's Department of Information was being extended in a way that presented a clear threat to the capacity of the CWMF to attract the best painters. Early in 1917 Francis Dodd, William Orpen, C.R.W. Nevinson, Eric Kennington, Paul Nash, and James McBey joined Britain's first war artist, Muirhead Bone, there. By July they had been to the front and their resulting work was shown along with twelve other British artists in an exhibition, Britain's Efforts and Ideals, devoted to 'the practical aspect of Britain's physical and material efforts.'[35] Their work also appeared in group and solo exhibitions as well as in the Department of Information's elaborate publications. When the Americans entered the war in April 1917, they immediately established a division of Pictorial Publicity under the well-known commercial artist Charles Dana Gibson and attached eight illustrators with the rank of captain to the American Expeditionary Force.

If there were competing organizations to worry about, there was also trouble in Canada. The reaction of Canadian art officials to the news that the CWMF had been established without their knowledge posed a particular problem; news of the Fund came to officials of the National Gallery of Canada, for instance, six months after the scheme was under way.

While convalescing from wounds received at the Second Battle of the Somme, Ernest Fosbery visited the Royal Academy's 1917 spring exhibition at Burlington House. As a Canadian and a portrait painter, he was struck by a painting of Arthur Currie, who had just become the first Canadian to command the Canadian Corps. The picture was the work of Richard Jack, who, though English, was still Canada's only official war artist. Assuming it to be 'one of the portraits of Canadian Generals painted by the British artist for the Canadian Government,' Fosbery wrote to Sir George Perley: 'We have in the Canadian Academy some good portrait painters ... and I think it probable that there would be considerable feeling in Canada if in a matter of this sort Canadian artists were entirely overlooked. Canada is taking its place as a nation and Canadian art has more than kept pace with the developments of the country. Would it not be possible to have this essentially Canadian series of portraits done by Canadian artists?' Fosbery pointed out that there were at least two associates of the Royal Canadian

Academy serving as privates with the forces: A.Y. Jackson and J.L. Graham. The employment of these men, he suggested to the acting high commissioner, would keep 'out of the trenches two of the best of our younger group of landscape painters.'[36]

Fosbery was quite wrong in assuming that Jack's portrait of Currie had been commissioned by the Canadian government. In the first place, the CWMF was independent of the government. Secondly, the Fund had commissioned only one picture: Jack's *Second Battle of Ypres*. His portrait of Currie was, it seems, a private affair between portraitist and subject. This misunderstanding of the situation did not, however, diminish the effect of the letter upon Beaverbrook. He took its contents very much to heart, and, as in the case of Arthur Doughty a year earlier, quickly moved in his customary way to co-opt the idea and its originator. He asked the OMFC's chief military adviser, Major-General Turner, to have Jackson, Graham, and Fosbery himself report to his office. He also approached Sir Edmund Walker, the chairman of the Advisory Arts Council, which since 1907 had advised the government on all matters concerning the selection and purchase of art for the National Gallery of Canada and the adoption of plans and commissions for public buildings and monuments. On 26 July Walker was invited by cable to comment upon the 'capabilities' of the three artists as well as another Canadian, H.J. Mowatt, a gunner in the British Royal Garrison Artillery, who had been seeking employment as a war artist. He was also asked to submit the names of any other Canadian artists who might be willing to join the CEF in France.

Walker replied four days later: Fosbery and Graham were both 'good draughtsmen,' Jackson an 'able impressionist,' but of Mowatt he knew nothing. As to the possibility of employing other Canadians, he assured Beaverbrook that 'at moment no Canadian artist available and willing to go except the landscape painter J.W. Beatty.'[37]

Walker's response was none too helpful, but later the same day he cabled again, informing Beaverbrook of a recent Advisory Arts Council's recommendation in answer to Sir Robert Borden's request of November 1916 'that material be obtained for the painting of a few important canvases in connection with the war.'[38] That recommendation, made to the prime minister just two weeks earlier, had suggested that three Canadian artists 'proceed to France, upon some salary basis, and there make sketches and drawings of the country during the war, of war events, and generally of the life and work of our soldiers.' The council would then inspect the 'sketches and from them commission the painting of certain pictures commemorative of Canada's part in the war.' Walker and Eric Brown, the director of the National Gallery, were in the process of selecting the artists envisioned by this proposal when Beaverbrook's cable arrived.[39]

Mindful of Fosbery's warning that there might be trouble should Canadians not be included, Beaverbrook requested through the OMFC – before receiving Walker's reply – that permission be obtained for Jackson, Graham, Fosbery, and three other artists to be attached to the Canadian Corps. Perley consented to this a few days later. By mid-August, however, Beaverbrook had viewed the work of Graham and Fosbery and found it unpromising. Mowatt and the Winnipeg printmaker, Cyril Barraud, a lieutenant with the corp's 14th Reserve Battalion, were still under consideration. But only Jackson was taken on immediately. Favourable consideration of him was probably assisted by articles from *Studio* magazine describing him 'as the coming man' and as a 'young artist of unusual promise,' which he himself produced. Helpful, too, would have been the announcement of the National Gallery of Canada's recent purchase of his painting *The Red Maple*.[40] He had also read – a fact that no doubt impressed Beaverbrook – *Canada in Flanders* in preparation for his interview. On 13 August Jackson was given a temporary honorary commission as a lieutenant; he thus became, along with Richard Jack, one of two CWMF artists.

Fulfilling his mandate to employ six artists in addition to Jack, Beaverbrook then hired the Canadians Cyril Barraud and James Kerr-Lawson and the British Augustus John, David Cameron, and Gyrth Russell.[41] Percy Wyndham Lewis, Alfred Bastein, and James Quinn were shortly afterwards loaned to the CWMF from the British, Belgian, and Australian forces. The numbers involved were increased still further by the fact that Laura Knight, Clare Atwood, Anna Airy, Charles Shannon, and many other civilian artists were commissioned to paint, for a set fee, specific works relating to the CEF in Britain.

Artists in fact came to the CWMF committee's attention in widely varying ways. Mowatt, Wyndham Lewis, William Roberts, and David Bomberg offered their services, while Leonard Richmond, Dudley Hardy, Harold Piffard, and Norman Wilkinson made themselves known through their contributions to CWRO publications. Others came to the committee's attention as a result of their participation in private or public art exhibitions. Haphazard though its selection of artists might have seemed and however negligent it was of Fosbery's warning to include more Canadians, the committee did manage to infuse some expertise into its hiring procedure. This was accomplished thanks almost entirely to the arrival of Paul G. Konody as art critic, adviser, and honorary secretary.

Konody was the art critic of two Harmsworth publications, the *Daily Mail* and the *Observer*, and for some time had been Lord Rothermere's personal art adviser (as Arnold Bennett put it, 'Rothermere collects, but employs P.G. Konody to collect for him'). The author of books on Velasquez, Filippino Lippi, the brothers Van Eyck, and Walter Crane, Konody had also edited the prestigious *Artist* (1900–2) and *Connoisseur* (1902–9) magazines.[42] In addition to his roles as scholar, art adviser, and critic, he was married to Isabel Pyke-Nott, sister-in-law of the well-established Pre-Raphaelite decorative painter, John Byam Lister Shaw.

Though resident in London since 1889, the Hungarian-born Konody still spoke 'with a dramatic mit-european accent.'[43] To one artist he was 'a charming and most entertaining person' with a fluency in several languages. Others viewed the suave, well-dressed, pipe-smoking art historian with more ambivalence. Arnold Bennett found him 'extremely able in absorbing other people's ideas' yet 'very unreliable' so far as his own taste was concerned (he was, moreover, 'not English'). The British artist Alfred Munnings 'did not see eye to eye' with him on matters of art, but nevertheless considered him to be 'the leading critic of the day.'[44]

No records exist to indicate what remuneration Konody received for his service to the CWMF, nor do we know when he began his work. He was attached in a casual way to the CWRO's publications department in the autumn of 1916. In September of the following year Augustus John remembered having spoken to him 'some months ago' about employment as a war artist. Konody wrote repeatedly of the CWMF's getting under way in the summer of 1917, seemingly ignoring its establishment in the autumn of 1916. But whenever he did become involved, he brought with him an ability to 'enlist men and women of capacity';[45] he also contributed an intelligent understanding of the artist's relationship to modern war and of modern war's visual relationship to previous wars.

Konody articulated his ideas in the columns of the *Daily Mail* and the *Observer*, in the prefaces of exhibition catalogues devoted to war art, in monographs on war artists, and in several articles dealing specifically with the CWMF. In all of this work, produced from the early years of the war to well after it, he stressed the uniqueness of the Great War. Conducted simultaneously on land, sea, and in the air, it had a vast significance for the life of nations. Immense, overwhelming, it rendered individual acts of heroism insignificant, yet elevated the dignity of the ordinary soldier. Dominated by the new engines of war, by 'giant guns and tanks, aeroplanes and submarines, poison gas and liquid fire,' it required a new artistic method and a new style. Paintings recording modern warfare had to be created, Konody believed, 'from actual impressions whilst they are fresh on the mind, whilst emotions and passions and enthusiasm are at their highest.' It was imperative that art be fashioned in a style that departed from 'stale allegorical imagery.' 'The painter who could successfully grapple with the unprecedented conditions of modern warfare' should, he felt, 'be an adherent of the modern school,' an artist who had assimilated the styles of Post-Impressionism, Cubism, and Futurism.[46]

Konody's modernist prescription for painting the Great War did have

limitations. He could not fully embrace Vorticism, the most radical move-
ment in British painting, as useful in depicting the war (he condemned the
Vorticist work of David Bomberg and Wyndham Lewis as 'geometrical
obfuscations' and permitted both to work for the CWMF only on speculation).
The kind of art Konody could accept lay between conventional illustration
and the Vorticists' 'picture puzzles.' He admired line, order, and harmony.
He wanted to see the artist 'express the poetry and rhythm behind his subject.'
In doing this he allowed for a wide ground between description and 'obfus-
cation.' He liked Nevinson's compromise of 'clear illustration and futurist
abstraction' because it was 'absolutely intelligible without being in any sense
of the word literal representation.'[47] With this relatively tolerant attitude,
his selection of artists was diverse, ranging from the near descriptive work
of John Lavery to that of the Vorticists whose painting he accepted on at
least a tentative basis.

Konody's preference for stylistic unity or, as he once put it, 'diversity
kept under control' was partly determined by the setting in which the CWMF's
pictures would eventually be displayed. Initially it was intended that
the collection decorate the new Canadian Houses of Parliament to be built
to replace those that had burned in 1916. But this idea changed after the
artists were consulted by Beaverbrook in the autumn of 1917: they 'strongly
held the view that a special building should be secured' because 'the lighting
in the new House of Commons would not be suitable and the pictures could
not be displayed there to the best advantage.' Their suggestions were taken
seriously and Konody announced in January 1918 that the collection would
'eventually be housed in a gallery specially built for this purpose on a prominent and suitable site in Ottawa.'[48]

Because the pictures were to form 'part of a homogeneous architectural
scheme' to consist of forty large in addition to numerous small panels,
Konody felt the work should possess a 'unity of scale and a broad decorative
treatment.' To accomplish this he boasted that 'only artists of the greatest
eminence and of universal reputation' were being invited to participate in
the scheme. Most, however, were Royal Academy associates or academi-
cians, teachers, or prominent society portrait painters who had come to
Konody's attention through exhibitions (their names appear again and again
in his weekly 'Art and Artists' column in the *Observer*). Not surprisingly,
the traditionalists outweighed the clique of artists who met at the Café Royal
to argue the merits of Vorticism over Futurism. As for Konody's opinion
of Canadian art, he believed it to be 'of comparatively recent growth' and
that it drew 'its strength from Parisian soil' (here he was in all probability
referring to the Canadian artist then living in Paris, J.W. Morrice).[49]

Konody's participation in the scheme did not end with the selection of
artists. He suggested the subject and size of the commissioned work and

frequently visited the artist's studio. As one artist wrote of him in a poem entitled 'The Konodian Army':

> In the case of a painter hard to beat
> I tell him his size is 20 feet;
> And major's rank and major's pay
> Are granted him on that very day ...

To the artists he was nothing less than 'the brain, the mind, the heart, / of the great Konodian Army.'[50]

Yet others had their roles too. Commissions and authorizations for painting at the front – secured through the OMFC and the War Office – studios, supplies, and transportation, were handled by Lieutenant J. Harold Watkins, the CWMF's secretary. Once in the war zone, artists came under the jurisdiction of CWRO employees Captain I.G. Robertson, Lieutenant W. Douglas, and three non-commissioned officers who designated automobiles and arranged lodgings. Overall responsibility for the CWMF remained with Lord Beaverbrook, whose organizational genius brought the whole scheme to fruition.

Beaverbrook gave much of his time during the autumn and winter of 1917 to overseeing the CWMF. He seemed to enjoy, too, the social company of the artists, giving dinners at the Ritz and luncheons 'in honour of the artists' in his Hyde Park Hotel residence, inviting Winston Churchill and others as guests. When the artists went to France the entertainment not only continued but, if anything, became more extravagant. Augustus John and William Orpen were among a group of CWMF artists Beaverbrook entertained in a suite at the Hotel Bristol in Paris. John recalled that ' "the guests were so spaced as to allow further seating accommodation between them. The reason for this arrangement was soon seen on the arrival of a bevy of young women in evening clothes, who without introduction established themselves in the empty chairs." ' Beaverbrook withdrew, as did Orpen, but John remained to drink champagne with the French ladies.[51]

There is no doubt that Beaverbrook enjoyed being the impresario of Canadian war painting. He never pretended to know anything about art – Konody had been hired to give him advice on that subject; but he did take more than a superficial interest in the artists and their work, even officiating at their exhibitions, though his off-the-cuff speeches unashamedly demonstrated how little he really knew about painting. Speaking at Nevinson's Leicester Galleries exhibition in 1918 he declared that 'Mr. Nevinson's art pleased him greatly, though he could not tell why by any process of reasoning. All he could say was that he felt its influence in his heart.' But while he may have been weak on painting techniques and styles, he did recognize the importance of having artists work at the front. 'Mr. Nevinson's work could never have been produced,' he continued, 'unless he had spent months in France. It was actual contact with the fighting which had given him that appreciation and realization of the realities of war ...'[52]

By December 1917, Jackson, John, Charles Sims, Barraud, Kerr-Lawson, and Cameron had had that contact too. Only four artists were authorized to go to the front at any one time, however, and Louis Weirter, Wyndham Lewis, James Wilson Morrice, Nevinson, Alfred Munnings, Gerald Moira, H.J. Mowatt, Leonard Richmond, Gyrth Russell, George Clausen, and Algernon Talmage were therefore kept in the wings. Of the forty-five artists employed by the CWMF in Britain during 1917, almost half were engaged in portraiture: Sir Robert Borden, Sir George Perley, Sir Edward Kemp, along with many distinguished admirals and generals as well as every Canadian Victoria Cross recipient, were to be painted. And despite Konody's antipathy to 'the colourless, academic reconstruction [of events] from descriptive material,' Louis Weirter, Edgar Bundy, and Nevinson were commissioned to reconstruct visually unrecorded land and air battles. The distinguished printmaker Frank Brangwyn was charged with the production of a series of lithographs on the horrors of war, Charles Sims with an allegorical work to be called 'Sacrifice.' Nor was this all. Beaverbrook planned to purchase historical portraits as well as commission 'contemporary portraits of Canadians who have been prominent in history.'[53] And a number of artists would be sent to Canada to paint munition factories, portraits, and training camps.

'The Canadians have robbed every artist of distinction in England,' exclaimed the British painter William Orpen in the autumn of 1917. C.F.G. Masterman was similarly awed by Beaverbrook's accomplishments: 'The Canadian Government ... alone seems willing to spend money on patronage of art in connection with the war and are paying large sums of money for work by Kennington, Nevinson, Orpen and others.'[54] Many saw the Canadian scheme taking a new step in the public patronage of the arts: 'For the first time a great art movement has been started in Great Britain, absolutely free from art officialdom; a movement without members of the RA or other official bodies being on the committee, a movement to give all groups, all schools of famous artists an opportunity to work for one purpose ... '[55]

The Canadian War Memorials Fund was, in fact, a vivid demonstration of quasi-official patronage. Salaries were paid by the military, but much of the decision-making was done by seconded civilians. No established artistic body such as the Royal Academy of Art had control over the selection of artists or subjects. In Britain, where there had been 'little official interest in further developing national facilities for art enjoyment and instruction' since 1900, and where no attempt had been made 'to apply public funds for artistic purposes in any innovative way,' the Canadian program was a revolutionary beginning, 'a new era of powerfully stimulating art patronage.'[56]

Yet Beaverbrook was not content to let the CWMF rest on its laurels. He wanted it to go on growing, and if funds were not forthcoming to hire more artists he promised that financial assistance would come from private subscriptions as well as from personal donations given by himself and Lord Rothermere. As he boldly told Sir Edmund Walker in December 1917, 'We shall not rest content until we have obtained £100,000 with which we shall be able to purchase a wonderful collection of pictures.'[57]

3 'Up in arms'

Throughout the summer and autumn of 1917 Sir Edmund Walker read of the growth of the Canadian War Memorials Fund. At first it seemed as though Lord Beaverbrook was engaging only a few artists: the scheme had, after all, been established in November 1916 and up to July of the following year only one artist, Richard Jack, had been employed. By mid-September, however, Beaverbrook informed Walker that several more, including A.Y. Jackson and Cyril Barraud, had been taken on. Walker was intrigued, 'anxious to understand' what Beaverbrook was doing, because in his capacity as chairman of the Advisory Arts Council he still owed the prime minister a detailed proposal to supplement the plan he and Eric Brown had submitted in July giving their own ideas about art and the war. He learned little from Arthur Doughty, who had returned from London in September though he did not see him until December. From a tired and broken Ernest Fosbery came a jaundiced account of Beaverbrook as a man 'altogether ignorant' of art and 'entirely in the hands of such people as Konody and others, who have no knowledge of Canadian art whatsoever,' while Richard Jack was 'at work on large battle pictures without having any knowledge of fighting conditions.'[1] Something, too, could be gleaned from newspaper reports. It was, however, from Beaverbrook himself that increasingly detailed letters, with appended lists of artists, eventually began to arrive.

As chairman both of the Advisory Arts Council and of the National Gallery's board of trustees, Walker viewed Beaverbrook's art scheme with a mixture of envy, helpfulness, and unconcern. He was amazed that someone who apparently knew nothing about Canadian painting had £15,000 to spend on art when the National Gallery's own acquisitions budget had been slashed. Furthermore, he and Brown shared an antipathy to the depiction of recent historical events, believing such renditions to smack of the 'special-artist-correspondent' sketches that filled the illustrated weeklies. They even felt that traditional battle pictures were 'not pictorial.' Yet neither showed any animosity towards Beaverbrook's operation.

Walker, certainly, had been impressed by Beaverbrook's apparent willingness to show him every courtesy, to keep in close contact, and invite him, from the beginning of their correspondence in July 1917, to make suggestions. He had sought Walker's opinion on the abilities of Jackson, Barraud, Fosbery, and Graham, before deciding whether to employ them, and of J.W. Morrice, the established Canadian artist, known for his low-hued tonal harmonies, then living in France. He had invited Walker 'to form an Advisory Committee in Canada to consider the question of housing and other matters which may arise from time to time.'[2] Beaverbrook had even offered to place the CWMF under Walker's sole direction and control.

Walker was willing to be helpful. He answered the enquiry about the merits of the Canadian painters in London and sent the address of Morrice, though he could 'hardly imagine him as being useful to the creation of war pictures.' And he was free with his advice about the actual production of the works. He objected, however, to the commissioning of large and finished canvases during the course of the war. Consistent with his and Brown's July proposal to Borden, he told Beaverbrook that the artists should not undertake paintings 'in the larger sense but ... come back with material drawn upon the spot'; in this way their sketches 'might be as realistic, as terrible or as horrible, as the facts.' The question of whether or not the sketches warranted developing into major works could be left to a later time. Walker did not doubt the ability of every CWMF artist to bring about 'some compromise with the facts of war' or to produce work that would be of lasting interest to the public. He was impressed that Beaverbrook had secured Orpen, Cameron, and other artists of that calibre: 'Whether they give us material in the form of sketches or finished work, we must in any event be thankful to obtain it.'[3]

Beaverbrook did not agree with Walker's suggestion that large works be produced only after the cessation of hostilities and only on the scrutiny of the CWMF's art advisers. His scheme depended upon quick action. In times to come he might not be able to find artists so willing to participate, honorary commissions so freely given, or war-charity money so easily raised. 'By securing these pictures at the present time,' he assured Walker, the CWMF was 'benefiting by the flood of patriotism now existent, which inspires the highest efforts. If we left the question of purchase until after the War, I am sure they would cost us tens of thousands more than they are costing us now.'[4]

Walker remained unconvinced, the more so when the realities of the scheme unfolded in the late autumn and winter of 1917. Augustus John's proposed forty-foot mural was, he felt, a rather doubtful concession to that artist's 'peculiarities.' Photographs of Jack's *The Second Battle of Ypres* (Fig. 1) and Nevinson's four oil paintings, *The Roads of France* (Figs. 9–12), sent to him by a proud Beaverbrook, left him unimpressed. 'Whatever its merits,' he wrote of Jack's picture, 'the public of the future is not likely to appreciate such realistic treatment of war.' Nevinson's mildly futuristic paintings were, on the other hand, not realistic enough. 'How much better a photograph is than the effort of the second-rate painter,' he grumbled. Walker also objected to Beaverbrook's intention of sending British artists to Canada, where they would paint military portraits and home-front activities. 'There are some very able artists here who could execute some of these commissions,' he bluntly told Beaverbrook.[5]

But while Walker disagreed with many aspects of Beaverbrook's scheme, he felt that its result would be 'important whether we like the way it is done or not.' By the autumn of 1917 his opposition was moderating. He no longer had a plan of his own before the prime minister. Doughty did not seem interested and, with Beaverbrook's program operating at such a level, offering rival suggestions would be like attempting to compete with a steamroller. The Canadian War Memorials Fund might, moreover, be of very practical benefit: as he told Beaverbrook in October, 'What you are doing will help us very much in the creating either of larger Archives buildings or of a National Gallery.'[6]

This, in fact, was a critical consideration. After the centre block of the Houses of Parliament was destroyed by fire in February 1916, the National Gallery was forced to move into one room of the Victoria Memorial Museum; its previous location in the museum's east wing had never been regarded as permanent, because the gallery expected to have a building of its own. Eric Brown, who became the gallery's first curator in 1910, felt its future lay in the 'building of a beautiful and permanent home on one of the finest sites of the city.' The prospect of obtaining that building now seemed possible through the acquisition of the CWMF collection. Brown and Walker were thus induced to put aside some of their prejudices against 'unpictorial' war paintings. When the CWMF collection came into the future gallery it could be hung in rooms of its own, apart from the rest of the collection; eventually, 'like all records of things that the world will want to forget,' it would, Brown assured Walker, 'steadily decline in popularity, if not in value.'[7]

With his own plans for a war art scheme now dormant, all that remained for Walker to do was to accept Beaverbrook's invitation to join the CWMF. But he still hesitated, not so much because he believed that war art was antithetical to a gallery of fine art and that major works should not be commissioned during wartime, but because he was reluctant to become involved in selecting Canadian painters and sculptors. As he told Beaverbrook, 'Owing to the rather irritable minds of most artists, I have been quite unwilling in the past to suggest the names of men suitable to do the work for the Canadian War Records Office.'[8]

Artists in Canada were probably no more irritable than anyone else. Their activity was, however, characterized by a kaleidoscope of styles and approaches, cliques and factions, and their ideas about public galleries, especially the National Gallery of Canada, varied considerably. Criticism of the National Gallery's buying policies had begun in 1913, the year it was incorporated and given its own board with Eric Brown as director. 'Rumor has it,' the *Toronto Star* reported on 9 June, 'that the board sometimes leans unduly to old masters, and spends a disproportionate amount of money on them.' A.Y. Jackson blamed this on the board's isolation from the artistic community, and had 'no faith in a system which appoints three laymen who are not in touch with either Canadian or European art or artists.' Lawren Harris also complained that the board displayed no sympathy, enthusiasm, or belief in the future of Canadian artists, except 'to keep us on the beaten track, which, so far as the artist is concerned, leads to oblivion.' Of the board's chairman, Sir Edmund Walker, opinion was mixed. 'Some say he is the sure friend of the struggling painter,' Augustus Bridle wrote in 1916, 'others that he is misled by a bigoted enthusiasm into bulling the stock of one artist – probably a dead one; some that he is a real connoisseur; others that he is not.'[9]

Much of this criticism was true. The gallery's board of trustees were laymen. The annual reports did show that far more European than Canadian works were purchased. This buying policy partially reflected Walker's own preference for the dark landscape paintings of the Barbizon School painters and their followers, the 'modern' Dutch 'dealer-made' masters, and his liking for Japanese woodcut prints.[10] It reflected, too, the gallery's concern over building a prestigious collection – no easy task when few important works came onto the international market at a price the gallery's small budget could afford – and in possessing works that would serve as an exemplary study collection for Canadian artists.

For most Canadian artists Europe was, after all, still the home of the Grand Tradition and of the great painters, ancient and modern. The influence of Paris and London saturated Canadian art. Most fledgling Canadian artists studied in Europe: the masters at the Julien, the Slade, and the South Kensington schools were their mentors, the standards of the Royal Academy and the Salon were their standards. When they returned home they transferred what they had learned in Europe to what was familiar to them in Canada. This approach usually resulted in paintings heavily indebted to European Impressionism, the anachronistic Barbizon School, or to the English Romantic-Realists. Though by the early 1910s a small group of young painters, later known as the Group of Seven, were using as their subject matter the unpeopled northern Ontario wilderness, their pictures, like those of the more conservative painters, remained reflective of a European style and sensibility.

Walker fully understood the derivative nature of Canadian painting and, as mentioned, preferred to collect Japanese and European pictures. He did, however, possess strong nationalist sentiments (he was a founding member of the Champlain Society and the Art Gallery of Toronto) – along with a distinctly imperialist bent (he was a strong supporter of the Round Table Movement in Canada) – a fact reflected in 1909 in his urging the other members of the Advisory Arts Council to purchase Canadian works 'which may not be attractive to us as individuals, but would be fair expositions of the condition of art in Canada.'[11] Three years later he reinforced the point, suggesting that the Advisory Arts Council purchase work annually from the Royal Canadian Academy of Art's exhibition.[12] After he became chairman of the National Gallery's board of trustees in 1913, the gallery continued to acquire proportionally more European works but 'did much more than usual in the way of purchasing Canadian pictures.' As *Maclean's* magazine reported in 1915, 'in spite of the war having reduced the buying of pictures to a minimum some appreciation of the work of Canadian artists has been shown by the Trustees who have recently purchased 80 pictures.'[13]

The attitude of Walker and Brown to Canadian and European painting was perfectly manifested in their ambivalent response to Beaverbrook's CWMF. On the one hand, they criticized him for failing to admit more Canadian artists; on the other, they praised him for acquiring the services of prominent English painters – Shannon, John, Rothenstein, Moira – from whom they had purchased work for the gallery's permanent collection that very year. They balked at the idea of participating themselves because that would mean confronting artists, commissioning works, and visiting studios – a much greater undertaking than that involved in acquiring pictures from exhibitions. Yet Walker was so tantalized by the possibility of obtaining a building that he continued to give Beaverbrook his views. At the moment, his involvement in the CWMF went no further. When all was said and done, his experience with Canadian artists compelled him to believe that a closer association with them through Beaverbrook's art scheme would be 'intolerable.'[14]

News of the Canadian War Memorials Fund came to most Canadian artists through the press. On 18 August 1917 the *Toronto Daily News* reported incorrectly that Jackson and Fosbery had 'been commissioned by the Canadian government through Sir George Perley, acting High Commissioner in England, to paint a series of pictures, depicting Canada's activities at the front.' Three months later another Toronto newspaper reported a plan to paint the war for Canada in an article headlined 'Canadian Artists Not Included.' These and other reports caused Canadian artists to protest. J. Gibbon, representing Montreal's Pen and Pencil Club, complained to Eric Brown of the 'attitude taken by the Canadian Records Office to Canadian Artists.' 'At a time when the Government has withdrawn its usual purchases,' he continued, 'it seems absurd that Canadian Artists should be overlooked.' Speaking for the Ontario Society of Artists, Brittan Cooke told both Walker and Beaverbrook of the 'very keen resentment felt among the senior artists in Canada [that] painters who are not known in Canada are being sent to record the work of Canadian troops.' With no further knowledge of the scheme beyond the participants' names, the complaints of the artists could not be more specific. But one thing was clear: someone else was being paid to paint their soldiers and they were 'up in arms.'[15]

Following the letters of protest, a special committee charged with 'making representations to the government, urging them to give Canadian artists an opportunity of getting pictorial material relating to the war,' was formed by the Ontario Society of Artists and the Royal Canadian Academy.[16] Two of its members, E. Wyly Grier, former president of the Ontario Society of Artists and founding member of the Arts and Letters Club, and Royal Canadian academician J.W. Beatty, met with Sir Edmund Walker on 19 December. Both men expressed their disapproval, then listened to Walker. What they heard revealed Walker at his characteristically ambivalent best: he told them of his reluctance to select artists for the scheme and of his preference, in opposition to what Beaverbrook was doing, for commissioning large works after the war had ended; at the same time, he was anxious they co-operate in some measure with the work being done. Grier and Beatty agreed with everything he said, and then offered to put forward the names of three or four artists who might be willing to go to France, and to suggest rank and pay. Walker was much relieved. He had swung the artists from absolute opposition to qualified support, and had got the Royal Canadian Academy and the Ontario Society of Artists to assume responsibility for selecting the artists; at the same time, he had not committed himself to any further involvement in the CWMF.

Ten days after Walker's meeting with Beatty and Grier he received their list suggesting artists. The moment was propitious: Beaverbrook had again asked for his assistance. This time Walker responded enthusiastically by cable, with a concrete suggestion: 'Some dissatisfaction regarding inadequate employment of Canadian artists and because of your letters have tried avert criticism and create harmony by obtaining from the whole body of artists suitable names. They suggest four who could go immediately Cullen, Beatty, Simpson and Varley. Rank of Captain, total remuneration $2,500 per annum with free transportation. All material resulting property of War Records. These stand very high among fellow artists, hope you will make appointments as this will clear difficult situation here.'[17]

The four suggested artists were representative of 'the whole body of artists in Canada' only to the extent that their names had been put forward by the two most powerful art associations. Yet, not withstanding the exclusion of French Canadians and artists from seven of Canada's nine provinces, Beatty, C.W. Simpson, Maurice Cullen, and F.H. Varley almost miraculously embodied four different kinds of painting. Beatty, having fought as a private with the Royal Grenadiers in 1885 against Big Bear and Poundmaker, had some military experience as well as a facility for drawing figures. Simpson had no war experience and was less a realist and painter of figures; he was, however, known as 'the cleverest decorative artist on this side of the water.' Cullen and Varley were the modernists: Cullen was an Impressionist renowned for his snow scenes of rural Quebec; Varley did double duty as a portraitist and landscape painter. Despite the diversity of their painting, these artists had one thing in common: they were 'all non-studio painters; men of the out-of-doors.'[18]

Walker had told Eric Brown that 'it goes without saying' that he would have to approve of the selection of artists.[19] The director of the National Gallery gave his consent. So, too, did the Canadian critics. Beaverbrook, who was extremely grateful for Walker's recommendations, agreed to the suggested salary, and asked Sir Edward Kemp, who had taken over the ministry of OMFC from Sir George Perley, to instruct the new minister of militia and defence, General S.C. Mewburn, to give the artists a nine-month temporary rank of honorary captain. He also sent £500 to help defray their initial expenses.

Beatty, Simpson, Cullen, and Varley departed from Halifax for Britain in March 1918. They 'had a fine passage over,' sailing up the Clyde on the morning of their arrival past 'wonderful' shipyards, then travelling from Glasgow by train, on which they had 'a cold and cheerless trip down to London by night.' Walker's and Brown's initial plan to send three Canadian artists to the front to 'acquire material' had come to fruition. And it had happened without Walker's having to make invidious choices. Eric Brown congratulated him 'for having brought harmony into the situation.'[20] Yet Walker's involvement with the CWMF had not ended. In Britain several things were occurring that would cause him to become even more of a participant in its activities.

In January 1917, Lord Cawley of Prestwich resigned the chancellorship of the Duchy of Lancaster and Sir Edward Carson relinquished the directorship of the Department of Information: the first resignation left vacant a sinecure that carried cabinet status; the second an office that had the potential of becoming a ministry. Partly because of Beaverbrook's splendid work for the Canadians, and because of his participation on the Department of Information's Advisory Committee, Lloyd George offered him Carson's position. Having just declined a post in the Ministry of Munitions as director of finance, Beaverbrook wanted more: an actual portfolio, a position in the cabinet. The prime minister gave in, inviting Beaverbrook on 10 February 1918 to become the chancellor of the duchy responsible for a Ministry of Information created from the Department of Information.

The appointment was not universally welcomed. The King disapproved, and so did Austen Chamberlain, soon to join the war cabinet, who questioned the ethics of appointing a newspaperman (especially of the *Daily Express*) to ministerial office. Lloyd George was not himself happy with the appointment, but he could no longer ignore the energy and the ability of Beaverbrook, or his influence in and out of the House. As Frederick Guest, chief whip of the Liberal Party, put it to the prime minister: 'He is bitten with it, knows it and I want him anchored.'[21]

Lord Northcliffe took over propaganda in enemy countries and Lord Rothermere propaganda in neutral countries, until replaced by Robert Donald. Beaverbrook was responsible for propaganda in Allied countries and in the British Dominions. The organization he inherited was inefficient. Under C.F.G. Masterman and John Buchan, the British propaganda effort from 1914 to 1917 'was ill-organized' with 'wastage of material, duplication of effort, and slowness to exploit opportunity ...'[22] The ineffectiveness of British propaganda at Wellington House and then at the Department of Information offered the indefatigable Beaverbrook the kind of challenge for which he had been looking throughout 1917.

Beaverbrook was confident that the methods he had used for the Canadian War Records Office could be applied to the new ministry, and he felt also that British war painting could be modelled on the scheme that he, Rothermere, and Lima had devised for Canada. On 6 March, within two days of the establishment of the Ministry of Information, the British War Memorials Committee, with Masterman as chairman and members Arnold Bennett, Lord Rothermere, and Beaverbrook himself *ex officio*, came into being; Alfred Yockney became secretary-treasurer while Paul Konody, Robert Ross, Thomas Derrick, Muirhead Bone, and Campbell Dodgson were appointed art advisers. At its first meeting the committee and its advisers drew up a list of thirty artists. More names were added in June when Sir Alfred Mond and his group from the Imperial War Museum joined. When this happened, the British War Memorials Committee was renamed the British Pictorial Propaganda Committee.

Beaverbrook was proud both of the British scheme and of the credit it gave to his Canadian one. 'You may have seen,' he told Borden, 'that I have succeeded in setting up an Imperial War Memorial Fund modelled on the Canadian precedent.'[23] As with the Canadian arrangement, artists were given either temporary commissions and a salary according to their rank in exchange for their total output, or were paid for the completion of a specific work; a third category, retained from the Department of Information, provided artists with facilities in exchange for the ministry's right to purchase their work. The ministry adhered to Beaverbrook's view that artists must create from their experiences at the front. The pictures were to be 'of certain uniform sizes' so that 'the whole collection could be made to fit into and decorate a definite building,' to be called the Hall of Remembrance.[24] Money would be raised for purchases and materials through the showing of films and the organizing of exhibitions of paintings and photographs. It was also hoped that the Treasury would contribute to operating costs; until this happened, Rothermere and Beaverbrook personally guaranteed a sum of £20,000.[25]

Beaverbrook retained his responsibility for the CWRO and his membership on the CWMF's committee, but his energies, his administrative staff, his artists, and even his purse came to rest almost exclusively with the Ministry of Information. What little attention remained for the CWMF was largely devoted to the acquisition of historical pictures.

It was not difficult to procure important works of art during the war. Christie's and Sotheby's auction houses had closed down during the first ten months of the war, but when they reopened they, along with second-hand booksellers and private galleries, soon enjoyed a booming trade. Beaverbrook was among those who took advantage of the availability of pictures. Through private purchase and auction sales he was able to acquire for the CWMF during 1918 four works of significant historical interest to Canadians: Sir Thomas Lawrence's portrait of *Sir Alexander Mackenzie*, the first person to lead an overland expedition to the Pacific; Thomas Phillips' *Sir John Franklin*, the arctic explorer; George Romney's *Joseph Brant (Thayendanegea)*, the Mohawk chief; and Sir Joshua Reynolds' *Jeffrey, Lord Amherst, 1717–1779*, the first governor-general of British North America. Most important of all, however, was the Duke of Westminster's donation – a tribute to the part played by the Canadians in the war – of Benjamin West's famous painting *The Death of Wolfe*. These pictures at once raised the prestige of the CWMF collection. They also pleased Sir Edmund Walker, who had been 'trying to discover the whereabouts of the very celebrated portrait of Joseph Brant' as well as the portrait of Mackenzie by Lawrence.[26] Walker, who had long dreamed of establishing an historical gallery modelled on London's National Portrait Gallery, saw the purchases as a step in that direction.

The Death of Wolfe rose far above the other historical works in importance. The significance of West's painting lay neither in its historical accuracy (most of the people represented had not been present at Wolfe's death and were only included because, as C.P. Stacey has suggested, the artist 'chose them on the basis of a not altogether nominal admission fee') nor in the work's uniqueness (three subsequent copies were made).[27] The picture was artistically significant because it had 'caused a revolution in history painting by applying the same principles to the reconstruction of the recent past as he used for the recreation of scenes from classical antiquity.' It apotheosized 'a contemporary hero without the apparatus of allegory.'[28] Of even greater significance was its role in shaping the founding myth of English Canada, by depicting the martyrdom of the dauntless hero at the moment of his great victory for the Empire.

Sir Edmund Walker felt that West's picture was 'not very valuable artistically,' even though it was 'almost invaluable to Canada.' Beaverbrook saw the tradition begun by West being carried on by his CWMF artists. The painting, he wrote, gives 'us a means of comparing the new battle pictures with one of the greatest of the old, bringing the Second Battle of Ypres into touch with the Battle of the Plains of Abraham.'[29] The acquisition was a coup. And, being a gift, it cost the Fund nothing.

The CWMF did not, however, confine itself to acquiring historical pictures. More artists were attached to it early in 1918. Almost fifty-five artists of British, Canadian, Belgian, Australian, Danish, and Serbian nationality now worked for the Canadians. Organizing this number was no easy task for the Fund's secretary, J. Harold Watkins, now promoted to captain. CWMF studios sprang up in Earl's Court, South Kensington, Chelsea, and St John's Wood, and they overflowed with artists transposing their field sketches or portrait studies onto canvas. But while the majority could complete their commissions in Britain, some twenty-eight artists – thirteen of whom were Canadian – had to travel to the war zone. With so many artists working for the Fund, the list of those waiting to go to France was enormous. Attempting to ease the situation, Watkins asked the Permit Office to increase the authorized number of artists at the front from four to six. His first request was made in August, but it was not until October that he received permission.[30] Nothing, however, hampered the work of the CWMF so much as Beaverbrook's own British Pictorial Propaganda Committee.

Before that committee's inception the Canadians, who had employed virtually every prominent painter in Britain, were accused of stealing artists from the Department of Information. Yet as artist William Orpen, who made the accusation, admitted, the British and Canadian operations had in fact complemented each other. The British had wanted immediate propaganda, the Canadians permanent memorials. After Beaverbrook assumed the Ministry of Information, however, British war art policy shifted in emphasis from immediate propaganda to the accumulation of works for a permanent pictorial record. This pitched the British scheme against the Canadian. Yet there could be no rivalry over artists or advisers because Beaverbrook headed both organizations. His position as minister of information none the less became more important as the need for Canadian propaganda diminished, thanks to conscription's implementation after the victory of Sir Robert Borden's Unionist government in December 1917. The British scheme was also a new one to develop, and Beaverbrook's love and talent lay in creation and merger, not in administering something already 'on its legs.' So he simply drew ideas, money, and manpower from the CWMF and directed them towards the Pictorial Propaganda Committee.

Before assuming his post as minister of information, Beaverbrook had told both Sir Edmund Walker and Major Edmund Bristol of the Department of Militia and Defence that he expected the CWMF to earn £100,000, a sum that would enable him to make 'a wonderful collection of pictures.' The Fund's financial standing at the end of 1917, however, showed a balance of only £14,391. An anticipated third exhibition of photographs, along with additional numbers of CWRO publications scheduled for the spring, would enhance the Fund's standing; so, too, would the private donations and subscriptions promised by Beaverbrook and Rothermere. Following the establishment of the Ministry of Information, however, the third exhibition of Canadian war photographs scheduled for March was cancelled, reputedly at the request of the War Office, and in its place an exhibition of British war photographs was held.[31] Reporting the cancellation of the Canadian exhibition, the CWRO's *Canadian Daily Record* blandly announced on 5 March 1918 that the Canadian organization wished to devote its energy to an exhibition of colour photographs to 'acquaint the people of Britain and the world with what the British soldiers were doing.'

The CWMF had lost its major source of revenue; and Beaverbrook and Rothermere did not come forward with their own money or attempt to raise any through private subscription. By May the Fund was 'short of money.' 'Until more profits had been made,' Beaverbrook told Eric Brown, 'we are not free to commit ourselves to any further expenditure.'[32]

The CWRO's photography facilities and ideas were not all that Beaverbrook borrowed for the Pictorial Propaganda Committee. When he established the new ministry at the Howard Hotel in the Strand, he took his private secretary, S.W. Alexander; his art adviser, Paul Konody; the Canadian War Records officers Captain W. Holt White and Sir Bertram Lima; and the CWMF's chairman, Lord Rothermere. Even the Fund's secretary, J. Harold Watkins, became a liaison officer for the British outfit.

Many of the artists also divided their time between the two organizations. Of the Pictorial Propaganda Committee's original list of thirty artists, Anna Airy, Clare Atwood, David Cameron, George Clausen, Augustus John, Wyndham Lewis, Algernon Talmage, William Wood, Charles Sims, William Roberts, and many others were already employed by the Canadians. This did not work to the CWMF's advantage. Augustus John failed to take his forty-foot mural beyond cartoon stage partly because he was sent by the Pictorial Propaganda Committee to paint portraits at the Paris Peace Conference. John Lavery, also at work for the British, never got around to serious business for the Canadians until after the war; by the time *Troops Embarking at Southampton for the Western Front* was finished, no funds remained to purchase it.[33]

Even pictures went from one side to the other. William Wood's painting of an aerodrome in Salonika, acquired by the CWMF early in 1918, was given to Sir Alfred Mond at the Imperial War Museum in June (while no Canadian contingent fought in the eastern Mediterranean, the Number One Canadian Stationary Hospital was located at Lembet Camp in Salonika). *A Howitzer in Action at Roisel*, painted by William Rothenstein, was also transferred to the Imperial War Museum.[34]

The attrition of funds, the lending of administrative and advisory staff as well as of artists, and in a few cases the transfer of works, thwarted the CWMF's expansion. Yet while the Fund was being eroded in England, the employment of artists to paint the home front in Canada was just getting under way.

Now that Beaverbrook's time and energies were being devoted to the Ministry of Information, the CWMF and the CWRO became an albatross around his neck. To make matters worse, questions were again raised in the Canadian House of Commons about government funding of the CWRO, about 'the nature of services rendered,' and about 'the nature of the campaign of propaganda.' Borden, however, did come to Beaverbrook's defence: he assured the House that the Canadian War Records Officer received no salary and that apart from an initial £25,000 the CWRO had never been given any money by the government. He did, nevertheless, ask Beaverbrook for a report on the CWRO and its operation, and Beaverbrook was not pleased, feeling that he had already been given little credit for his activities. Borden mollified him to some extent a few weeks later by praising his work, particularly his purchase of historical pictures.[35] But further difficulties arose in the spring of 1918 when Beaverbrook decided to carry out his earlier plans of extending the CWMF's activities to the Dominion. The English artist Harold Gilman prepared to sail for Canada in the spring for the purpose of recording wartime activity in Halifax harbour. This was an insensitive move, one against which Walker had warned Beaverbrook in December. When news of Gilman's imminent departure reached Canadian artists, they were once again 'up in arms.'

Beaverbrook wished 'to avoid all criticism,' but he did not cancel Gilman's orders. Instead, he attached Canadian artist Captain Kenneth Forbes to the CWMF and promised an annoyed Sir Edmund Walker not to send the British artist Charles Ginner in Gilman's wake. He also asked Walker to put forward the names of Canadians who might be prepared to work for the British scheme. This was the smooth co-opter at work – a strategy further extended when he again offered Walker greater responsibility in the CWMF. This time his supplications for help were backed by promises of monetary assistance: 'desire have largest possible proportion of whole work done by Canadian artists. Anything you do in connection with employment Canadian artists will be approved by Committee and necessary funds will be placed at your disposal.'[36]

Beaverbrook had already asked Walker to purchase any Canadian pictures of home front activities that came onto the market. Before that, he had invited him to suggest subjects and artists who could produce work relating to the same theme. But Walker had remained determined not to be responsible 'as far as the public here is concerned, for the selection of Canadian artists,' and he turned to Wyly Grier and C.W. Jefferys for names and subjects which would then be passed on to Beaverbrook for final approval (he did play a part in selecting Grier himself as Canada's best known portraitist to paint General S.C. Mewburn's portrait, but only after receiving 'rubber-stamp-approval' from Beaverbrook). Despite his caution, Walker was slowly being drawn into the CWMF. The artists saw him as a channel to Beaverbrook, someone to whom they could complain about the employment of Gilman or through whom they might secure employment. Beaverbrook, for his part, saw Walker as his successor. Moving the Fund to Canada under his direction would, moreover, release artists, administrators, and advisers for employment in the British scheme.

Walker was still reluctant to become involved, and even wondered about the ability of Canadian artists to fulfil commissions (he warned Beaverbrook that he should see how Varley, Cullen, Beatty, and Simpson performed before enlarging the number of Canadian participants). He had, on the other hand, already mentioned the possibility of giving work to several Canadian artists and felt 'the situation would be very embarrassing to me' if they were not employed.[37]

Beaverbrook had made it clear in his cable of 20 May that the CWMF was moving onto Canadian territory; it was, that is, going to occupy Walker's own ground. Funds from the CWRO exhibitions of photography in Canada and the United States were even promised to support a Canadian-based operation. Walker thus received from Beaverbrook an offer he could ill afford to refuse: money for acquisitions. Following Beaverbrook's cable, he received a cheque for $5,000 and following that another for $10,000, with promises of more. With funds in hand, amounting to half again that of the National Gallery's annual budget, Walker's direct and active involvement in the affairs of the CWMF began. It had, after all, been a long time since he had had money for acquisitions. As he later put it to a friend, 'fortunately

I was able to control a large amount of money raised in England ... and ... give some of the Canadian artists a chance to do work both in France and at home.'[38]

Walker moved with characteristic caution. In June 1918 he employed two artists: Grier to paint the above-mentioned portrait of General Mewburn and Arthur Lismer to complete a set of lithographs of Halifax harbour. The scope of his activities was, none the less, gradually broadened. He asked Beaverbrook to send him a list of the subjects and sizes of the CWMF's work. He consulted Colonel A.[?]C. Osborne about artists' permits for sketching in military establishments, and asked Eric Brown about Grier's and Jefferys' suggestions for subjects and artists.[39] His usual salmon-fishing holiday in Newfoundland in June interrupted these activities, but when he returned in July he commissioned Frank Johnston to make studies of Canadian flying schools and Jefferys to sketch troops drilling on the grounds of the University of Toronto. But, though by early July Beaverbrook's $10,000 had been added to the original $5,000, Walker commissioned no further artists until September.

The list presented by Grier and Jefferys was to provide the basis for both subjects and artists. Eric Brown, now into the scheme with all the enthusiasm that the availability of patronage money commanded, played no small part in suggesting additional themes for consideration. 'Coming into Toronto I saw shipbuilding going on at the harbour front,' he told Toronto artist Robert Gagen, 'and it struck me there was material for a good war records picture.' At Toronto's Canadian National Exhibition he noticed the women munition workers in their overalls; surely, he told sculptor Frances Loring, 'they were very fine subjects for a series of small bronzes.' Arthur Crisp learned from Brown that 'the last time I was in Boston I was immensely interested to see recruiting on the Common enlisting British soliders'; and a few weeks later Crisp in fact travelled from his New York home to Boston to record the scene.[40]

One might have thought from the list of subjects to be painted that wartime production, which had brought the Canadian economy out of its pre-war slump giving it aircraft, munitions, and shipbuilding industries, was restricted to one area of the country: central Canada. One might have thought, too, that every recruit in the CEF was trained at Valcartier or Camp Borden and drilled on the lawns of the University of Toronto. There was nothing of the wheat production that allowed prairie farmers to keep their sons out of the trenches; nothing of the training camps in British Columbia and Alberta; nothing of the copper and nickel mines on the Canadian Shield; and nothing of munition production in the provinces east and west of Ontario and Quebec (these provinces had, indeed, to fight hard with the Imperial Munitions Board to get what contracts they had managed to secure).

This central Canadian exclusiveness was characteristic of the Brown/Walker pattern of patronage. The artists who worked for the CWMF in Canada came almost entirely from the art societies of anglophone Montreal and Toronto. No Maritime artist (Lismer, a temporary resident of Halifax, hardly counted) and no Westerners got access to the CWMF largesse. When there was work to be done outside the Toronto–Montreal–Ottawa triangle, someone was sent from central Canada. 'Our subjects would be incomplete without a series of winter pictures of lumbering either for shipbuilding or aeroplanes,' Brown told Walker, who then suggested that a central Canadian artist be sent to Prince Rupert in British Columbia. A portrait of Private M.J. O'Rourke, VC, in Vancouver was required, but as Walker told Beaverbrook 'in confidence,' 'there is practically no portrait painter of quality in the West'[41] – the picture was done by Fosbery from a photograph.

Equally striking, no French-Canadian artists were hired (Suzor-Côté refused to join the scheme).

Walker boasted that the artists were paid salaries 'no higher than those earned by skilled mechanics.'[42] Most received a set fee plus expenses, or were put on a monthly salary of $250. For this they produced sketches, in keeping with Walker's and Brown's antipathy to the commissioning of finished works. If these met with the approval of Walker and Brown, a new fee was established for a canvas.

It was Brown who most often examined the work; in many ways his functions were similar to Konody's. As for Walker, he secured artists' passes from militia and naval authorities, from the Royal Air Force, and from the Imperial Munitions Board. Beaverbrook, still trying to draw him into the scheme as fully as possible, suggested that he form a committee to handle its affairs in Canada. Upon his refusal, his name was added, along with Lady Perley's, to the general committee of the CWMF; in this way Walker continued to avoid what from his point of view would have been too great a measure of responsibility for its operations in Canada.

In their concern to compile a comprehensive record of war activity in Canada, Brown and Walker were intent on drawing on the talents of the most distinguished Canadian artists. When the wealthy young painter, Lawren Harris, refused to join the CWMF, they were furious. 'We want the War memorial stuff to be the very finest collection of commissioned art that Canada has produced,' Brown told Harris, 'and if it is not to include any of your work, it will be lacking to that extent.'[43] Harris, who had left the army after suffering a nervous breakdown, stood firm in his belief that the work ought to be done by the less established and less financially well-off artists. Brown had purchased Harris' pictures for the National Gallery and was warming up to the young Canadian 'moderns'; he felt let down and only reluctantly struck Harris' name off the list.

Walker and Brown soon discovered that their participation in the CWMF gave them more than funds. It was the first time that either man had worked so closely with the art community. Previously they had bought Canadian pictures largely from exhibitions or through dealers. Now they were visiting studios and commissioning pictures directly. It was the first time, too, that public art patronage in Canada had been directed exclusively towards Canadian artists. As a result their opinion of Canadian art and artists began to change. Like almost everyone else in the English-speaking part of the country, they began to be caught up in the new sense of identity being heightened by Canada's participation in the war. They were anxious to show that Canada's artists could do as well painting munition factories as her soldiers had done fighting at Vimy Ridge.

It was particularly fortunate that they were involved in the painting of home front activity, for Brown especially continued to doubt there was much point in dealing with the war itself on canvas. In two essays – 'Painting the War at Home' and 'Canadian War Art to Order' – he made it quite clear that he had not changed his thoughts about the unpictorial qualities of modern warfare. The home front, however, was quite another matter. As a subject for art, it 'had vastly more pictorial possibilities than the front line trenches.' Future Canadians would look back upon the cutting of lumber by the Canadian Forestry Corps in Windsor Great Park with more interest than upon 'a no-man's land nocturn.' Home front pictures formed 'a preface, as it were, to the sterner epic which was being written within the sound of guns.' They also possessed their own pictorial quality: Mabel May's sketches of munition plants were 'sufficiently striking in design and explanatory of various munitions processes to be worthy of enlarging'; a snow scene of lumbering 'could be treated in a large and decorative way'; and Manly MacDonald's landscape paintings incorporating farm workers could be 'picturesque.' Such themes not only fit into preconceived decorative categories, but according to Brown they possessed a heroic quality of their own. 'Men, women, and girls laboured day and night like Trojans' in Montreal munition factories; young women workers offered 'a beauty of subject worthy of fifth century Greece'; the Toronto flying schools 'were an epic in themselves.' Even recruits could be portrayed as 'future heroes of world famous activities.'[44]

The painting of war was thus, in Brown's view, no longer to be concerned only with the depiction of battles. It ought to encompass 'every phase of the changed life of the people during the great struggle, from the farmer girls plowing in the fields to the sittings of the War Cabinet, and from Canadian lumbermen cutting historic timber in Windsor Park to the camouflaging of soldiers' huts behind the lines in France.'[45] It ought, that is, to be deployed not only in celebration of the nation in conflict; it had also to serve as a demonstration of the qualities that would make it strong and unyielding in peacetime. It must, in sum, show not only that the nation could fight but also that, once the war was over, it could live in peace, prosperity, and growth, thanks to the very qualities of human enterprise and commitment that were making successful prosecution of the war possible.

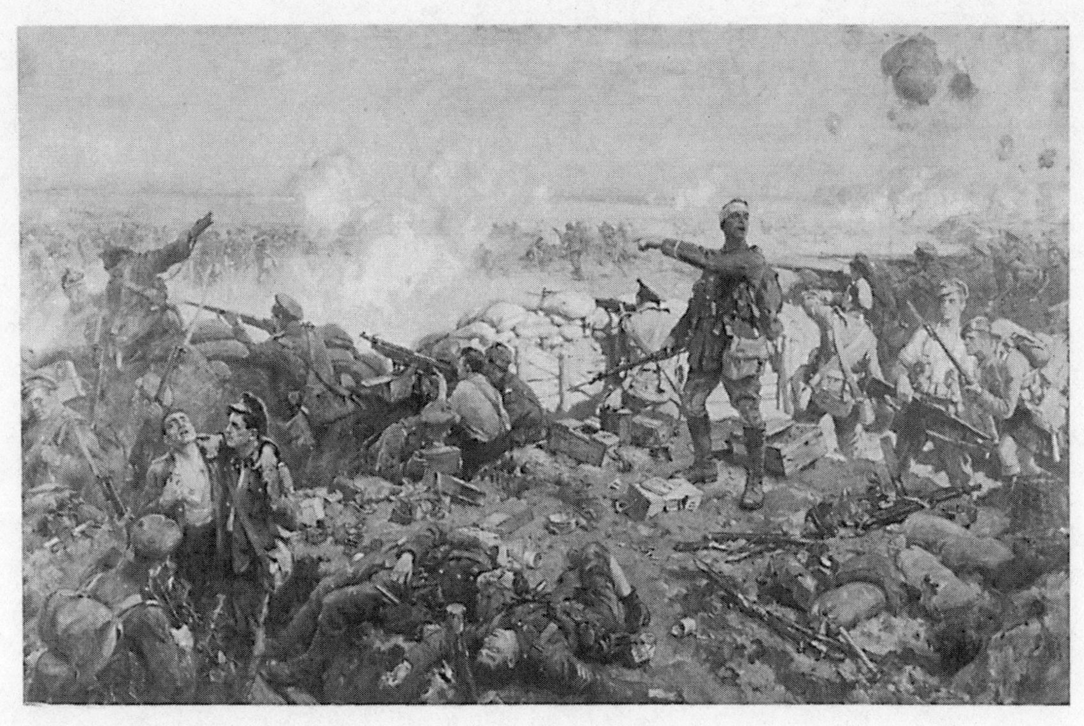

1 Richard Jack, *The Second Battle of Ypres, 22 April to 25 May, 1915*
canvas 146 × 234¹/₂ in / 371 × 596 cm CWM 8179

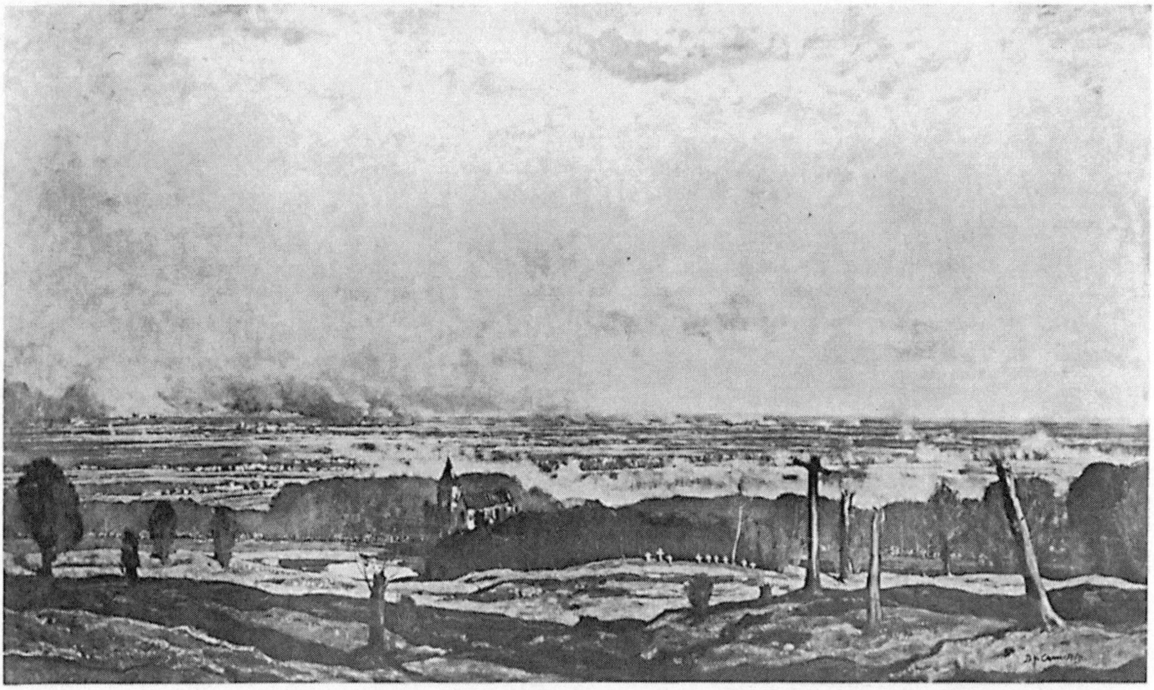

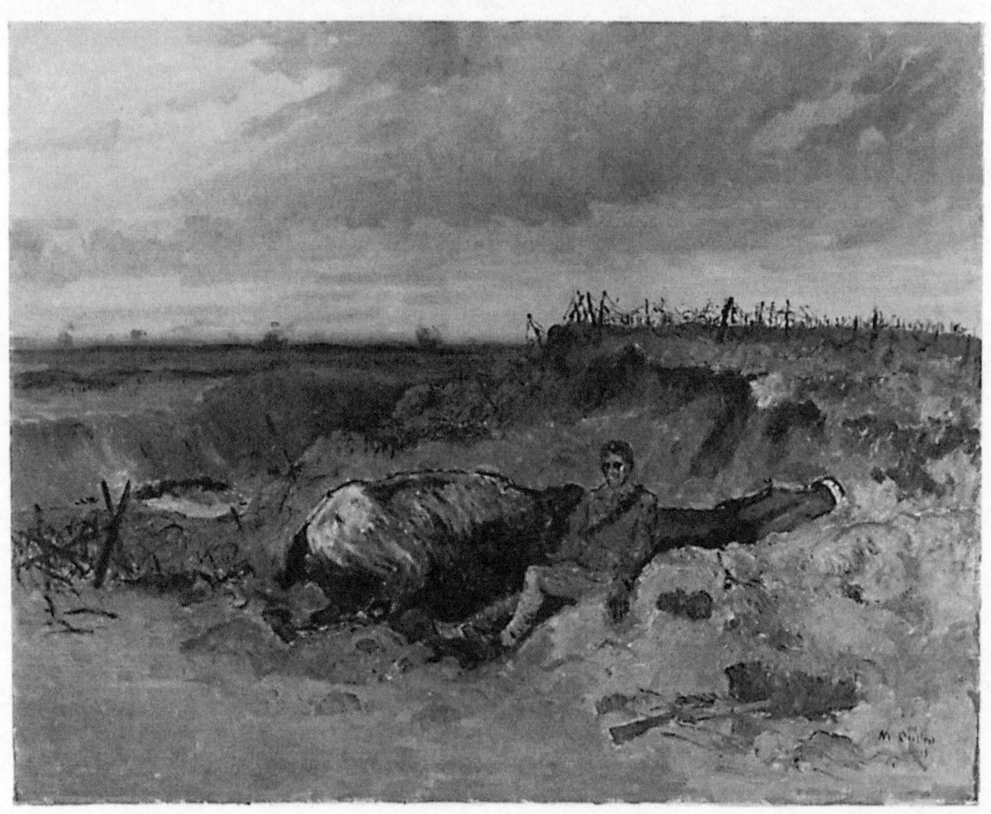

2 David Cameron, *Flanders from Kemmel*
canvas 77$^1/_2$ × 132$^1/_4$ in / 197 × 336 cm CWM 8129

3 Maurice Cullen, *Dead Horse and Rider in a Trench*
canvas 44 × 56 in / 112 × 142 cm CWM 8140

4 Maurice Cullen, *Ruined Village, France*
canvas 20 × 25$^1/_2$ in / 51 × 65 cm CWM 8144

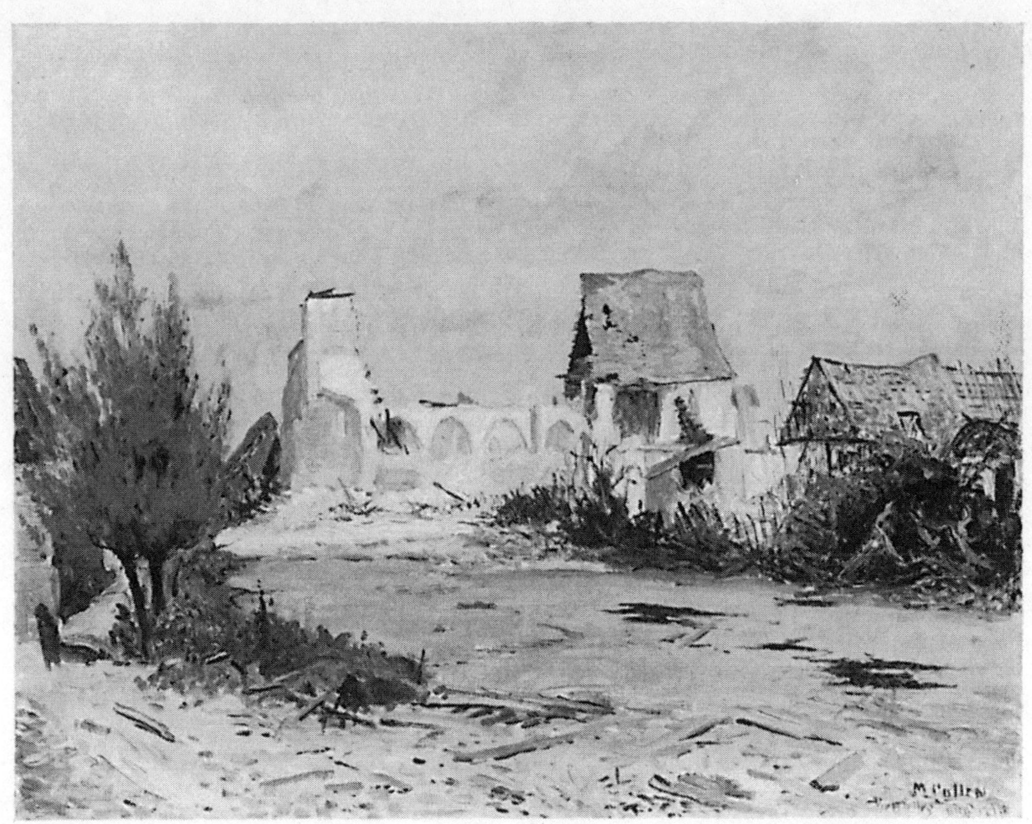

5 J.W. Beatty, *Liévin from Vimy Ridge*
canvas 30 × 40 in / 76 × 102 cm CWM 8103

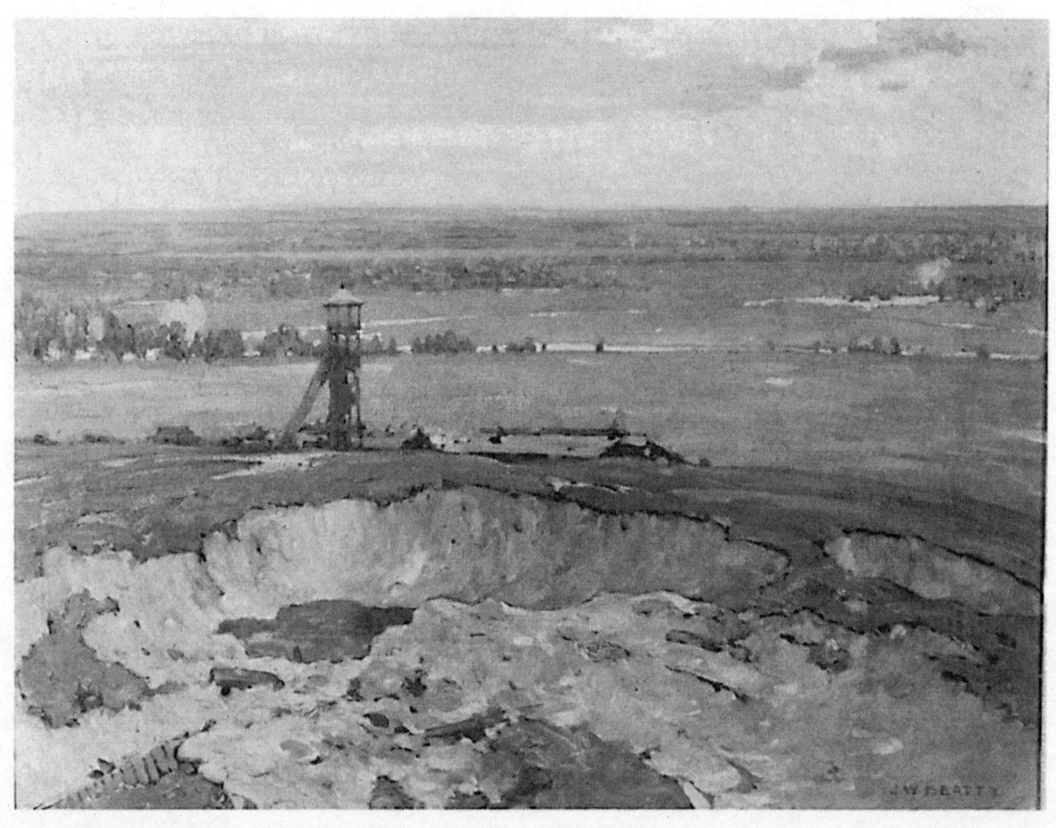

6 Paul Nash, *Void*

canvas 28 × 36¹/₈ in / 71 × 92 cm NGC 8650

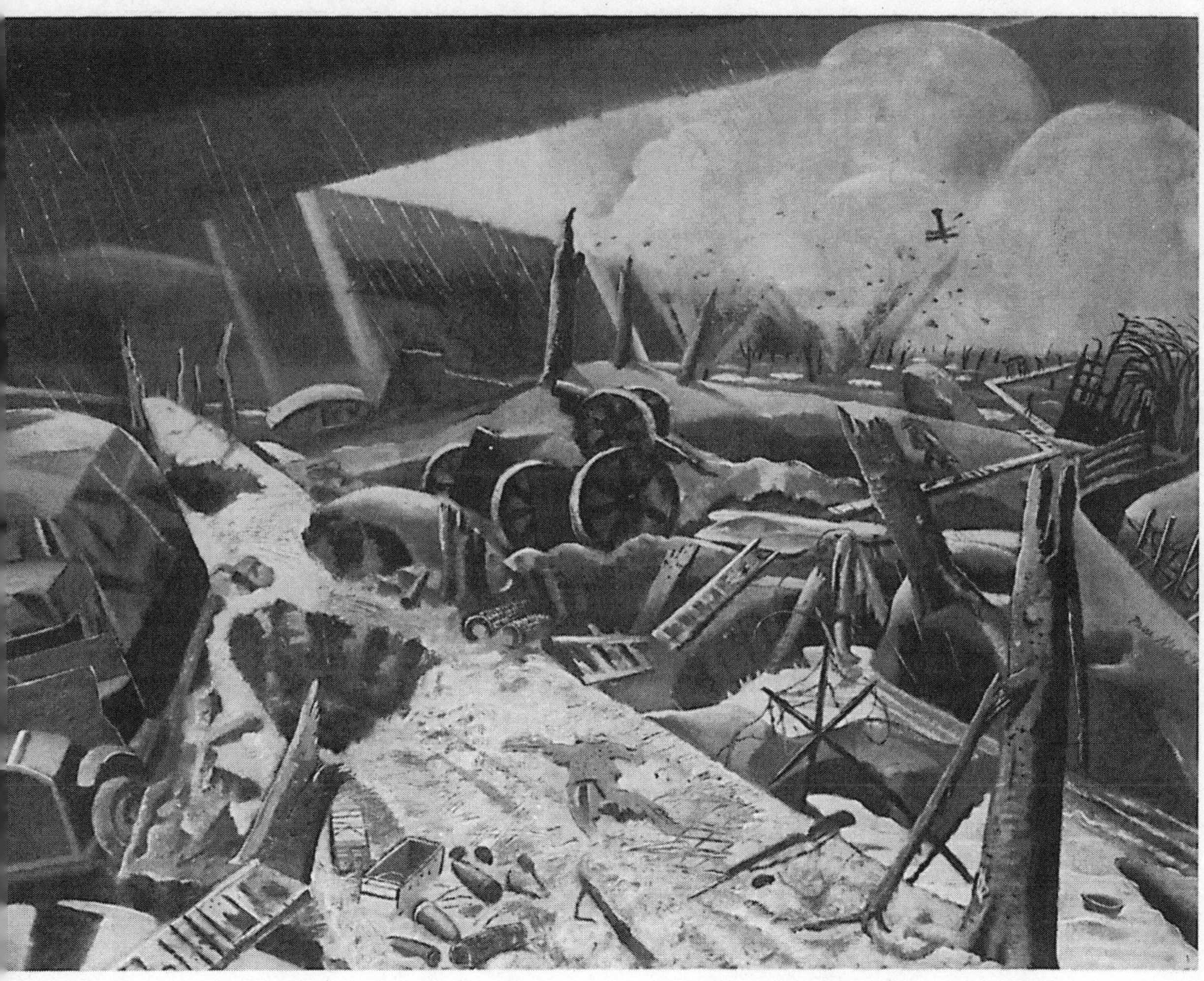

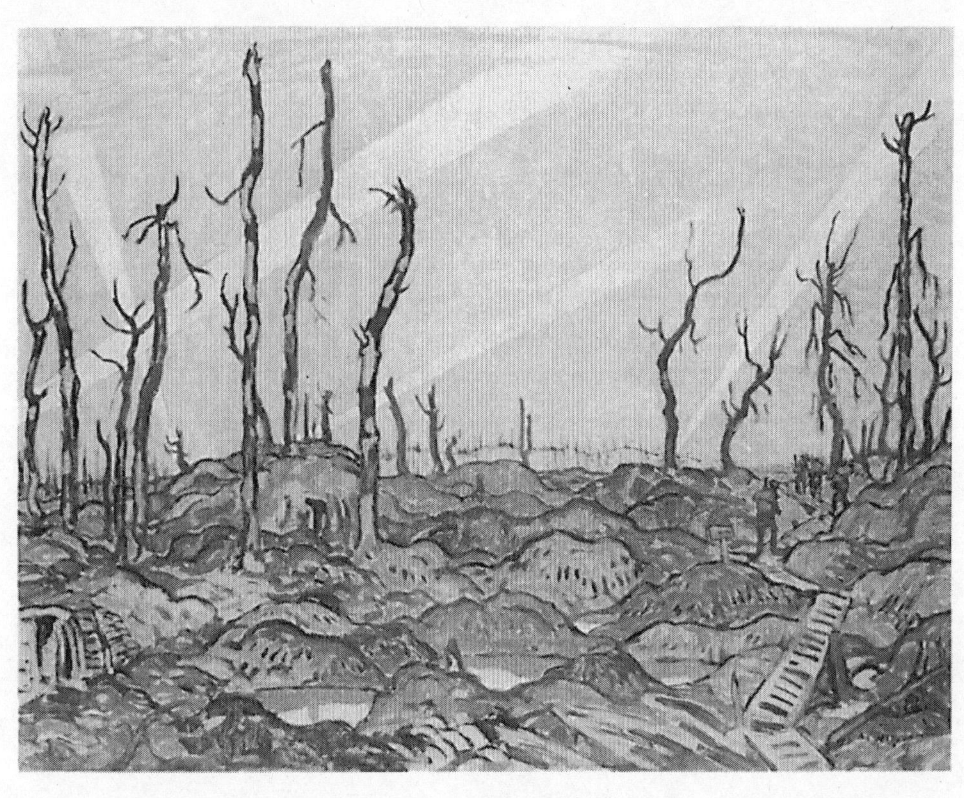

7 A.Y. Jackson, *A Copse, Evening*
canvas 34 x 44 in / 86 x 112 cm CWM 8204

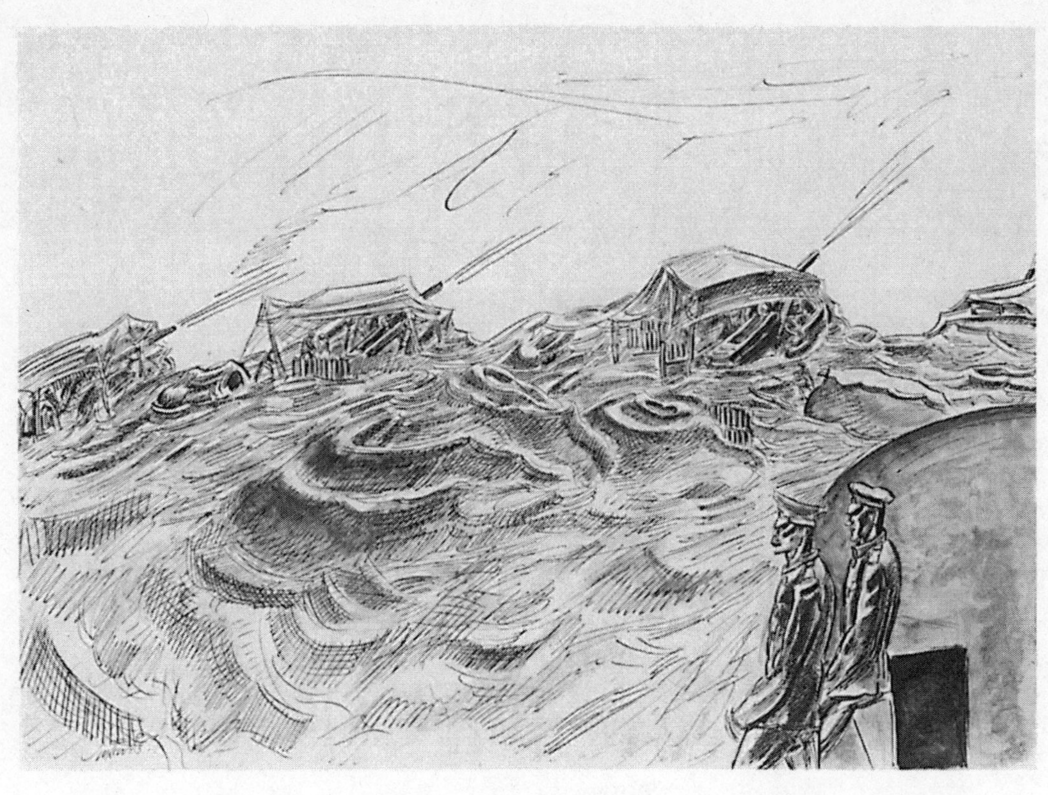

8 Percy Wyndham Lewis, *A Canadian Gun Pit*
  ink and watercolour 14 x 20 in / 36 x 51 cm NGC 8357

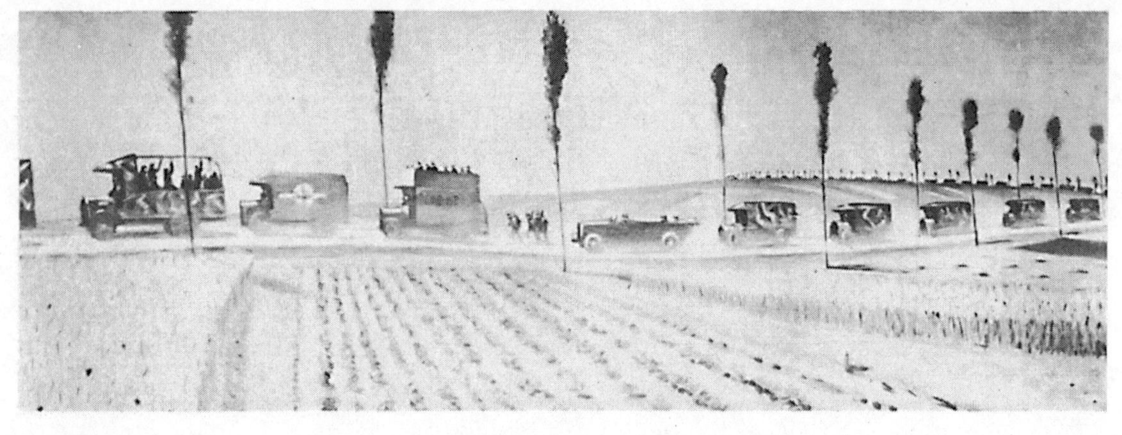

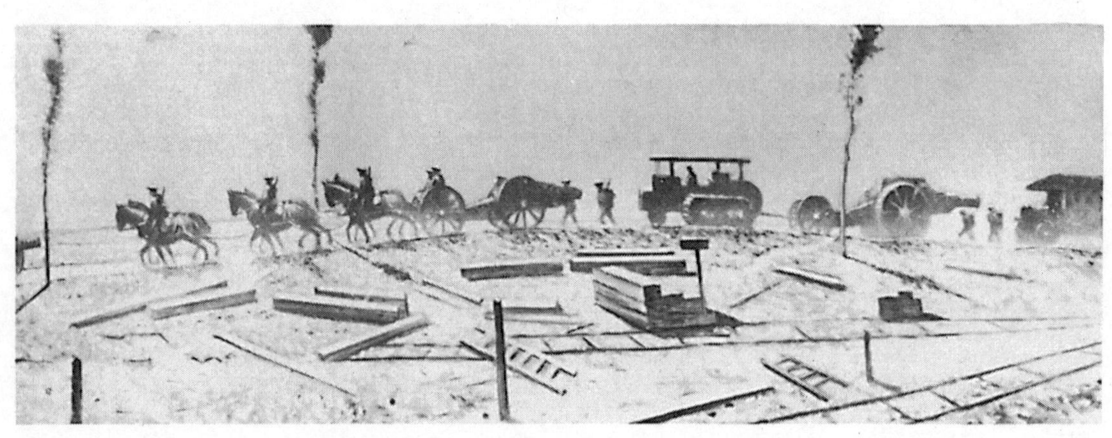

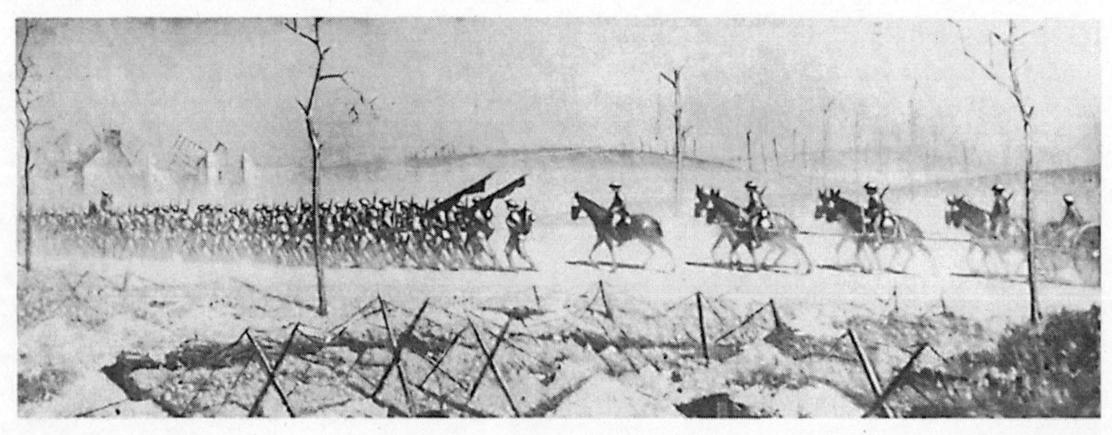

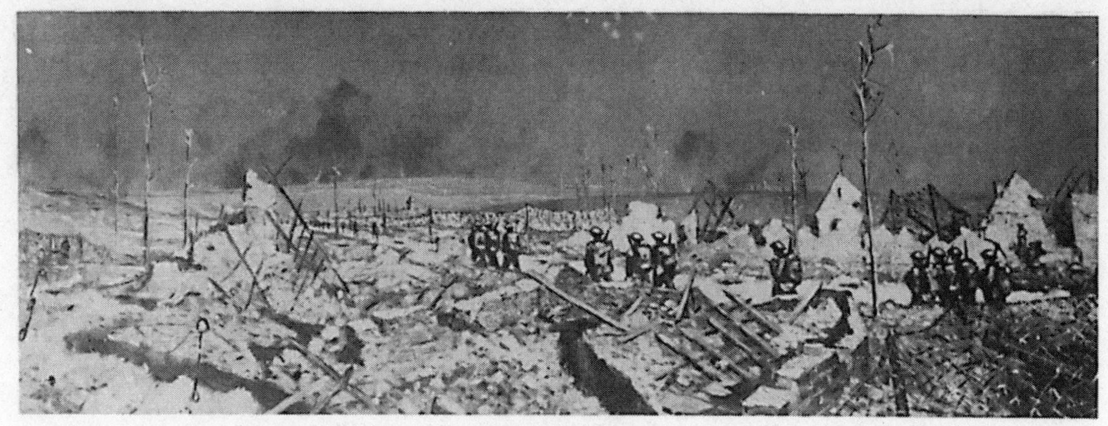

13 F.H. Varley, *The Sunken Road*
    canvas 52 × 64½ in / 132 × 164 cm CWM 8912

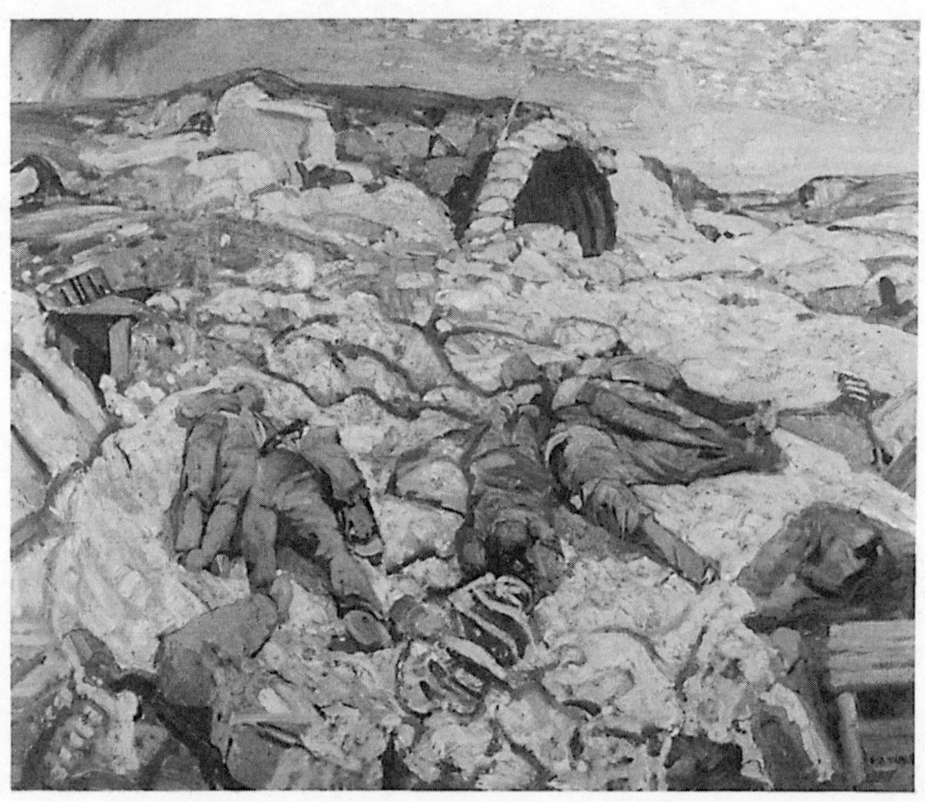

14 The battlefield after a Canadian charge, October 1916
Public Archives of Canada PA-868

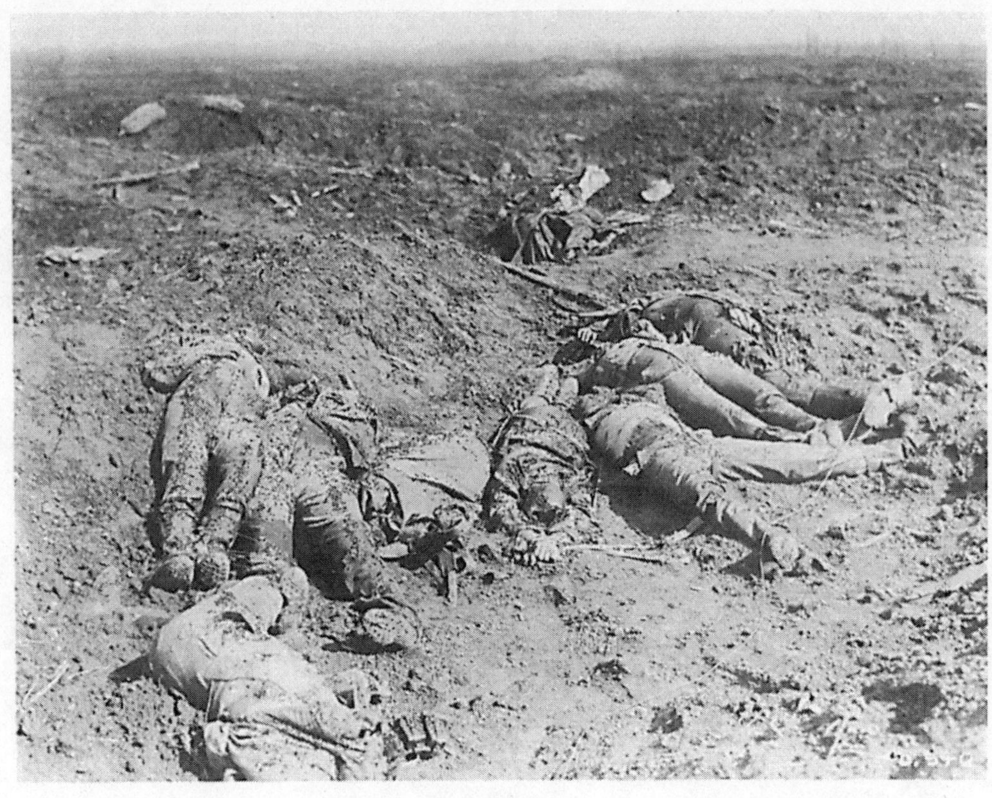

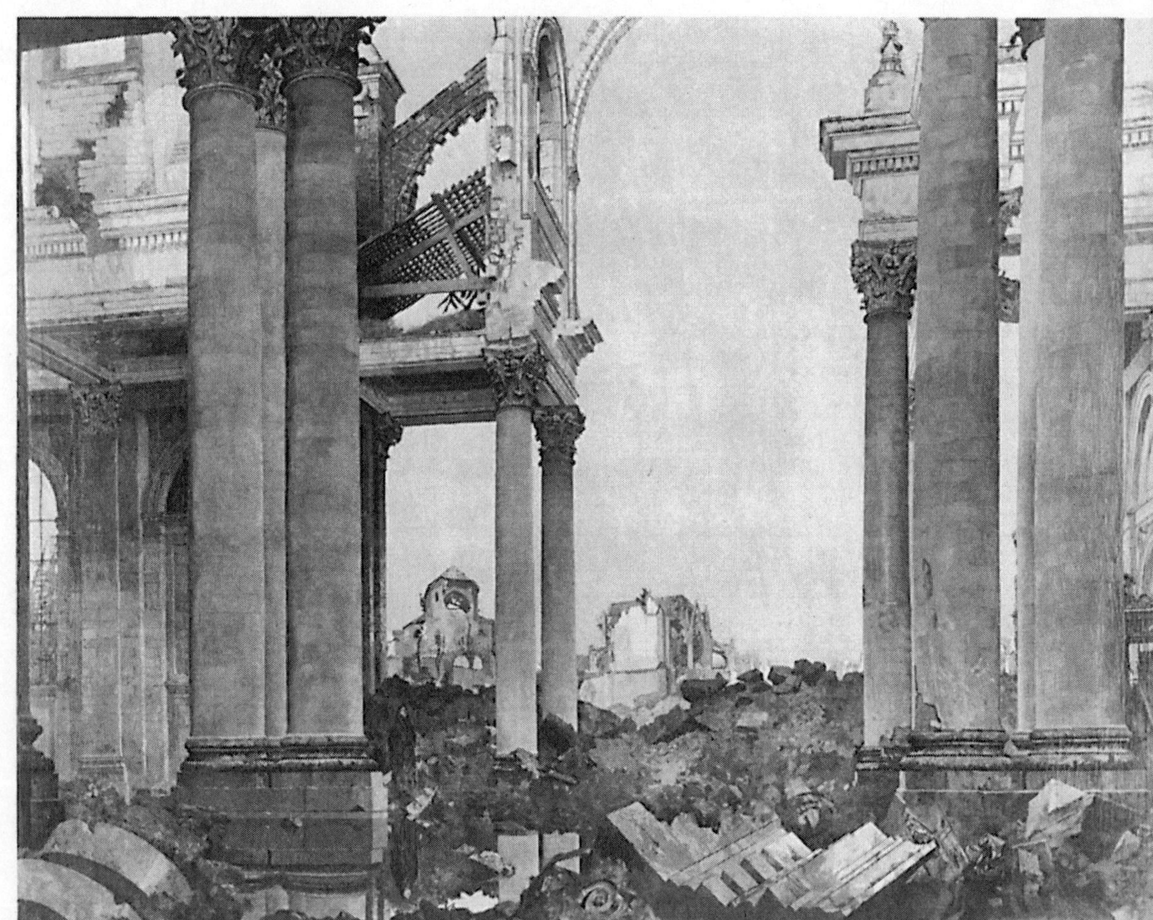

15 James Kerr-Lawson, *Arras, the Dead City*
    canvas 109 x 145 in / 227 x 368 cm CWM (Senate) 8353

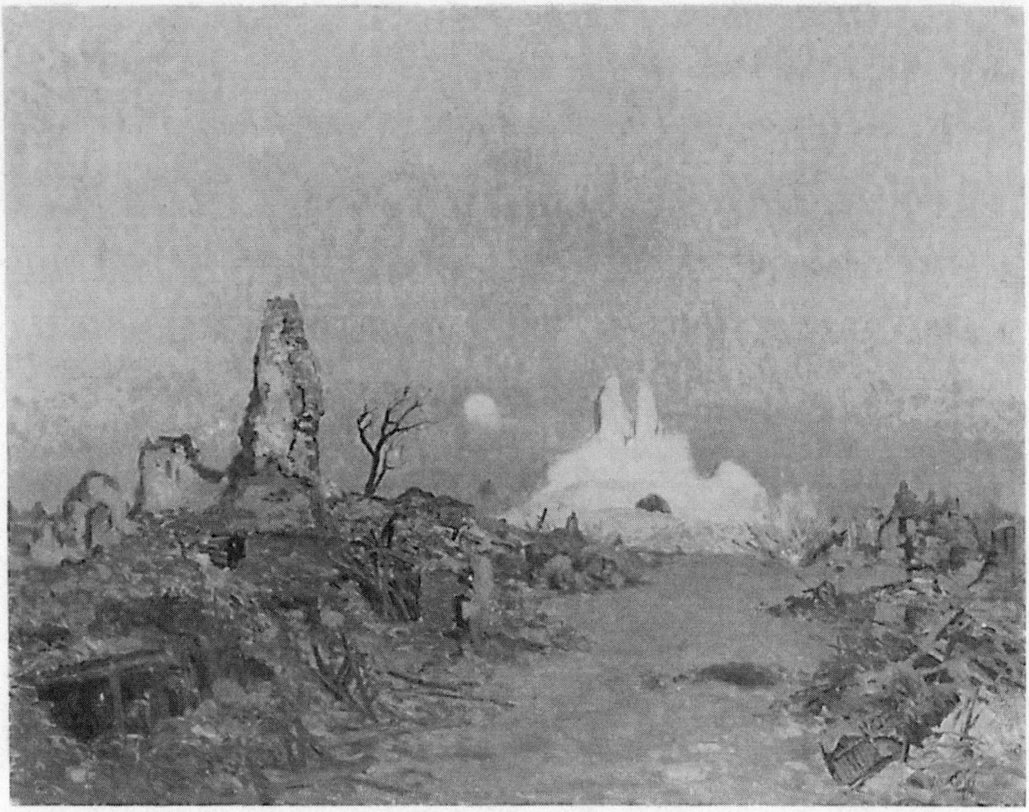

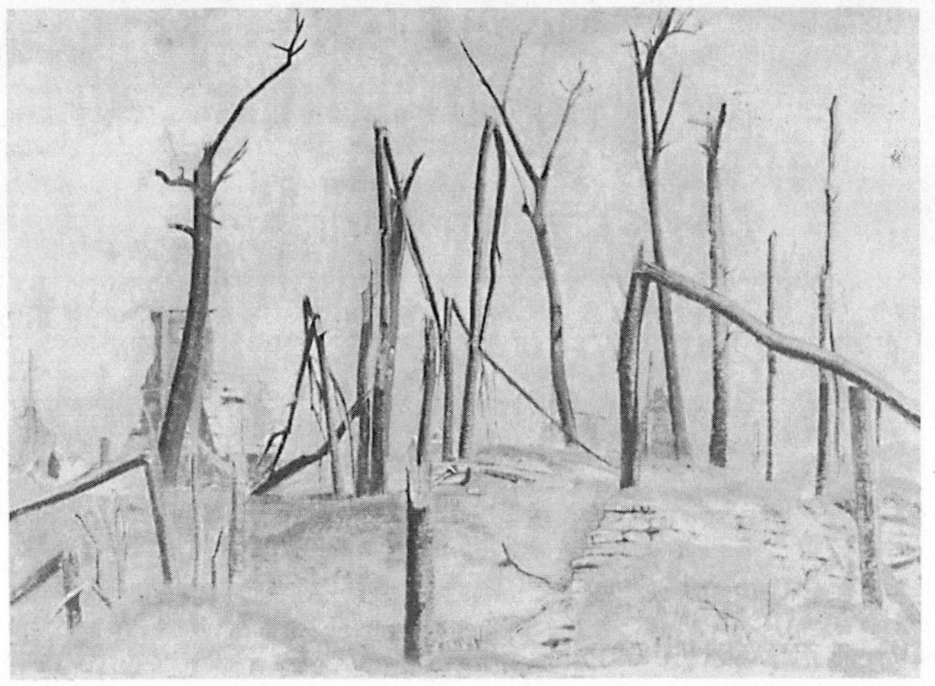

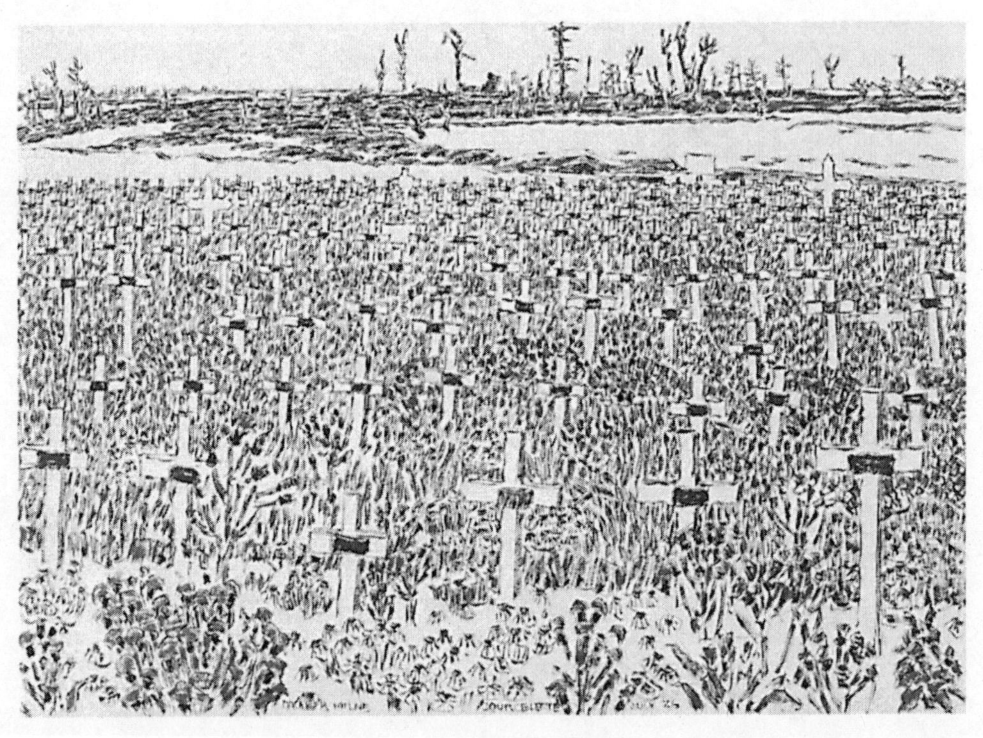

18 David Milne, *Courcelette from the Cemetery*
watercolour 13⅞ × 19⅞ in / 35 × 50 cm NGC 8478

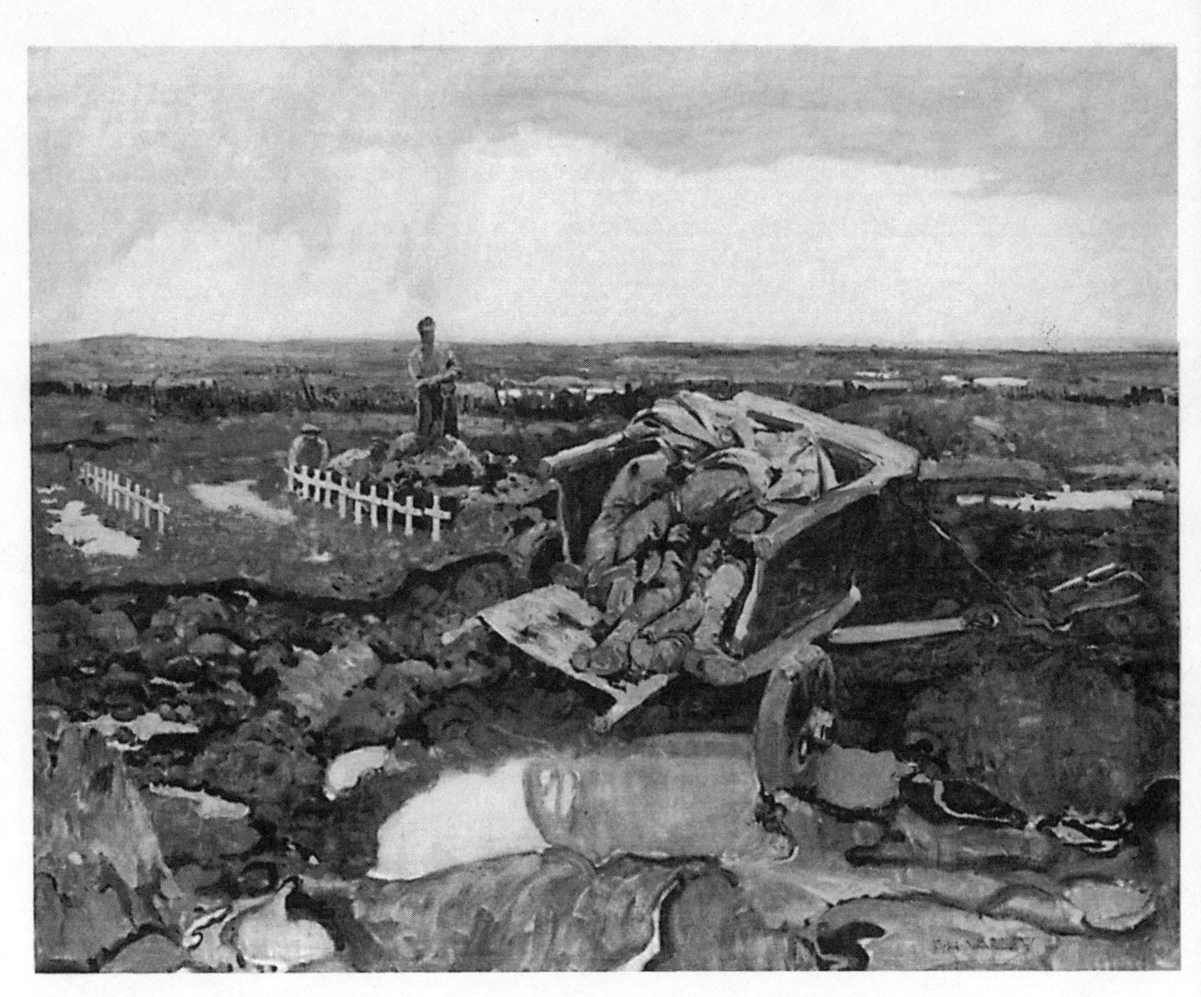

19 F.H. Varley, *For What?* canvas 58¹⁄₄ × 72¹⁄₄ in / 148 × 184 cm CWM 8911

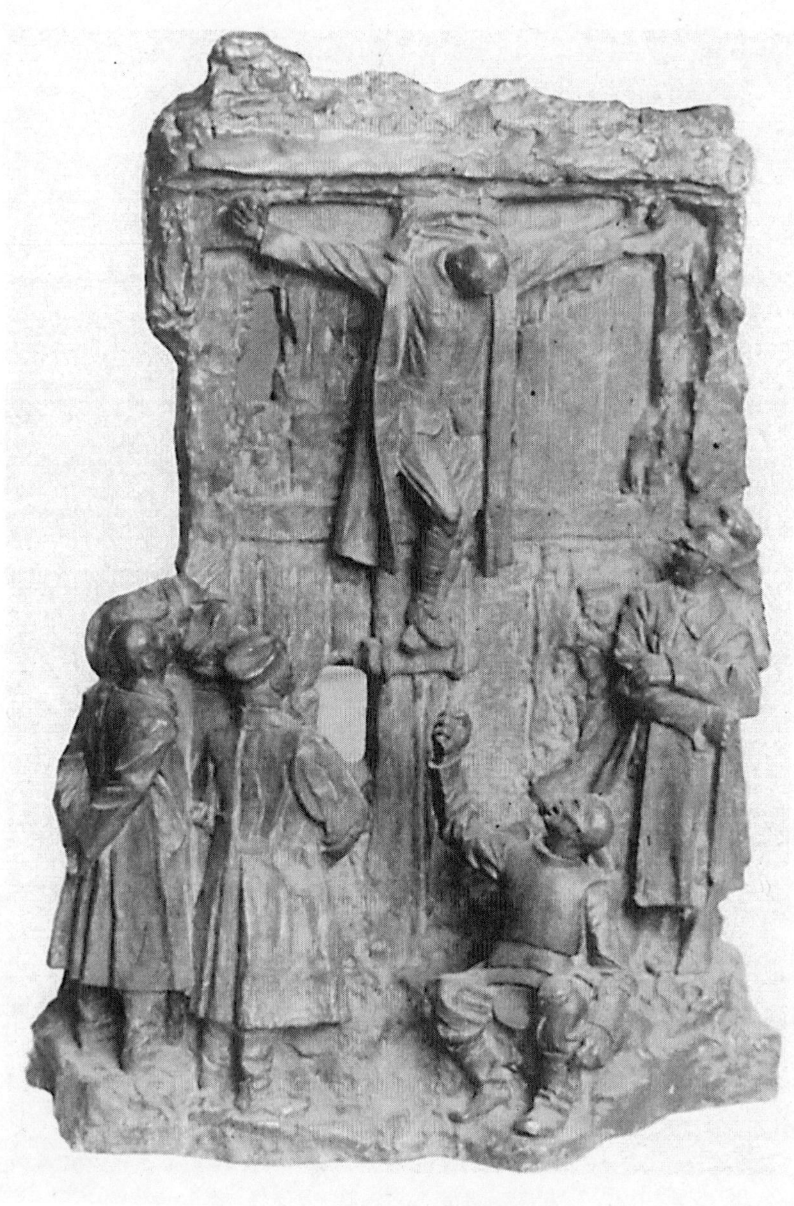

20 Derwent Wood, *Canada's Golgotha*
bronze 32 x 25 in / 81 x 64 cm CWM 8940

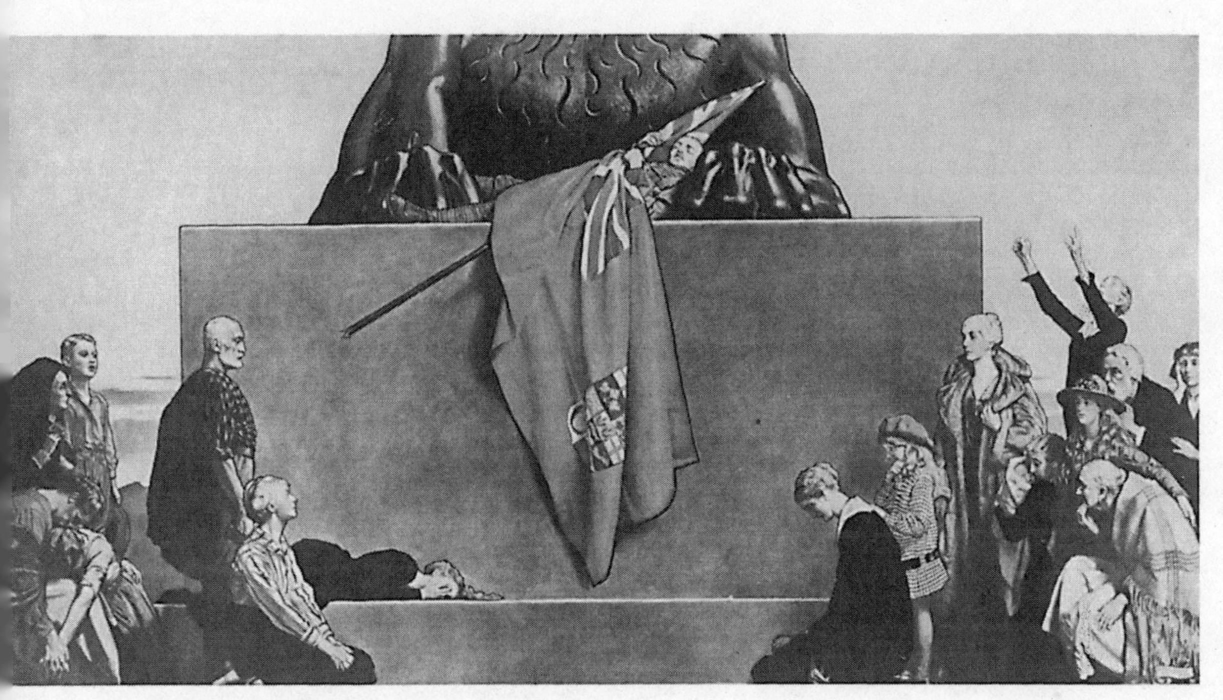

21 John Byam Lister Shaw, *The Flag*
   canvas 78 × 144 in / 198 × 366 cm CWM 8796

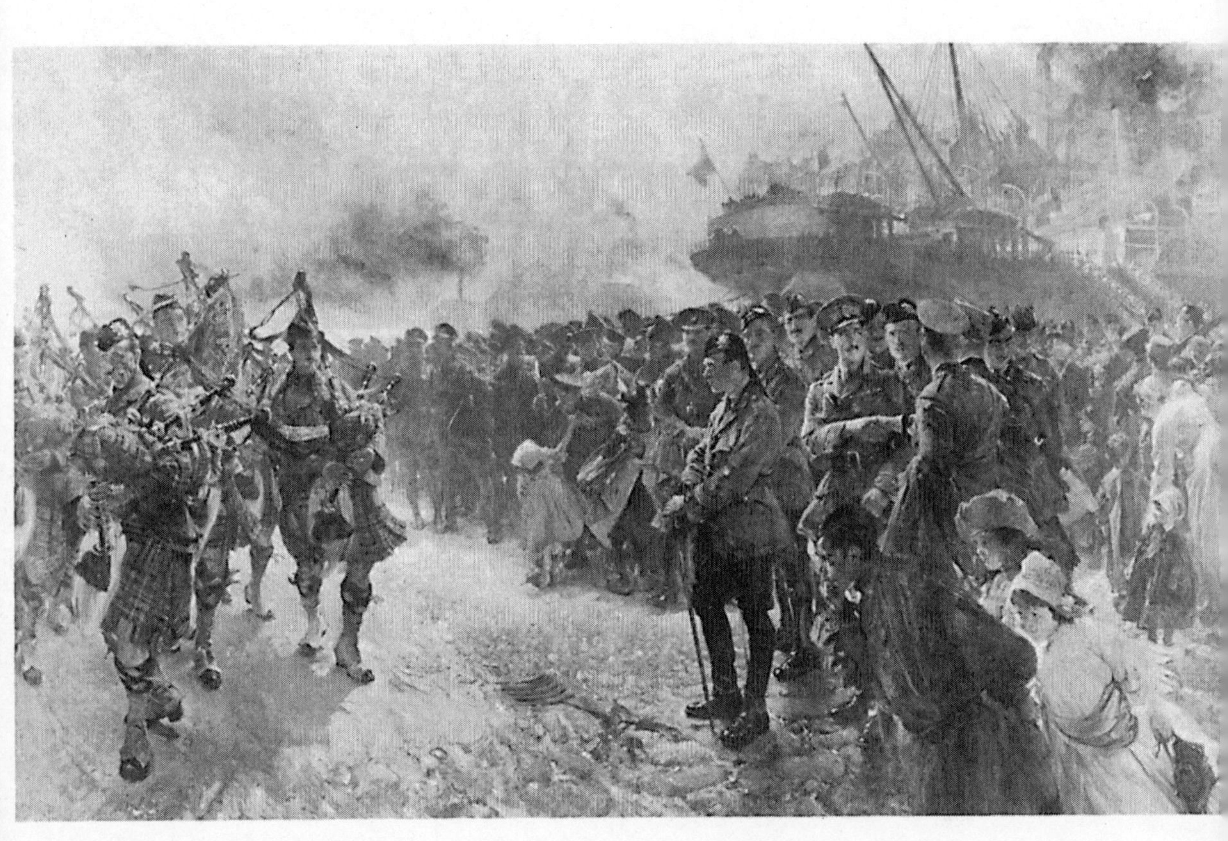

22 Edgar Bundy, *Landing of the First Canadian Division at Saint-Nazaire, 1915*
canvas 102 × 180 in / 259 × 457 cm CWM (Senate) 8121

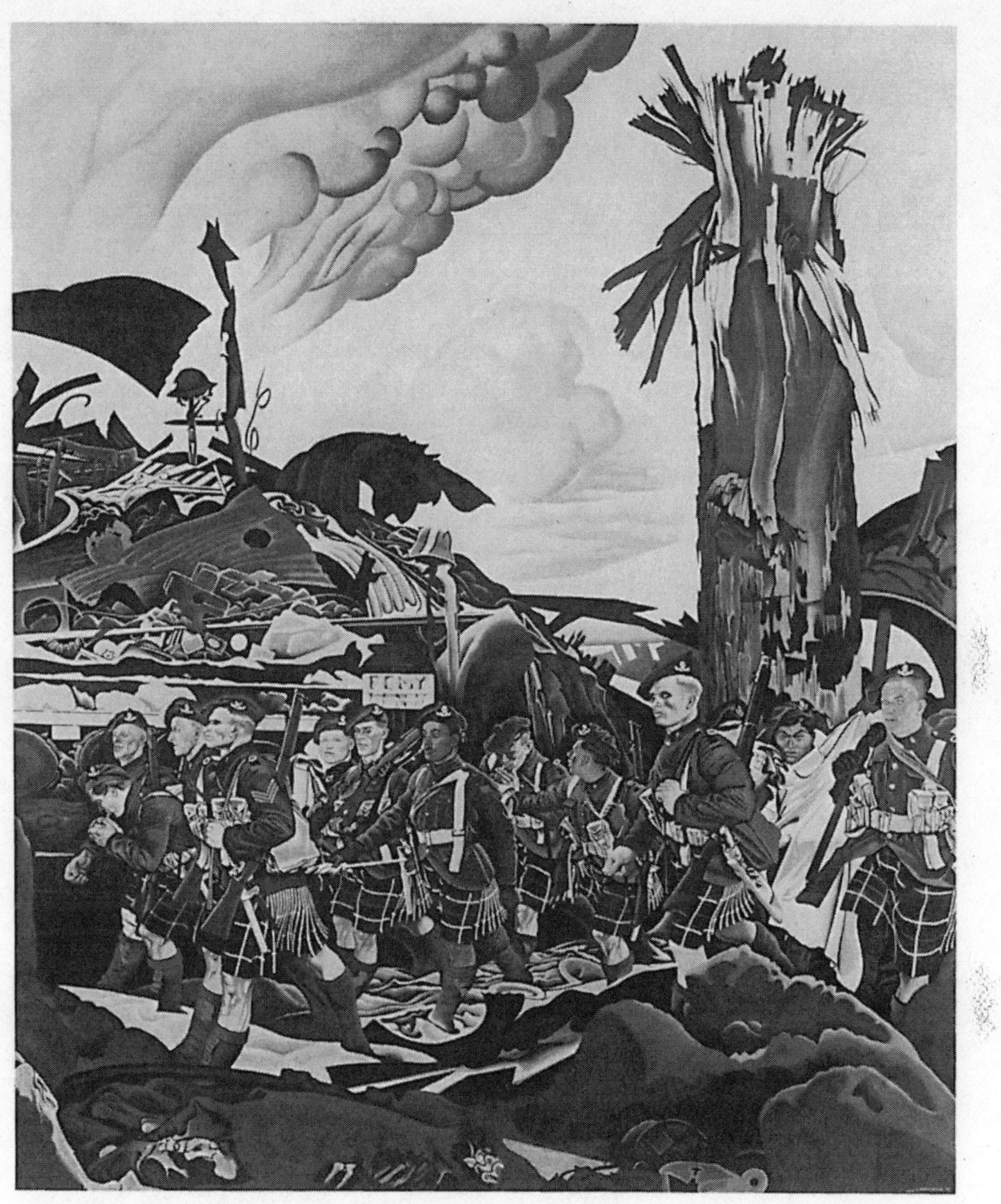

23 Eric Kennington, *The Conquerors*
canvas 116½ × 95½ in / 296 × 243 cm CWM 8968

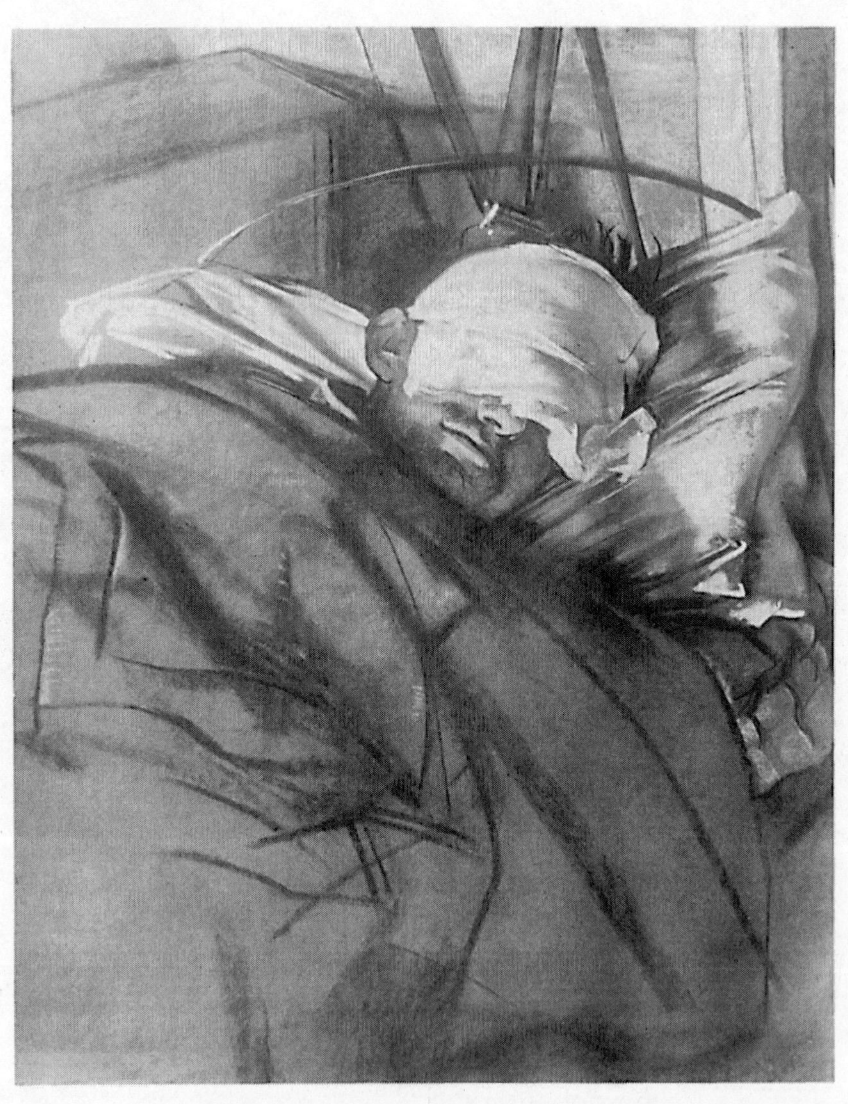

24 Eric Kennington, *Mustard Gas*
pastel 25¾ × 19¾ in / 65 × 50 cm CWM 8350

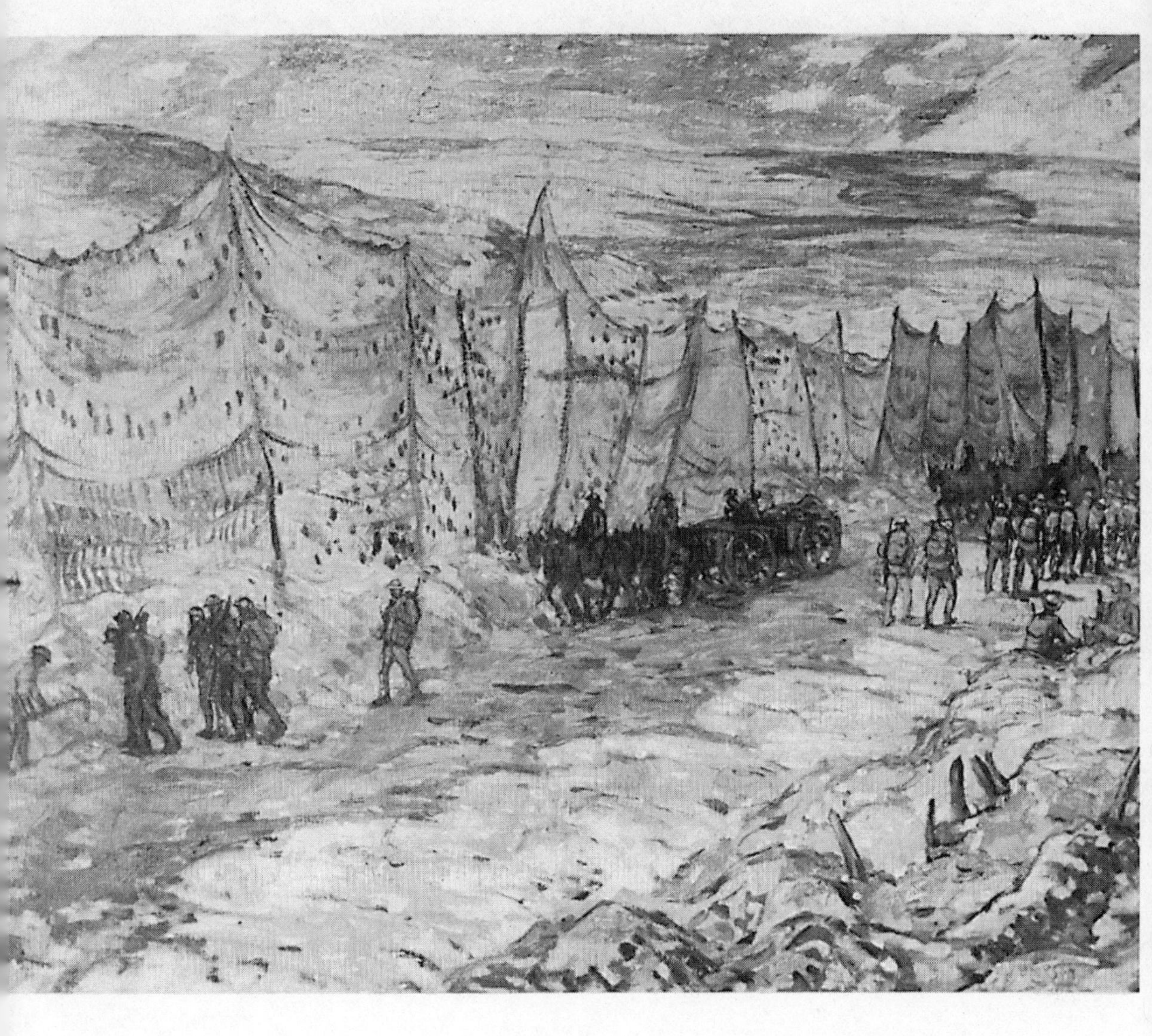

25 A.Y. Jackson, *Screened Road 'A'*
unfinished canvas 44 x 34 in / 112 x 86 cm CWM 8188

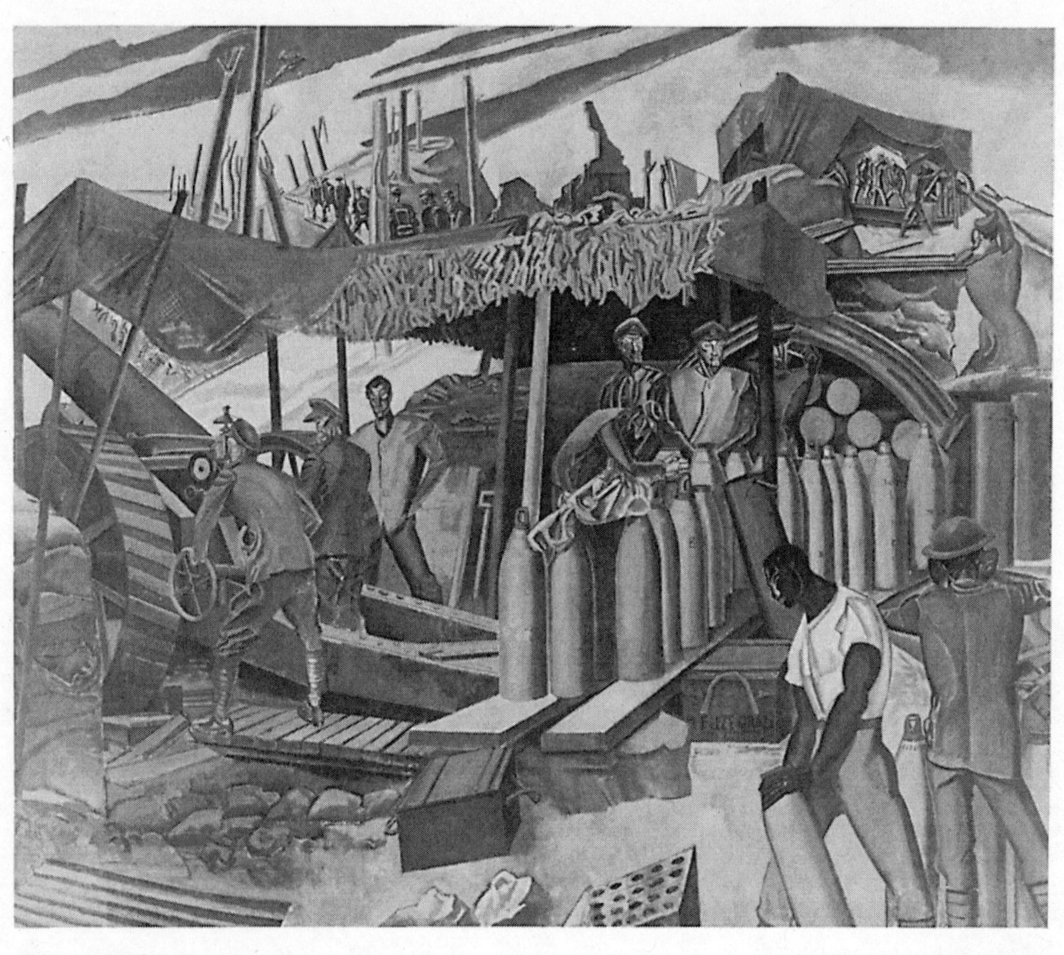

26 Percy Wyndham Lewis, *A Canadian Gun Pit*
canvas 120 x 142¹/₂ in / 305 x 362 cm NGC 8356

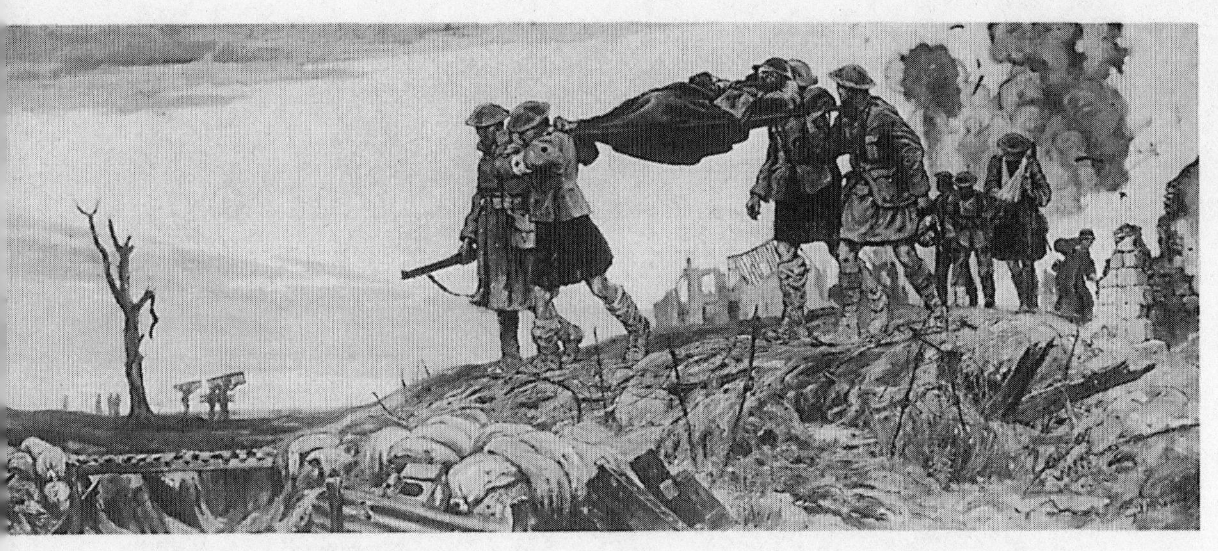

27 Cyril Barraud, *The Stretcher-bearer Party*
    canvas 34¹/₂ x 54 in / 88 x 137 cm CWM 8021

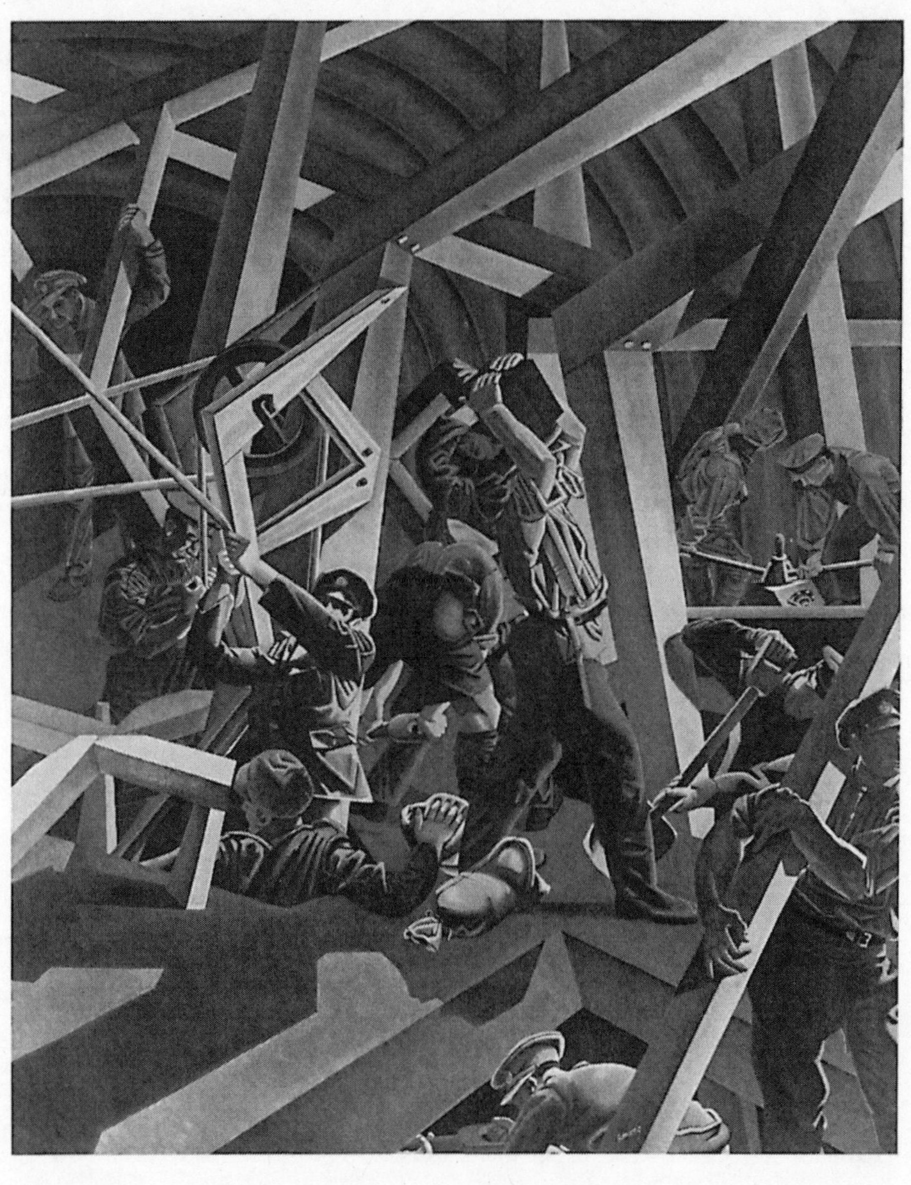

28 David Bomberg, *Sappers at Work: A Canadian Tunnelling Company*
canvas 120 x 96 in / 305 x 244 cm NGC 8108

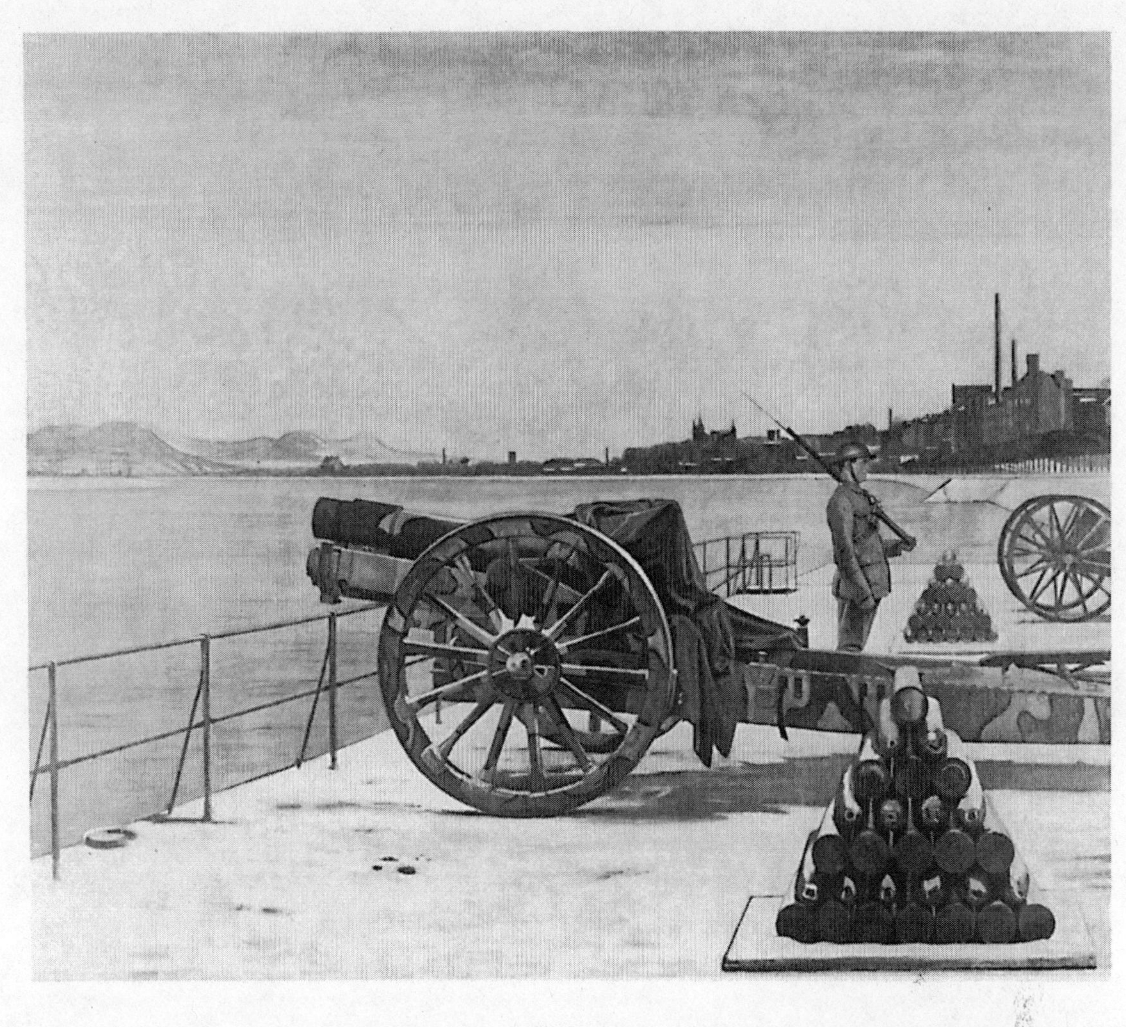

29 William Rothenstein, *The Watch on the Rhine (The Last Phase)*
canvas 120 x 142 in / 305 x 361 cm CWM (Senate) 8740

30 Louis Weirter, *The Battle for Courcelette*
canvas 120 x 240 in / 305 x 610 cm CWM 8931

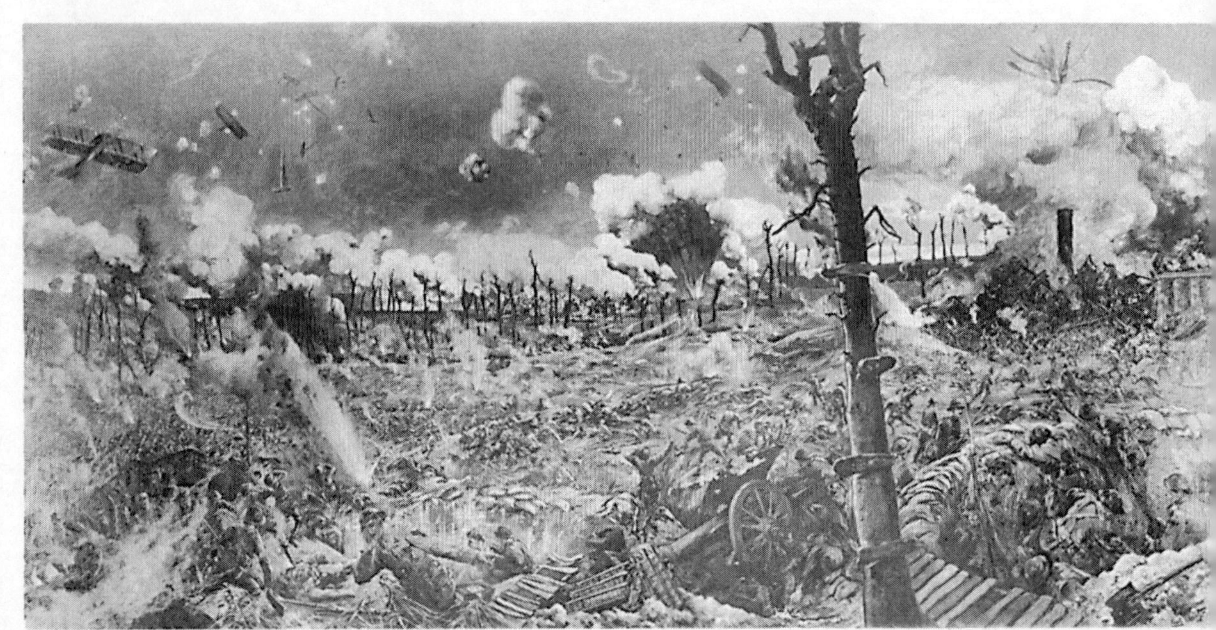

31 William Roberts, *The First German Gas Attack at Ypres*
    canvas 120 × 144 in / 305 × 366 cm NGC 8729

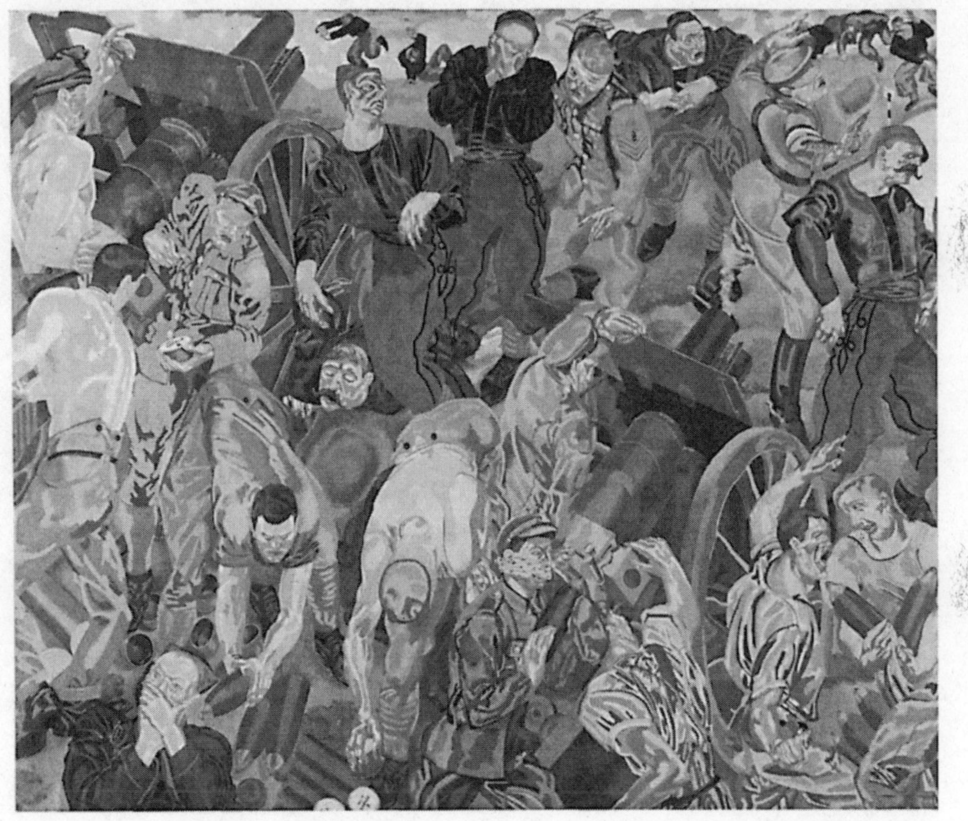

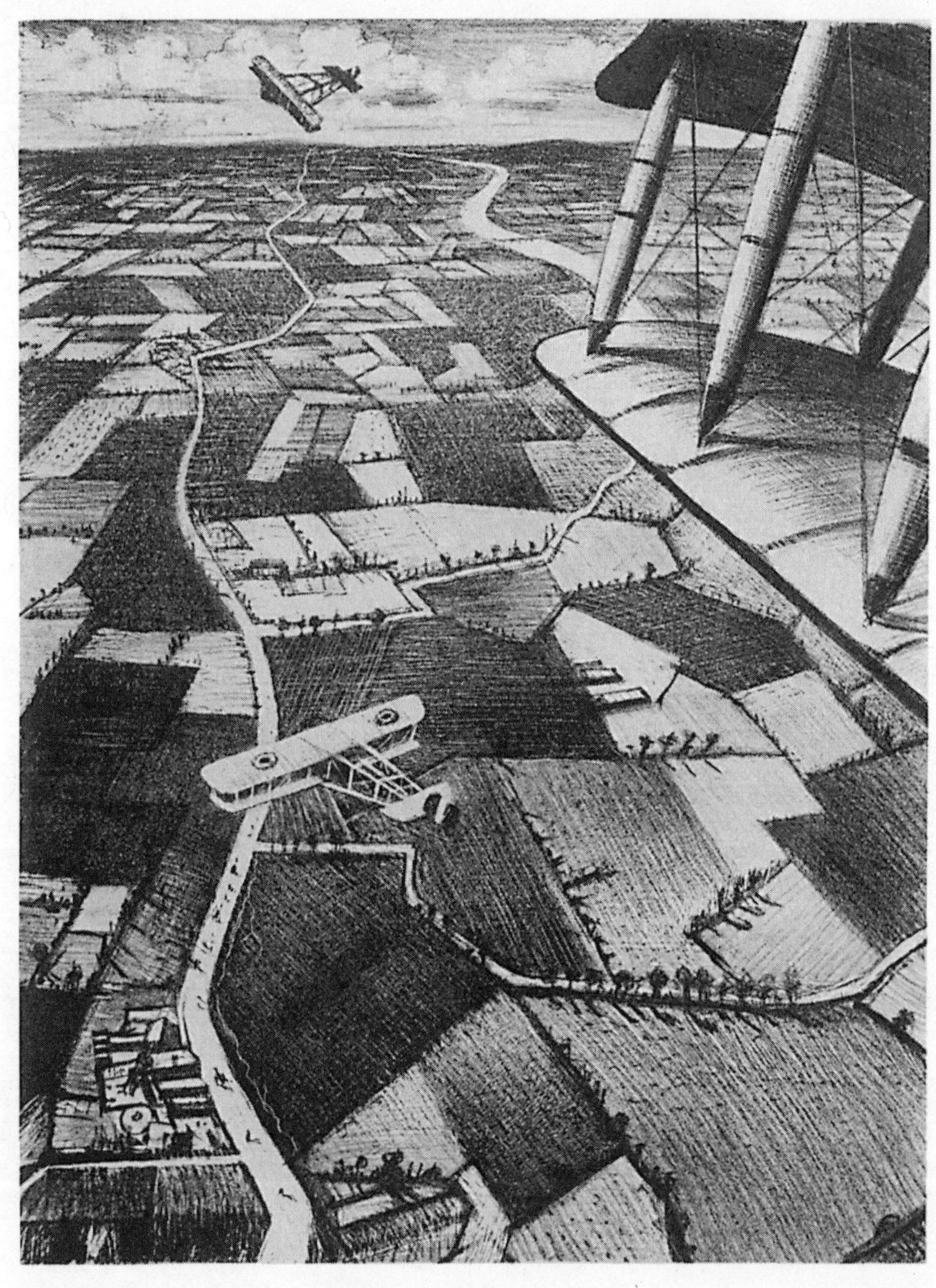

32 C.R.W. Nevinson, *In the Air*
lithograph 15¾ × 11⅞ in / 40 × 30 cm CWM 8668

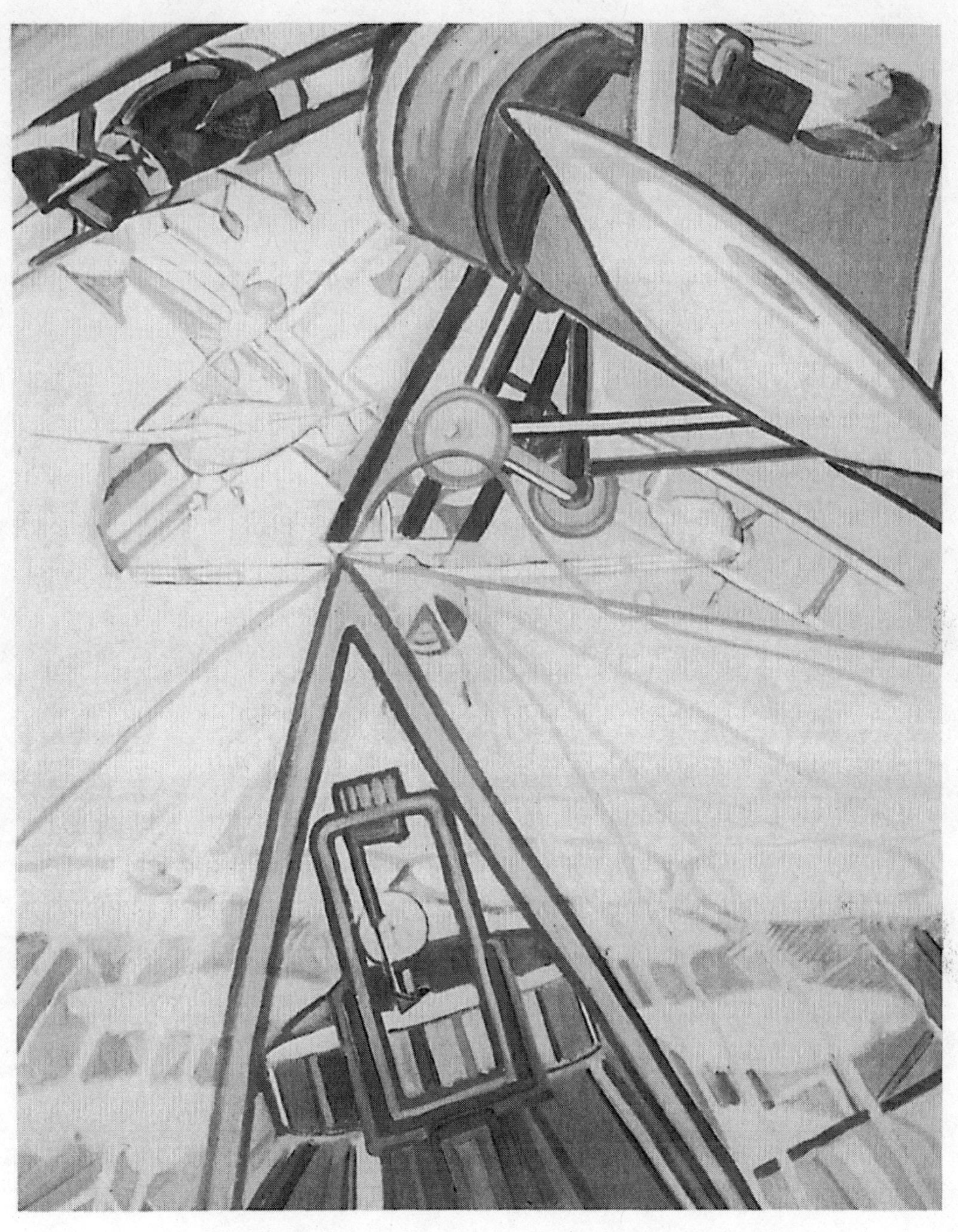

33 John Turnbull, *Dogfight* canvas 35¹/₂ × 28 in / 90 × 71 cm CWM 8904

34 Alfred Munnings, *Charge of Flowerdew's Squadron*
    canvas 20 × 24 in / 51 × 61 cm CWM 8571

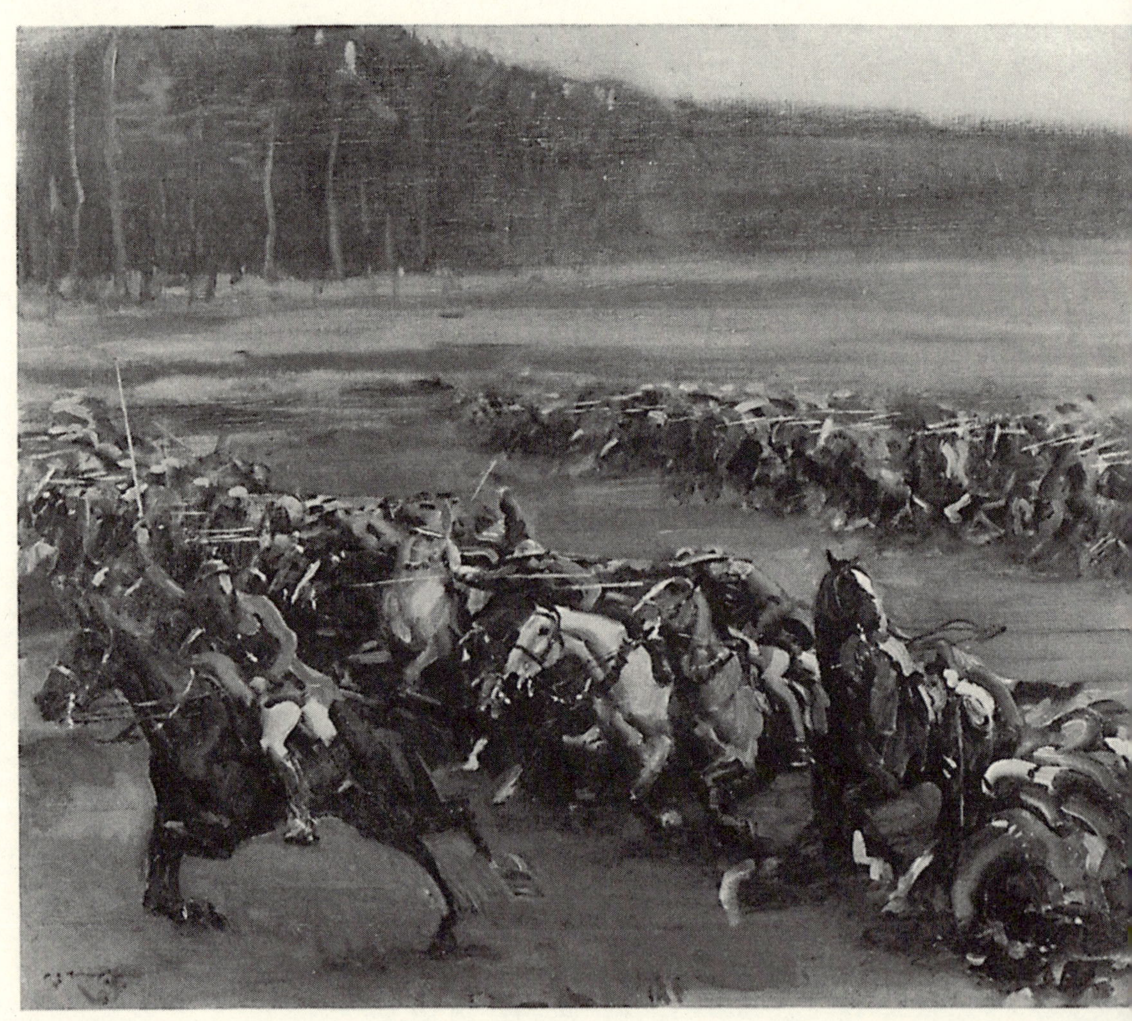

35 H.J. Mowatt, *Trench Fight*
   crayon 18 × 12¹/₄ in / 46 × 31 cm CWM 8562

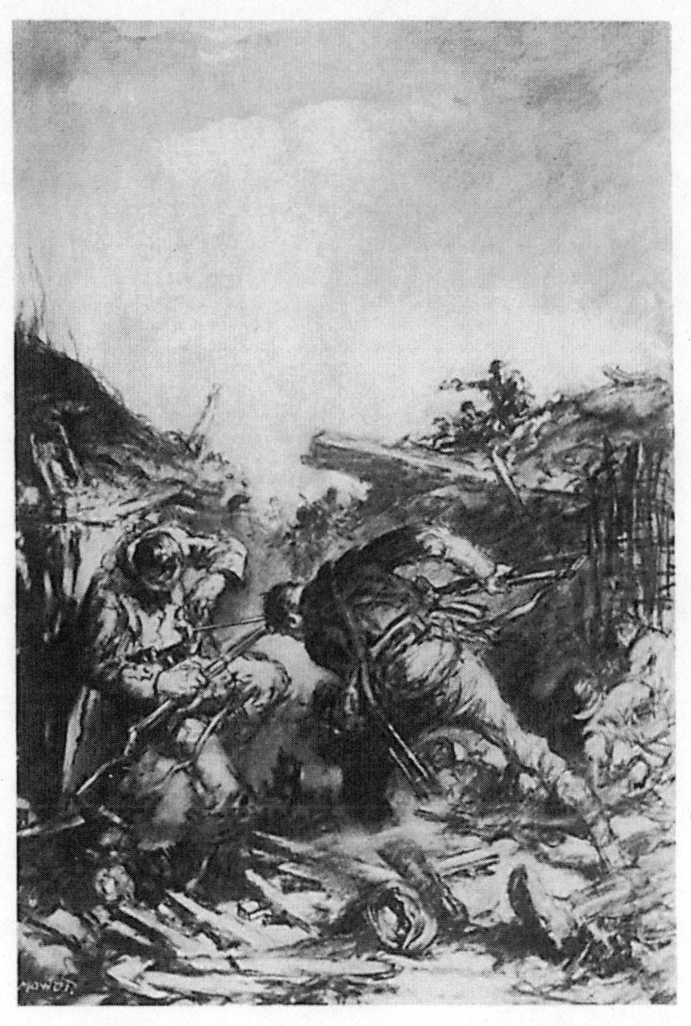

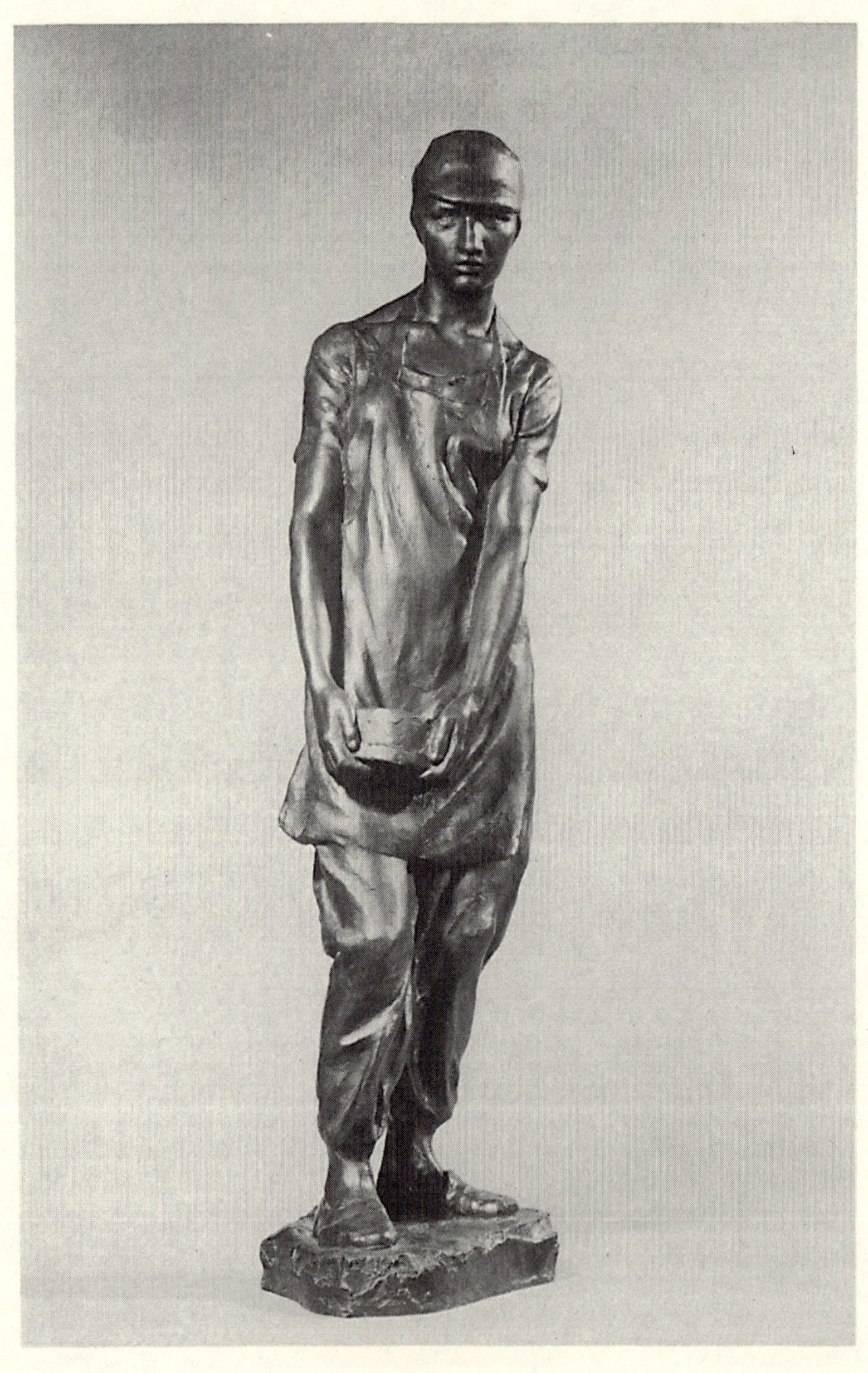

36 Florence Wyle, *Munitions Worker* bronze 26¼ in / 67 cm high CWM 8521

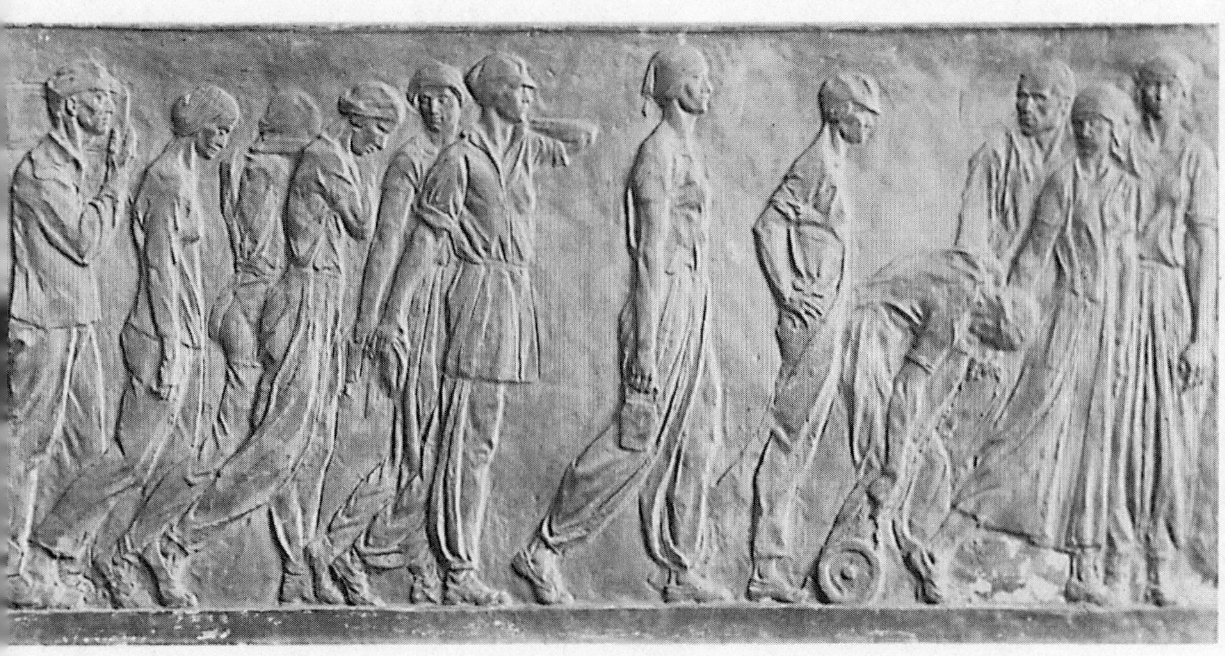

37 Frances Loring, *Noon Hour in a Munitions Plant*
    bronze relief 35 x 73½ in / 89 x 187 cm CWM 8505

38 Mabel May, *Women Making Shells*
    canvas 84 x 72 in / 213 x 183 cm CWM 8409

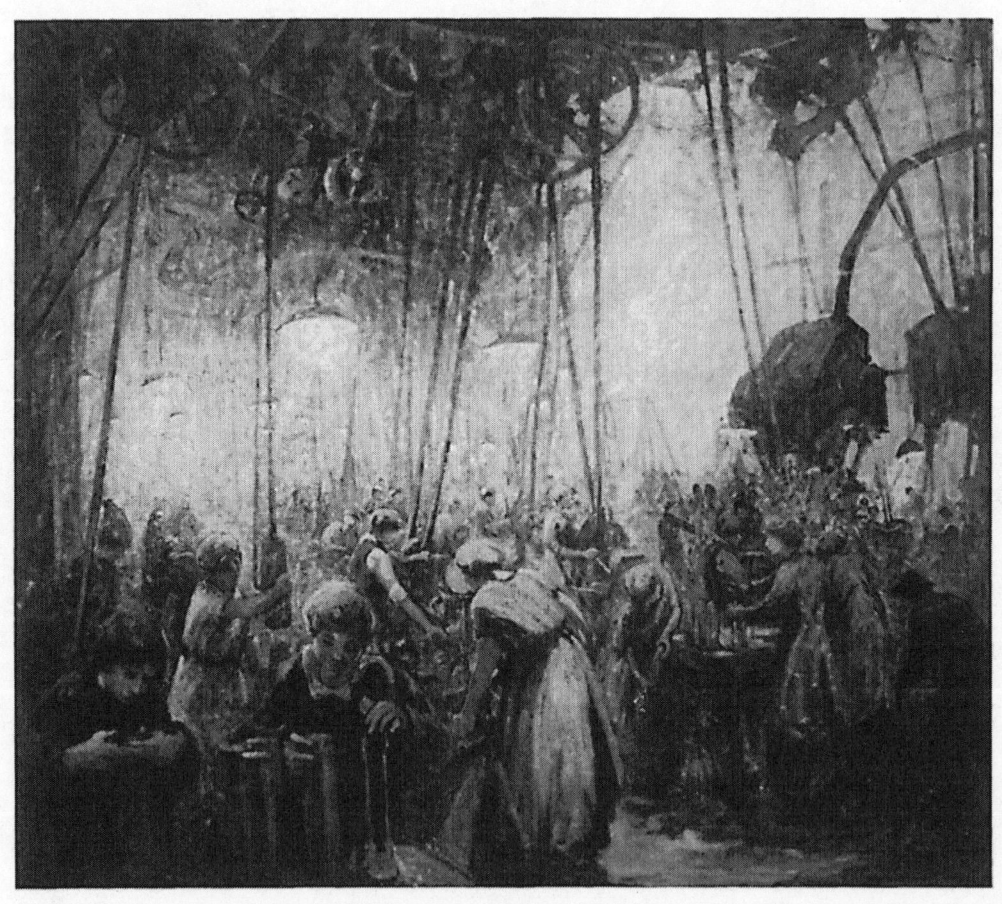

39 Frederick Jopling,
Forging the 9-Inch Shell
mezzotint 17¹/₈ × 12³/₈ in /
43 × 31 cm CWM 8330

40 Charles Ginner,
The Filling Factory
canvas 120 × 144 in /
305 × 366 cm NGC 8173

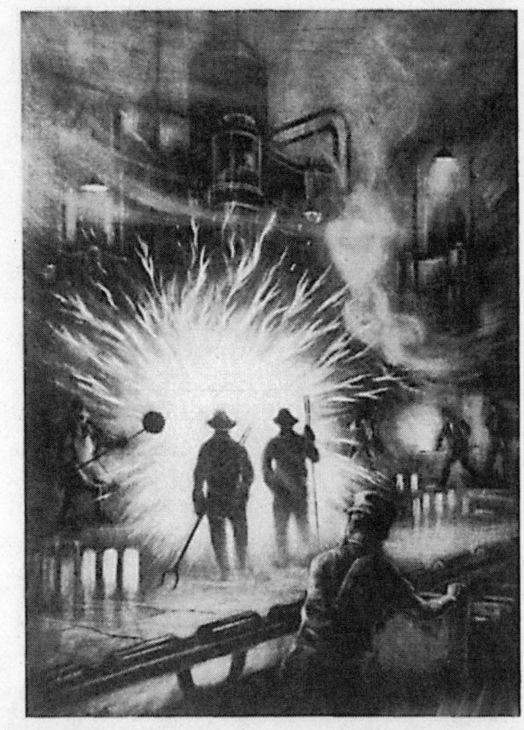

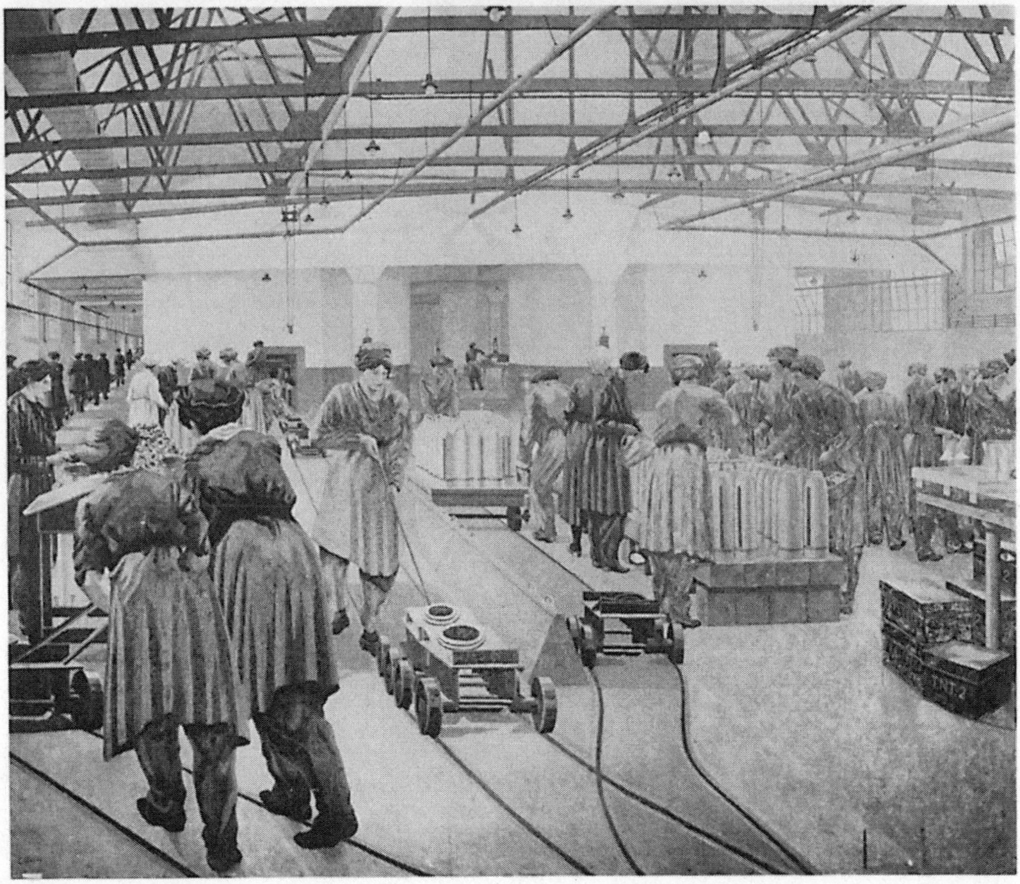

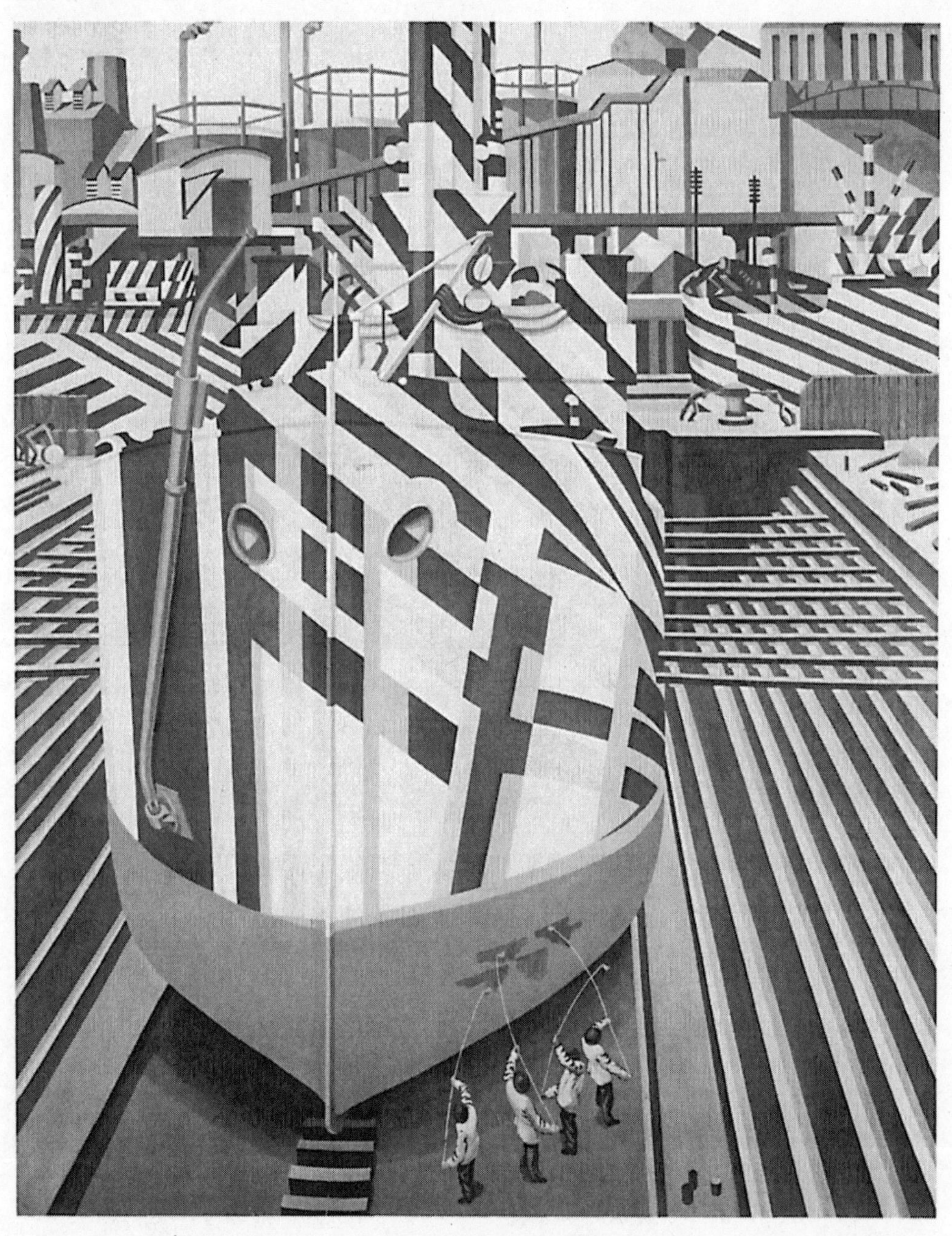

41 Edward Wadsworth, *Dazzle-Ships in Drydock at Liverpool*
canvas 119¹/₂ x 96 in / 304 x 244 cm NGC 8925

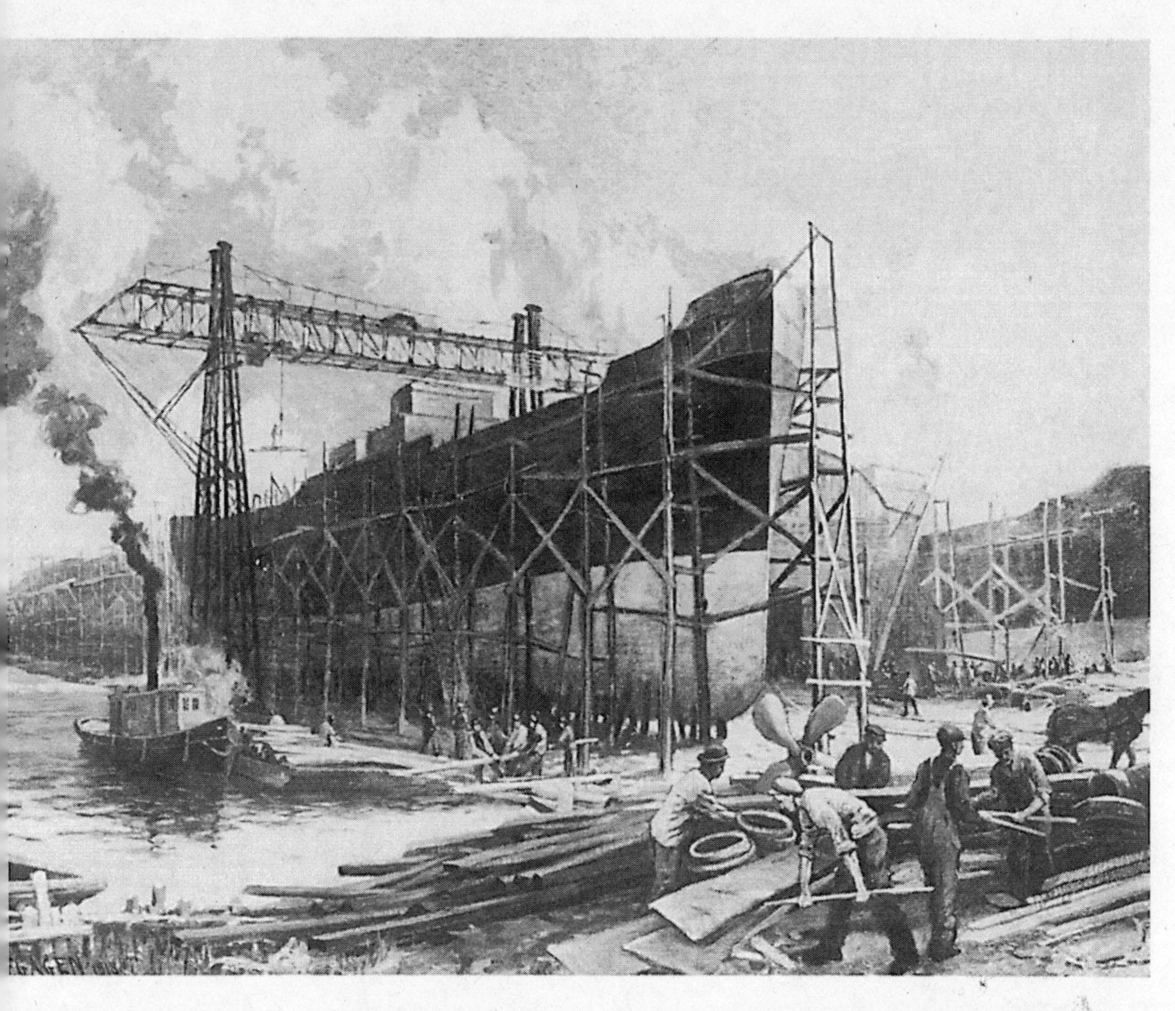

42 Robert Gagen, *Shipbuilding in Ashbridges Bay, Toronto*
watercolour 57 x 81 in / 145 x 206 cm CWM 8167

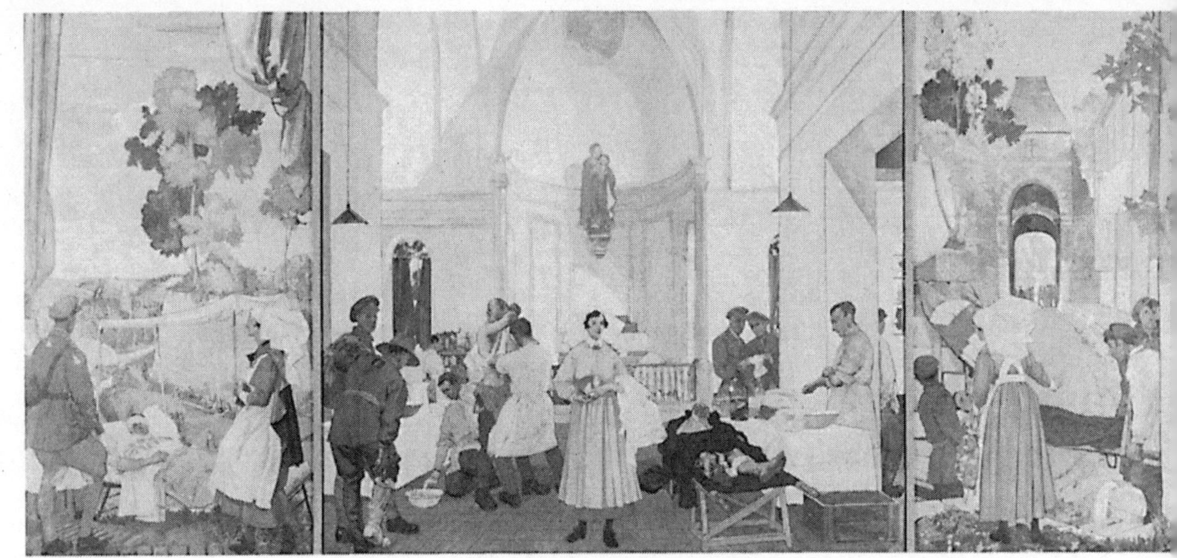

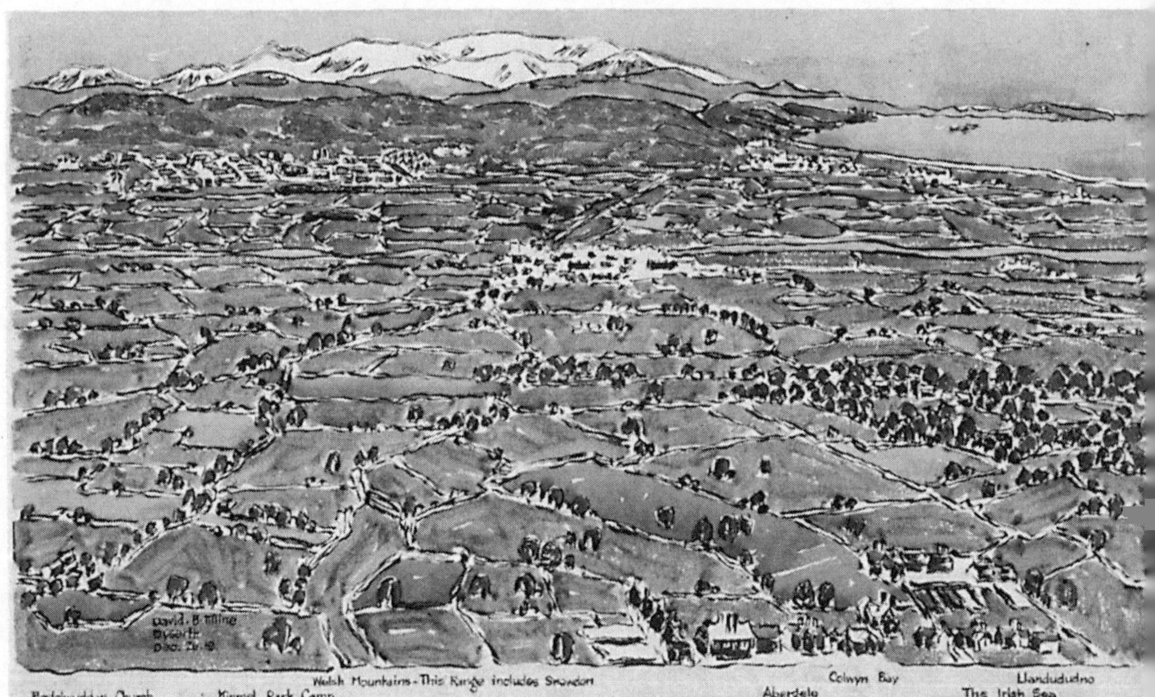

David B. Tilling
Dyserth
Dec. 24.18.
Welsh Mountains - This Range includes Snowdon
Colwyn Bay
Llandudno
Bodelwyddan Church
Kinmel Park Camp
Abergele
The Irish Sea
River Clwyd - The flat land on either side of
the river was once the famous
Rhuddlan Marsh.
Rhuddlan Castle and Town
River Clwyd
Dyserth Village

OPPOSITE

43 Gerald Moira, *No.3 Canadian Stationary Hospital at Doullens*
canvas 120 × 264 in / 305 × 671 cm CWM 8555,6,7

44 David Milne, *Location Sketch of Kinmel Park Camp from the Hills about Dyserth*
watercolour 11³∕₈ × 17⁷∕₈ in / 29 × 45 cm NGC 8515

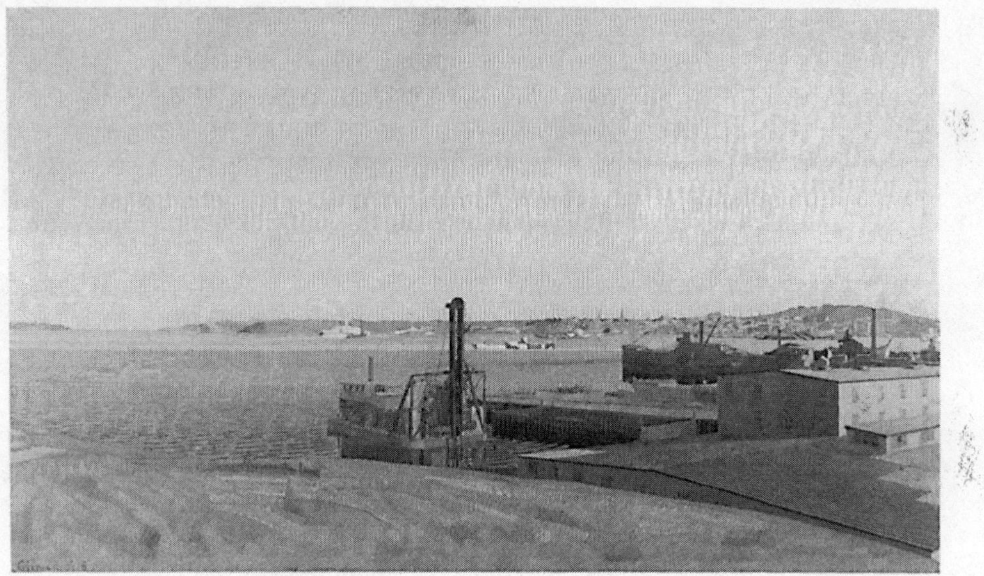

45 Harold Gilman, *Halifax Harbour at Sunset, 1918*
canvas 77 × 132 in / 196 × 335 cm NGC 8172

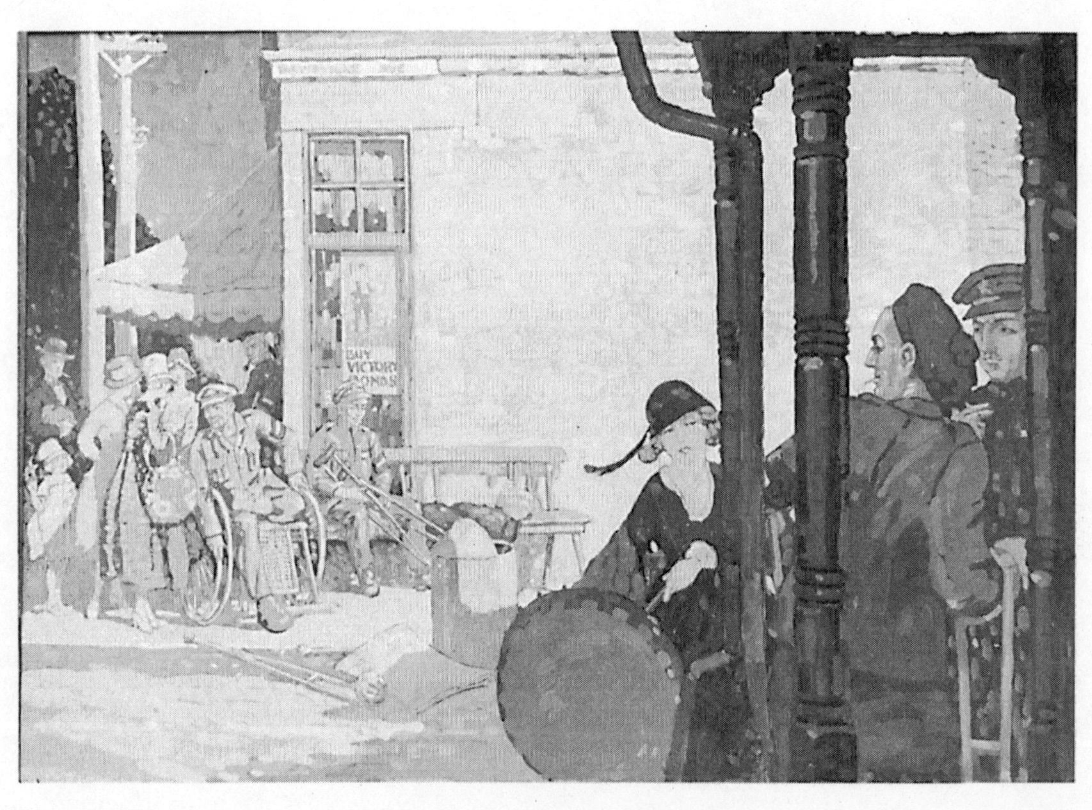

46 Stanley Turner, *A War Record*
    oil on board 26 x 38 in / 66 x 97 cm CWM 8907

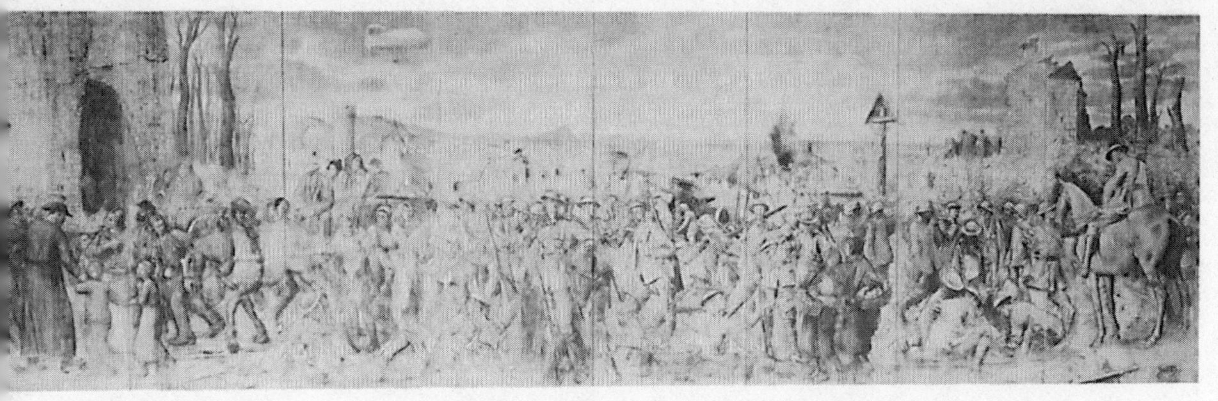

47 Augustus John, *The Canadians Opposite Lens*
charcoal 12 x 40 feet / 366 x 1219 cm NGC 16989

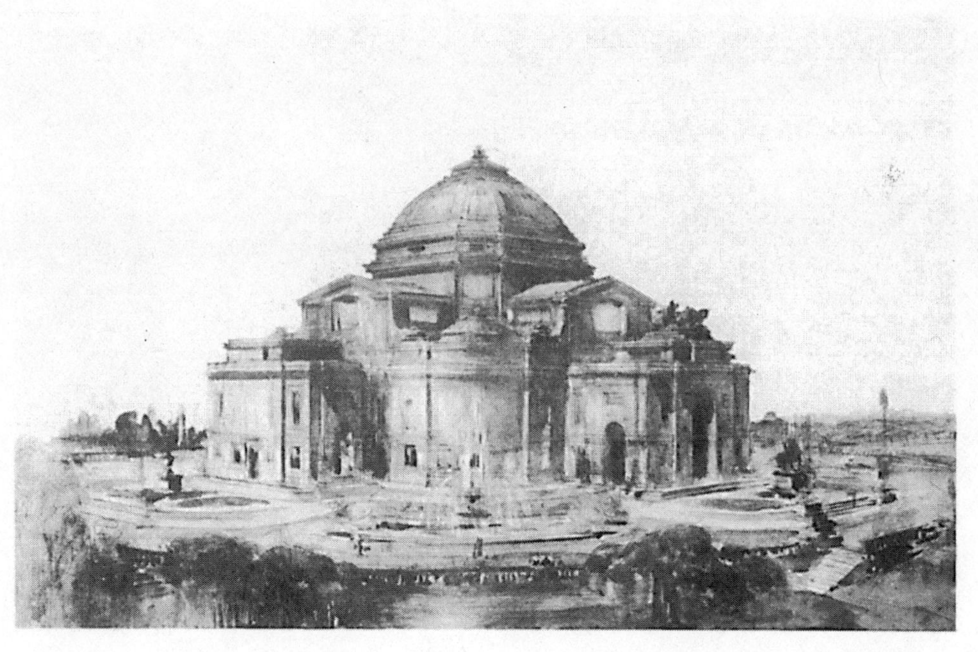

48 E.A. Rickards, *Design for the Canadian War Memorial*

49 George Clausen, *Returning to the Reconquered Land*
canvas 106¹/₂ × 154 in / 271 × 391 cm CWM (Senate) 8135

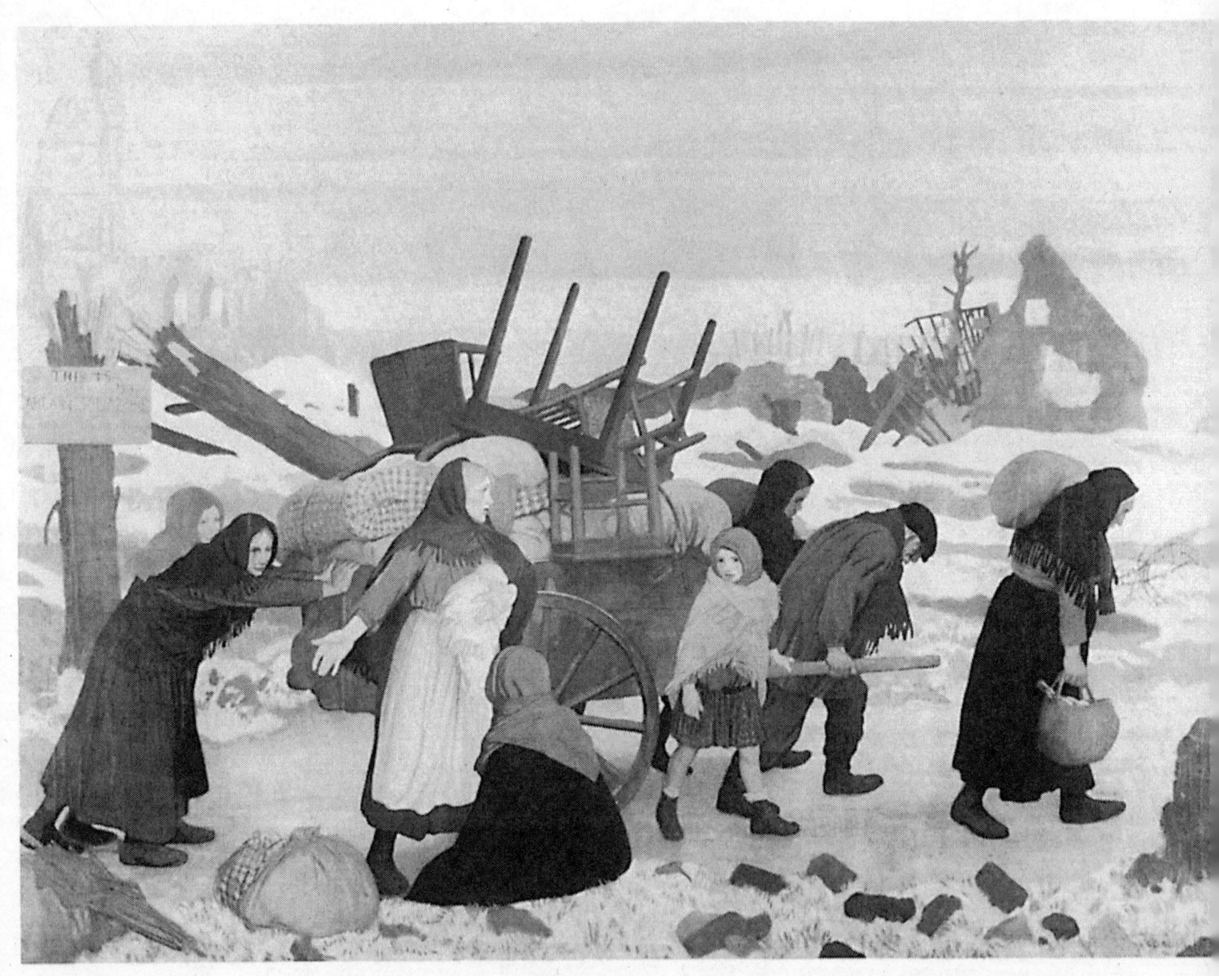

50 Paul Nash, *Night Bombardment*
   canvas 72 × 84 in / 183 × 213 cm NGC 8640

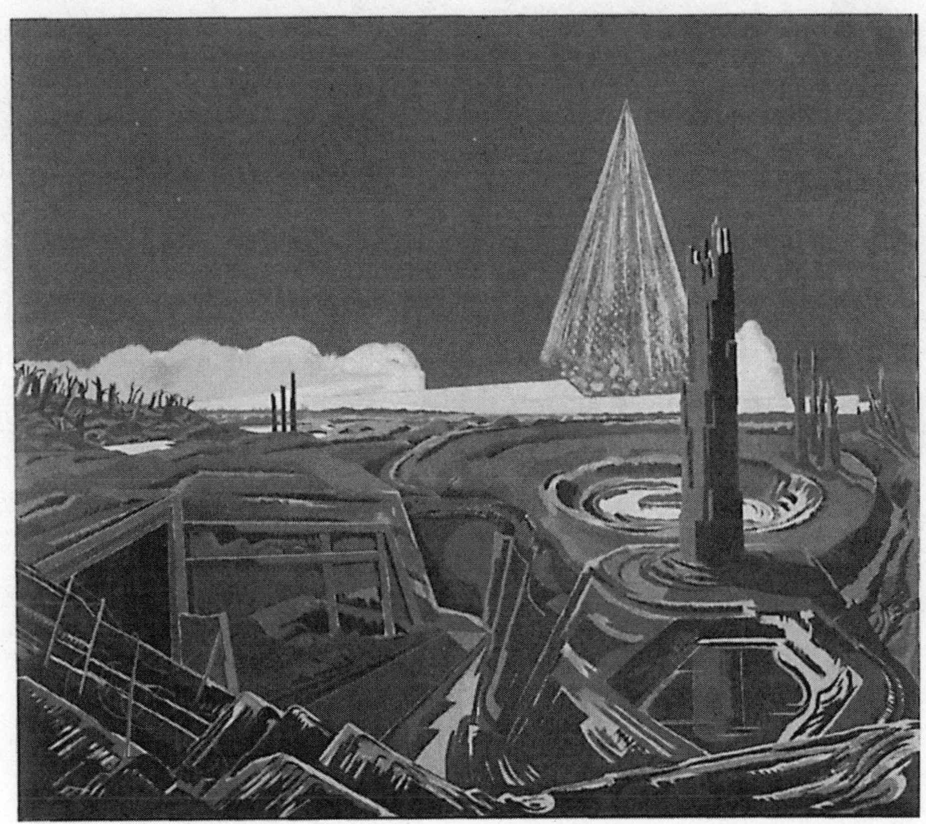

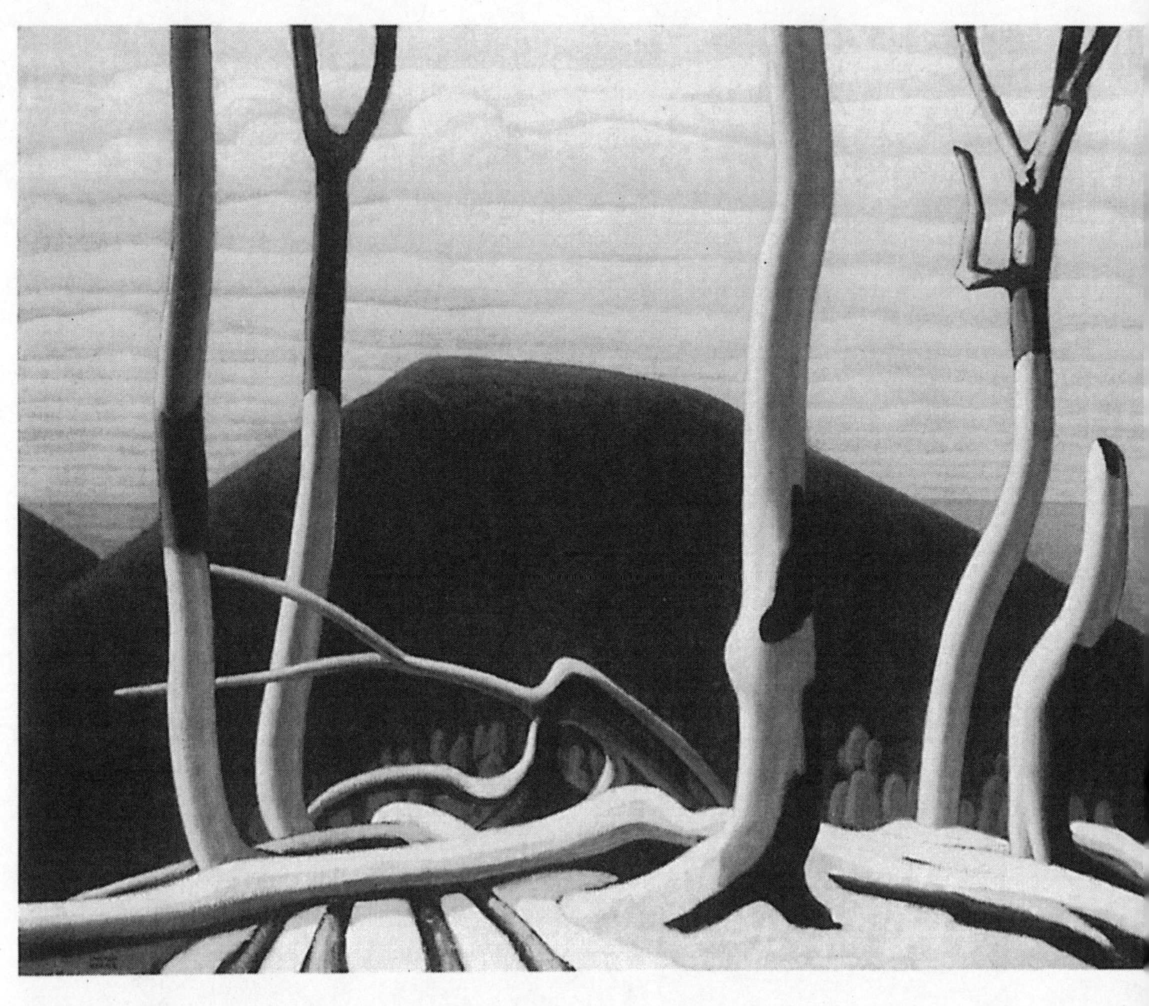

51 Lawren Harris, *Above Lake Superior*, c. 1922
oil on canvas 48 x 60 in / 121.9 x 152.4 cm Art Gallery of Ontario,
Toronto, Gift from the Reuben and Kate Leonard Canadian Fund, 1929

4 'Work which cries to be done'

The war artists joined the Canadian troops at Passchendaele in October 1917, followed them in November down to the Vimy-Lens front where they remained until late spring, then over the summer of 1918 further south to Amiens, northeast to Arras, southeast to Cambrai, and in early autumn northeast to Mons where they joined the hundred-day advance. They were, for the most part, onlookers. They lived in CWRO headquarters generally located well behind the lines. As officers they had a batman and usually a driver, and a car to transport them to and from their chosen sketching ground. But, unlike most officers, they had no set duties and no immediate superiors to whom they were responsible. William Rothenstein described the life as 'a kind of simple State Socialism: and an official artist [as] a kind of official parasite, with nothing to do but to draw and draw and no material worries to prevent him working all day and every day save such transitory things as shells.' Whenever Rothenstein visited the front, he 'felt a childish elation at sharing for a short space and in small measure ... the danger and discomforts in which these men lived hourly.'[1] Only A.Y. Jackson, Paul Nash, Percy Wyndham Lewis, William Roberts, C.R.W. Nevinson, and a few others who had served in some capacity on the line, had had any experience of day-to-day life in the trenches. And sometimes even these men, once they became war artists, viewed things with more distance. But however much artists might be onlookers, they were not exempt from danger. Nevinson, Wyndham Lewis, J.W. Beatty, Nash, David Cameron, Leonard Richmond, and Jackson all had to sketch under fire. Writing from 'somewhere in France,' Beatty told his friend Robert Gagen what it was like working two thousand yards in front of Canadian gunners: 'Our heavies were firing over our heads & the whistle of those shells going over was not so very disconcerting but old Fritz was trying to get a railway line that ran about four hundred yards in front of us & we could hear his stuff coming & watch the burst of it ... to make matters more interesting there were air fights going over our head & the Archies were pestering Hunny with shrapnel which was bursting just over us ... it is not conducive to steady draughts-manship to work under those conditions.'[2]

Without the help of a batman on one occasion, or a driver and car, Leonard Richmond had to make his way from Abbeville to Barlin, a distance of some forty-five miles, in a transport vehicle; during the course of the thirteen-hour, night-long journey the vehicle was lost, then shelled. Wyndham Lewis thought he would be safe painting a howitzer in a fairly inactive section of the line; then he opened his sketch-book, and 'a great angry shrapnel burst occurred spraying the ground all around.' A.Y. Jackson 'found it hard to manage a sketch box while shells were dropping here and there' in Belgium during the spring of 1918; billeted in an isolated house located near a railroad station in Poperinghe, he was the target of German bombers who hit the station during the night and then dropped the remaining shells on their way back across the lines. Even Nevinson, who was considered by most 'a desperate fellow ... without fear ... anxious to crawl into the front line and draw things full of violence and terror,' found the 'shelling most disconcerting for any actual drawing.'[3]

It was not, of course, always possible for the war artist to be a mere onlooker. While accompanying General Hubert de la Poer Gough's Fifth Army in March 1918, William Rothenstein reported being 'hard at it day and night helping nurses as well as I can and doing the little I am able to do to help in looking after some of the crowded wards ... I can't think of drawing now, while I can be of the least service, and people keep pouring in.' Eric Kennington co-operated in another way. 'I am making drawings of men and things for a picture,' he reported to Paul Konody, 'the result is jealousy the other colonels ask if I will stay with them & make drawings of their men.' But while there were difficulties, and the artists were not always flattered by such petitions – Richard Carline, a British artist who worked for the Ministry of Information, made it particularly clear that he was irritated by requests to do cartoons and portraits of the men – they generally complied with such requests.[4] Some, indeed, even went further: F.H. Varley, anxious to win acceptance, found an old piano behind the lines and entertained the men with Beethoven sonatas.

Such ways of gaining favour did not always work. Frequently the artists were looked upon with suspicion by the officers and men in the trenches and the staff behind them. As a war artist Jackson did not receive much of a welcome 'until they found that earlier I had been in the line with the infantry.' And it was not just the act of sketching that aroused suspicion and hostility but the artists' very appearance. Some general standards were, to be sure, maintained: most wore the uniform of an officer, though it frequently lacked regimental buttons and rank badges; some wore the insignia 'Official War Artist' or 'Canadian War Records Officer' on their shoulder;

and all carried a sketching permit in their pocket. But there was a good deal of variety as well. William Roberts, on loan to the Canadians for six months, continued to wear his Royal Field Artillery uniform. Alfred Munnings had no uniform at all: he joined General J.E.B. Seely's Canadian Cavalry in the Arras sector of the front in 1918 turned out in a chequered suit, cloth cap, and leggings, causing Seely to view with some apprehension the odd-looking figure who had been commissioned to paint his portrait. As it happened, Munnings quickly overcame the initially unfavourable impression the officers and men formed of him by showing that he was an excellent horseman. He also exhibited his sketches for them after each day's work. But if, as a result, he 'fitted comfortably into that unfamiliar milieu,' most of his colleagues did not. Artists were frequently arrested as spies by villagers or soldiers, then brought before the local mayor or nearest commanding officer; after producing their permit they would be released and allowed to return to their sketching. It was, none the less, an annoying business. 'Tired of being taken for a spy,' Nevinson found a solution: he wore motor goggles around his cap to hide the absence of a badge.[5]

If not arrested for spying, disturbed by bombs, or unable to get to and from the front, the artists often had to work in severe weather conditions. During the cold winter of 1917-18 Rothenstein's paintbrush froze on the way from the paintbox to the paper. That same winter Wyndham Lewis told Konody that 'Everything is under snow ... How I shall be able to hold a pencil I don't know.' Studio painter William Orpen was almost paralyzed by the cold; but even worse than the harsh weather was 'the sense of panic' he experienced when, upon losing his way from the front to his car, he found himself amidst a field of German dead.[6]

Artists also discovered that the war did not sit and pose for them. When there was something of interest it was either on the move, quickly over, or concealed under the cover of darkness. When a major offensive occurred, as in the spring of 1918, their billets and cars were needed so they were sent home. They also had to work quickly: the official time allotted them at the front ranged from three weeks to about two months. Though many received a few weeks' extension, they had little opportunity to make more than a cursory pencil or charcoal sketch. Details of equipment and uniforms had to be carefully studied and added later. Few possessed Nevinson's ability to complete studio canvases from memory.

Their work, moreover, had to meet certain standards. These ranged from what turned out to be the very loose requirements established by a Canadian military intelligence officer – 'all he said,' according to Jackson, was ' "so long as you don't publish gun positions or such objects in relation to a recognizable landmark, there is nothing to bother about" ' – to the much more precise limits set by the CWMF's organizers.[7] Konody gave most front-line artists specific subjects, among them military hospitals, lumber camps, railroad construction camps, veterinary units, and the Canadian Cavalry (only Augustus John, Jackson, and Cyril Barraud were allowed to 'wander about the Canadian lines ... making sketches in a "record" kind of way'[8]). Sir Edmund Walker and Eric Brown followed Konody in designating particular matters for treatment. Then, after viewing the finished product, the three would accept it, reject it, or suggest how it might be improved. Montreal portraitist George Horne Russell had, for example, to amend '2 or 3 rather bad military inaccuracies' in his painting of Sergeant Frederick Hobson because Brown feared 'unfavourable criticism from soldiers.' David Bomberg was told by Konody to repaint *Sappers at Work: A Canadian Tunnelling Company* (Fig. 28). Modernists Nevinson and Roberts, along with the decorative mural painter Gerald Moira, painted pictures at their 'own risk' with acceptance of them made contingent upon the approval of the CWMF committee. Many artists were, of course, uncomfortable with all of this, viewing it as an encroachment upon their artistic liberty. Sir Edmund Walker's scrutiny certainly made 'an artist of [Harrington] Mann's standing, rather hot under the collar.' Bomberg felt that in redoing his picture for Konody he had made 'one of the few compromises of his life.' Wyndham Lewis complained of having produced 'one of the dullest good pictures on earth' for the Canadians. Roberts simply regretted 'the impossibility at present to do some work that would be worth showing.'[9]

Artists painting on the English and Canadian home fronts also had their difficulties. Working in Halifax during the summer of 1918, Arthur Lismer had to cope with the ultimate problem: there seemed to be nothing to paint. Transports had ceased to come and go for no convoys had left for some time. And, when he did find something interesting to put in his sketchbook, the public made dealing with it unpleasant: 'One of the local papers is lashing up an argument against landscape painters having access to docks etc. & I have been frequently reported as a suitable subject for internment.' Toronto landscape painter Frank Johnston found himself in something of the same position: there was, he reported to Brown, 'little or no action in the training camps other than straight flying.' Albert Robinson had a problem of a different kind: obtaining access to the Vickers munitions plant. 'I cannot get into those works to save my boots,' he complained to Brown, who then arranged a permit signed by Sir Joseph Flavelle of the Imperial Munitions Board. Mabel May experienced difficulties gaining access to the Northern Electric Plant in Montreal; and Montreal artist Edmond Dyonnet arrived in post-war Winnipeg to paint the portrait of VC recipient Alexander Brereton only to encounter the disruptions caused by the Winnipeg General Strike. British sculptor Clare Sheridan, commissioned to do a bust of Canada's brilliant flying ace Major Billy Bishop, was treated to his 'flirts' during each sitting. The British allegorical painter Anna Airy had to work under a corrugated shelter in a munitions plant. 'They roll red hot shell cases in batches within 4' of me, to cool off!' she recounted; 'I can't describe the heat, but the general swelter and steam and the dust and the swearing are going to make a ripping picture I think.'[10]

Some of the artists, it was true, had a much more comfortable time of it. Laura Knight arrived at Witley Camp in the south of England in November 1918 with instructions to record physical training. Though no one had any knowledge of her commission, her studio soon 'became the central interest of the camp. The men spent all the time they could sitting around the big tortoise stove that had on it a large tin of water, serving to wash my paint-brushes in ... The dreary ugliness and monotony of camp life was stamped on the men's faces, sick for their homes and their own big country.' Frances Loring and Florence Wyle had no difficulty getting female munition workers to pose for their sculptures. Another Canadian, Florence Carlyle, was commissioned to paint a portrait of Lady Julia Drummond, the head of the Canadian Red Cross, and moved into her palatial residence near Westminster Abbey. 'I have been a great swell lately,' she wrote home, 'dining at nine o'clock in full dress.' Even Johnston and Lismer found what they were doing could have its bright moments. Johnston spent a week at the Beamsville flying camp during which he went 'through all the stunts that the machine is capable of barring a crash.' And in Halifax, Lismer 'found a naval commander who is really interested & I was put in the hands of one arm of the service & spent a night & a day at Sea.'[11]

Whether the artists found themselves dealing with problems or working in relative ease, they had to give up the age-old notion that it was necessary for them to paint in isolation, either out of doors or in the privacy of their studio. Bombs, 'flirts,' arrest as spies, red hot shell cases, going missing and getting frozen, had become part of their daily experience. So too had an unprecedented sense of camaraderie, a feeling on the part of artists who would normally have had little to do with each other that they were somehow bound together. Munnings and Orpen, engaged in painting General Seely and his officers, comprised what Seely called his 'Ecole des Beaux Arts.' John and Jackson, quite distinct from each other in style and never having worked together, spent a memorable evening watching an Allied gas attack, which Jackson later described as 'a wonderful display of fireworks with our clouds of gas and the German flames and rockets of all colours.'[12] And Laura Knight and Anna Airy, who were both painting at Witley Camp, spent pleasant evenings in each other's company.

For some, of course, the pleasure of being a war artist involved much more than sharing dinners or taking in the spectacle of battle. The society portrait painter Ambrose McEvoy found the battlefield to be 'the most thrilling sight I have ever seen.' Though initially hesitant about taking a war art commission, Rothenstein never tired of working all day, while Orpen reported that he had come 'up against the biggest thing I have or ever can cross – in this world.' After being in France for several weeks, Eric Kennington asked Konody for a three-month extension: 'I do not wish to miss the fast-disappearing marvels out here.' Even Augustus John, who felt 'like a fish out of water' and was (except for an occasional call to Amiens or Paris to relieve 'the monotony of life') generally bored, 'enjoyed painting the soldiers, and sketching around the various batteries, and was not insensible to the camaraderie that war engenders.' The effect of the cold, the noise, and the other discomforts at the front soon diminished for most artists. As Rothenstein reported to Konody, 'I know my way about here now and anyone will put me up anywhere. I work in cold & wind & rain eat anything & sleep on any bed without grumbling ... I have lost all vanity about my powers but I do believe I can do this work decently & that it is work which cries to be done.'[13]

When the art adviser acting for both the Imperial War Museum and the British Pictorial Propaganda Committee viewed the pictures of war artists during the summer of 1918 he was struck 'by the monotony of themes.' There were 'scarcely half a dozen.' And the paintings represented 'a ghastly sameness in treatment, even allowing for different temperament and degrees of merit.'[14] Thus Robert Ross, who had never been to the war zone, reacted to the handful of devices which by 1918 comprised the artistic iconography of the Western Front.

Nothing came to symbolize the war for the artist and the combatant as much as the land upon which it was fought. By the war's end one could gaze at 'a glowing red sun ... low undulant hills ... gun flashes and drifting smoke' and call it 'a genuine battle picture.'[15] No artist who visited the front could resist painting the landscape. For F.H. Varley the whole story of the war was told 'in the thousand and one things that mingle with the earth.' Edward Handley-Read thought there had never been a war that so lent itself to the art of the landscape painter. Indeed, as Robert Cortes Holliday was to point out in 1918, 'the idea of landscape as anything other than background for the spectacle' of war was 'a modern invention.'[16]

Pock-marked with gaping water-filled craters, strewn with bones, metal, and all the refuse of modern warfare, the topography of the front line offered few familiar associations. As Paul Nash observed of the Somme in 1917, it might have been 'a terrific creation of some malign fiend working a crooked will on the innocent countryside.' The machine had superseded God's handiwork; his landscape was being reshaped by man's instruments. Ypres and

Vimy Ridge were 'deliberately invented scenes, daily improved on and worked on by up-to-date machines.'[17]

If the landscape had changed its meaning, the character of the activity in it was different too. By day the front seemed deserted, at night it was full of activity. During the evening, noted Canadian artist Louis Keene, the 'trees seem to walk about.' Disoriented by an ungodly terrain, confused by the reversal of day and night, front-line soldiers clung to the familiar aspects of their surroundings: during their 'enforced leisure' on the line they charted the migration patterns of birds for British and French ornithologists and turned to 'the study of flowers, trees, birds and beasts'; behind the line they cultivated garden plots and adorned their shacks and Nissen huts with flowers. But still the 'ridiculous mad incongruity' that set man against nature enabled Paul Nash to see dandelions and a lilac bush, and permitted him to hear the throbbing of a nightingale amidst the rumble of the guns. Everyone on the front line found himself, to use Eric J. Leed's word, in a 'liminal' state of existence.[18]

It was, in consequence, difficult to portray the front through traditional landscape perceptions, for these were largely dependent on a Romantic-Realist style. Other approaches were also of limited utility: 'the impressionist technique I had adopted in painting,' A.Y. Jackson wrote, 'was now ineffective, visual impressions were not enough.'[19] Artists none the less persisted in their attempts to use familiar conventions. David Cameron, perhaps the most celebrated landscape painter commissioned to work for the CWMF, painted *Flanders from Kemmel* (Fig. 2) in a manner consistent with his already well-formed notions of what a landscape painting should be. Working in his London studio from pencil sketches made at the front in December 1917, he chose a high and distant viewpoint from which to render the scene. While he did not ignore the fighting, the thin layer of smoke rising from behind the far-off hills might just as easily be early morning fog or a low innocent cloud as the smoke from sixteen-pound howitzers. Although he did not overlook the war's effect upon the vegetation, his placing of branchless trees grouped in a symbolic trio in the picture's foreground hardly did justice to the devastating nature of its impact. He had attempted to paint a landscape of war, yet what he produced was not very much different from his Highland pictures. By adding a distant church, by exaggerating the rhythm of the undulating hills, by throwing a wide canopy over the land – the sky occupies three-quarters of the picture – he in fact managed to avoid the unpleasant aspects of the front and make a featureless landscape into an interesting, if not a beautiful, picture. Most artists who painted in the war zone did much the same.

Shell-blasted trees, such as those rendered by Cameron in *Flanders from Kemmel*, became one of the war artists' most popular devices. Canadian painter Cyril Barraud, whose graceful Art Nouveau trees had formed a screen across his behind-the-lines pictures, used the splintered and bare forms he found closer to the front in an effort to create a similar effect in his paintings of it.[20] Frequently coupled with the limbless tree was a dark palette; the nearer an artist got to the line, the darker his painting became. Maurice Cullen's *Dead Horse and Rider in a Trench* (Fig. 3) envelops the landscape in an impressionistic shroud of soft greys and browns, while his *Ruined Village, France* (Fig. 4), painted further behind the line, depicts the land in bright crisp dabs. And if he did not paint it clothed in mist, the artist frequently rendered the landscape as it appeared in the early morning or late evening. All was often vagueness and imprecision, a lack of clarifying and descriptive detail. For example, the only thing indicating that J.W. Beatty's painting of a grass-covered crater at *Liévin from Vimy Ridge* (Fig. 5) marks the spot where some of the worst fighting of the war took place is the title.

Many of the artists found a strangely congenial quality in what they saw. 'The beauty of places like Ypres is beyond words,' wrote William Rothenstein, who painted the shell-torn trees around Bourlon in gay colours and graceful rhythms. 'Hill Blast Corner could look serene and colourful on a spring day,' Jackson recalled, although he also warned that 'these were only minor truths, which confused one trying to render an equivalent of something crowding on all sides.' The disposition to see beauty even in the midst of horror reflected the influence of received opinions concerning what the artist should be doing. George Moore had, after all, written in his *Modern Painting* two decades earlier that the artist had an obligation to use the 'series of conventions' art provided to express his 'special sense of beauty.' Most artists working for the CWMF shared Moore's view. Frank Dobson felt no urge to reveal the unpleasant aspects of the war in his sculptures because 'a work of art that was beautiful in itself would pay tribute to those commemorated by the memorial more by the fact of its beauty than by virtue of any [emotionally exploitative] context.' Partly because it was easier to fall back on old associations and methods and partly because, as Varley pointed out, 'the whole thing is so intensely beautiful ... that you forget the horror and the reality of what it means,' most artists made no attempt to reveal the '*major* truths' that Jackson felt so poorly equipped to express. Many never even got close enough to where the machine was daily transforming the land to make preliminary sketches. The paintings they eventually worked up in their London studios possessed only an artificial vision, one corresponding to that of the visitor Arnold Bennett, who saw 'not a whisper of war' at the front but only 'a faint puff of smoke' that made 'no apparent impression on the placid and wide dignity of the scene.'[21]

While most artists working for the CWMF clung to the ideas expressed in Moore's *Modern Painting*, there were some who believed that 'modern art needs not beauty, or restraint, but vitality.' T. E. Hulme, spokesman for the small group of modernists that Konody had so boldly included in the CWMF, underscored the fact that beauty and a delight in nature and colour were not part of the new geometric artist's credo. Vorticists, Cubists, and Futurists alike, wrote Hulme, desired 'to avoid those lines and surfaces which look pleasing and organic.'[22] Nash and Nevinson might have seen beauty in the war zone, but they were not seduced into painting it. They took their task to be one of showing the discord, incongruity, bleakness, and dullness of light that pervaded the front.

Paul Nash, a superb interpreter of the beauty and rhythm of the English countryside, sought the 'character and form' and the 'reality behind the external' in his watercolour drawings of the war zone.[23] Shattered trees rendered by Beatty as graceful, balancing, and decorative elements appear in Nash's *Void* (Fig. 6) as stark, blasted images that deny the picture balance, symmetry, and beauty. The sky, a separate and dominating entity for many artists, is linked to the earth by great wide shafts of light. The viewer, moreover, is not left feeling detached from what he sees, for Nash thrusts him into the mud, shrapnel, and bone-bleached earth. Order and regularity are given over to chaos. Soft, rose-coloured clouds become clear, dark forms. Each jarring thrust and crevice of the broken land is emphasized. Nothing is veiled, everything is exposed.

Unencumbered by the desire to paint beautiful pictures and capable of revealing the structure of the land through his knowledge of the vision of such painters as Cézanne, Nash was able to execute paintings that won the approval of the soldiers. Stark, brooding, and eerie in their use of light and colour, his work, like that of no other artist, reproduced – Leed's term again – a liminal state of confusion and abnormality. In doing so, Nash wrote that it made him a kind of messenger whose brooding pictures of the land would 'bring back word from the men who are fighting to those who want the war to go on for ever.'[24]

A. Y. Jackson, having viewed Nash's work in London, tried for the same effect. In *A Copse, Evening* (Fig. 7) searchlights throw their great beams from the earth to the sky; a strangely luminous quality pervades the canvas. Yet the rhythmic undulations of the trees and the mounds of earth tied the painting to a style that was more concerned with expressing order than incongruity.

Wyndham Lewis was convinced that 'those miles of hideous desert known as "the line" ' presented him with 'a subject-matter so consonant with the austerity of that "abstract" vision I had developed, that it was an easy transition.'[25] When, in consequence, he depicted the stretch of land between a Canadian gun pit and an observation post in the pen-and-ink sketch *A Canadian Gun Pit* (Fig. 8), he was far from ignoring its jagged contours, but he did set aside the debris and detail that was so much a part of the landscape paintings of Nash and Jackson. The result was a much starker vision.

Nevinson, taking much the same view, felt the Futurist style offered 'the only possible medium to express the crudeness, violence, and brutality of the emotions seen and felt.'[26] What he thought should be done was plainly in evidence in the four panels of his *The Roads of France 'A,' 'B,' 'C,' 'D'* (Figs. 9-12). The first panel depicts orderly rows of vegetable fields through which trucks transporting men proceed. The last, portraying troops marching through rubble and ruin, dramatically underscores the extent to which a once tranquil countryside has been devastated by the instruments of war.

Part of the sense of E.H. Gombrich's dictum that 'artists tend to look for motifs for which their style and training equip them' was anticipated long before the first artist went to the front by Horace Taylor's observation in 1914 that 'the explosive style of the Futurists is eminently suited to the character of modern warfare, and battle subjects are the very thing that would appeal to them.' Nevinson, Wyndham Lewis, and other modernists certainly admired the power of the machine, and after the war began saw themselves, thanks to their particular technique, as the most obvious interpreters of its impact upon the land. Other painters, however, continued to focus on the landscape too. F.H. Varley, certainly, was more in tune with the land than the machine and more influenced by Impressionist and Art Nouveau styles than by Vorticism and Futurism. Yet even though his style did not permit exactly the sort of direct approach to the harshness and angularity of the machine-devastated landscape that was vouchsafed to Nevinson and the others – he wondered 'how the devil' one could paint anything to express the horror that made one's 'wildest nightmares pale before reality' – he none the less managed to do just that.[27]

Upon returning to Canada after two sketching trips to the front, Varley painted from a CWRO photograph and a sketch one of the most memorable works in the CWMF's collection, *The Sunken Road* (Fig. 13). In preparing this study of the remains of a German gun crew Varley relied heavily on the photograph (Fig. 14); but while this influenced subject and composition, it did not result in an absolutely realistic depiction of broken and decomposing bodies (this would, he said, have made the painting too 'deadly literal'[28]). By using the foreshortening technique of another war artist – the Renaissance painter Mantegna – to emphasize the dead soldiers, by bathing the entire work in a harsh light that allows nothing to be shrouded in mist or darkness, and by thinking 'about mud, and nothing but mud,' Varley was able to merge the figures with the wreckage of the earth.[29] The dead soldiers thus become in a double sense dehumanized, as intricate a part of the refuse of war as Nash's bits of iron, brooding skies, and water-filled craters.

The barren landscape of the front dominated most of these canvases, but devastated buildings also had their place in the iconography of the Great War. No small measure of Allied propaganda was devoted to making the battered cathedral, the shattered town hall, and the ruined farmhouse a symbol of what that propaganda's architects were anxious to have seen as the enemy's 'unhealthy desire for destruction.'[30] Believing the Germans to have been 'ordered from the outset to assassinate every work of art that stood within the path of their invasion,' the French placed sand-bags around the Vendôme column, the Italians removed the four bronze horses from St Mark's Cathedral, and the British insured their picture exhibitions against air attacks. The Canadians, having no art treasures in direct danger, none the less associated themselves with the assumed necessity to take precautions against the German onslaught on art and culture by producing sketches of the result of an imaginary bombing of St Paul's and the Houses of Parliament with the caption 'If London were Ypres.'[31]

Seen by thousands, war-devastated buildings seemed to tell 'the tale' of a nation bent on destroying civilization with particular force. The stately gate of St Martin's was a triumphant arch leading into the rubble that had once been Ypres. The golden virgin of the Basilica of Albert, hanging precariously from the steeple until the war's end, became 'an emblem of pathos, of the effect of war on the innocent.' And the magnificent façade of the cathedral in Arras stood like some 'ghastly figure bearing all the marks of modern warfare in the midst of all the horror and devastation.' So deeply did many observers come to believe that the 'destruction of private property by the German soldiers' had been 'deliberate,' that actions of this sort won a significant place in Lord Bryce's 1915 report on German atrocities.[32]

For those artists who felt it was their business to portray beauty and not destruction, there was no more telling a symbol of Germany's 'brute rage' than the remains of Ypres' medieval Flemish Cloth Hall. Almost as poignant were the ruined villages and châteaux that Rothenstein encountered, especially so in view of their resemblance to the ruined abbeys of his boyhood. The war-damaged houses Jackson sketched around Ypres were not unlike the picturesque farmhouses and barns that he had painted in the rural areas of Quebec. What had, in sum, happened to the buildings, large and small, grand and homely, in which men and women had lived, worked, and worshipped, might, as for Beatty, be made to represent 'an everlasting monument to the ruthless savagery of the abominable Huns.'[33]

Where paintings of 'no man's land' were almost always dominated by dark and gloomy colours, those of ruins were generally bathed in light and even airy colours. Augustus John found that ' "a good sun" ' could make beauty out of wreckage.[34] Rendered after the dust had settled, and in some cases after grass and foliage had softened their jagged contours, demolished buildings were treated in circumstances that removed them from the activity that had enveloped them during their destruction. Rarely were they depicted in the midst of being destroyed. Frank Brangwyn's etchings of burning buildings, their gaping walls exposing their shattered interiors, were an exception. For most artists the painting of damaged buildings offered an opportunity to recollect in tranquillity what the war had done; those wanting scenes of destruction in process generally looked elsewhere.

The peculiar detachment with which these war-damaged buildings were treated produced some striking effects. The devastated buildings in James Kerr-Lawson's monumental picture *Arras, the Dead City* (Fig. 15) might just as easily be a group of classical ruins. The rubble in Maurice Cullen's *The Sunken Road, Hangard* (Fig. 16) stands in splendid isolation, graphically outlined against the sky, infusing interest into an otherwise featureless scene. A pile of rocks and a few charred timbers in Rothenstein's *Entrance to Bourlon* (Fig. 17) indicate in a remarkably understated way the remains of a village. Only in Brangwyn's work is there a suggestion of horror, an indication that the bricks, timbers, and stones that once were buildings might now be human graveyards. Paintings of ruins are, for the most part, serene, calm, and as detached from the reality of war as the distant, wide-sky views of the front characteristic of the work of David Cameron.

The most frequently portrayed ruins were those of churches or cathedrals. Fraught with romantic associations, often the oldest building in the village, the church's destruction epitomized what was held to be the German's lack of respect for culture. For some, indeed, their devastation of 'the temples of God' placed the Germans in opposition to the Creator Himself. By destroying churches, as Arnold Bennett noted, they had 'accomplished nothing more austerely picturesque, more religiously impressive, more idiotically sacrilegious [and] more exquisitely futile.'[35]

Cemeteries and roadside Calvaries were also used to great effect. In Alfred Bastien's *Agny: Ruins of Shrine in the Wood*, the Christ figure hangs precariously from its cross like the golden virgin from the steeple of Albert. David Milne found several broken relics in Thelus Cemetery and, setting them against a white background, produced *Shattered Images in Thelus Cemetery*. Only infrequently were the Calvaries depicted as symbols of devotion as in Edward Saltoft's *A Woman at a Cross*. For the most part the cross meant self-sacrifice, not atonement; the soldier was a 'heroic fellow-sufferer' with Christ.[36]

It seemed clear from the hundreds of crosses that were nailed together from any two pieces of wood available that 'the war had stimulated religious awareness and prayer.' The cross assured the fighting man that his death would not be forgotten. Far from being that of a soldier dying the dreary death of so many victims of trench warfare, his parting would assume a dignity and stature hardly less than that of Christ's itself. After the armistice, David Milne, acting in conformity with this sense of the matter, painted several military graveyards in dry-brush watercolour. Varley encountered the neat-rowed crosses too, but was more interested in the disturbed contents of the civilian graveyards; in a kind of mockery of the Imperial War Graves Commission's assurances that every soldier's grave had grass, flowers, and shrubs, he did, however, depict two grave-diggers putting a cartload of limbs into a mass grave. Milne's *Courcelette from the Cemetery* (Fig. 18) counters this view by reinforcing the belief that every soldier had his own grave, whatever the exact condition of that grave might be. On the other hand, Varley's *For What?* (Fig. 19) not only denies the soldier a decent burial but questions the purpose of his sacrifice. The work also goes a long way towards bringing home the horror of the front. 'You in Canada ... cannot realize at all what war is like,' he wrote to his wife, Maud, in mid-October 1918: 'You must see ... your own countrymen unidentified, thrown into a cart, their coats over them, boys digging a grave in a land of yellow slimy mud and green pools of water under a weeping sky ... until you have lived this little woman – you cannot know.'[37]

The sculptor Derwent Wood returned to the notion that the soldiers' deaths could be likened to that of Christ. In a bronze sculpture, *Canada's Golgotha* (Fig. 20), he in fact extends the metaphor to its limit by depicting a Canadian soldier nailed to a barn door. The work leaves nothing to the imagination. Recreating the alleged crucifixion of a Canadian soldier by the Germans during the Second Battle of Ypres in April 1915, it shows its principal subject hanging in full view of five Germans pointing and jeering at his sagging corpse. Here the Germans are depicted as more than destroyers of culture, of churches, of the land; they are to be seen as nothing less than sacrilegious criminals, on a footing with the executioners of Christ Himself. No harsher indictment would be made by any CWMF artist. The truth of the charge that this terrible event had actually taken place would be challenged by the Germans themselves when the piece was finally exhibited in January 1919.[38]

The sacrificial nature of the soldiers' death was never made more explicit than in Wood's sculpture. Yet John Byam Lister Shaw showed, in one of the few allegorical works in the collection, that there was another way of dealing with that theme. *The Flag* (Fig. 21) places a Canadian soldier not on the cross or beneath it but athwart the paws of the British lion. Around him, standing in bowed reverence, are the friends, relatives, and countrymen for whom his sacrifice has been made; across his body is draped the Canadian Red Ensign. A particularly poignant note for those who came after lies in the fact that the models for the central figure in the picture and the boy in the foreground, both Byam Shaw's sons, were killed in the Second World War.[39]

The hero of the Great War was not always depicted in these dramatic, even overwrought, terms. Nor, as in traditional war paintings, was he to be seen as a high-ranking professional soldier. Long before the first artist had gone to the front, Fleet Street had 'taken "Tommy" in hand' by clothing 'him with emotions' and by giving 'him a manner and a physiognomy' – making the ordinary soldier into a popular hero. Nevinson claimed that this operation transformed him and his fellows into ' "castrated Lancelots," ' mild-eyed eunuchs who were 'unable to melt butter on their tongues and mentally and physically incapable of killing a German.'[40] Most observers, however, reacted more positively to the idea that the average soldier should in some way be celebrated.

Canadian troops, certainly, seemed worthy of such treatment. Arnold Bennett remarked that he liked 'to see Canadians walking about London' because they possessed a 'freedom and independence in their gait.' At the front, Robert Graves paid a group of recruits 'the compliment of telling [them] the real story of Loos, and what a balls-up it had been' because, since 'they were Canadians,' they deserved to be taken into his confidence. Considered rugged, easy-going, hard to discipline, likely to use artillery longer in their barrages than anyone else, capable of setting up the best barbed-wire entanglements, and in possession of the kind of initiative that allowed them to develop the raid tactic, Canadian infantrymen were seen as having injected an independent, frontier energy into the trenches. From this appreciation of their role arose the belief that they took on the hardest assignments of any fighting unit on the Western Front and that 'whenever the Germans found the Canadian Corps coming into the line they prepared for the worst.'[41] That over 60 per cent of Canada's recruits up to the beginning of 1916 were British-born, and that senior positions in the CEF were largely staffed by British officers, was immaterial. People, both in and outside the Dominion, wanted to believe that Canada's soldiers embodied the independent spirit that was thought to typify North Americans.

The popular mythology that came to surround the Canadian infantryman was not, as it happened, much evident in the work of most CWMF artists. Some, like the Australian war artist Will Dyson, did not believe that 'the soldier who is saving the world for us should provide us with a fund of light entertainment while doing it.' Others thought him largely incapable of performing heroic acts, for the overwhelming domination of the machine had made 'individual heroism … puny.' Still others believed that the soldier's relationship to senior officers, 'emphasized not merely by separate quarters and messes and different uniforms and weapons but by different accents and dictions and syntaxes and allusions,' helped to foster a sense of estrangement that bordered on alienation. Varley, for one, thought the ordinary soldier was a victim of forces beyond his control, caught up in a 'game of life and death [which was] nothing but a huge bluff conceived by some wise guys with business instincts.' No matter who was responsible – the machine, senior officers, war profiteers – the front-line infantryman was to be seen as dominated on all sides. As Jackson wrote in a letter home from the Somme in 1916, 'You feel at times so very insignificant. A private is nothing, unless he disobeys an order, then there is a big fuss made over him, and he probably gets shot.'[42]

Artists generally viewed the soldier in one of two ways: either they believed that 'a certain roll of his shirt-sleeves or a tilt of his helmet marked out the individual man almost as distinctly as if he had worn a special uniform all his own' or they felt that his unquestioning subservience to the guns, the officers, and the invisible forces that governed the war made one soldier indistinguishable from another.[43] Those who held the first view sought to reveal through their art the intimate experience of every man in the trench; those operating in terms of the second denied the soldier any individuality, believing that his experience and his response to it was no different from the next man's.

Eric Kennington was the most significant and the earliest of those painters who believed in the individuality of the ordinary soldier. As he told C.F.G. Masterman, 'it is the individuals that interest me.' His well-known *Kensingtons at Laventie, Winter 1914*, painted on his own before he was an official war artist, thus pays close attention to the faces, posture, and deportment of the soldiers with whom he fought during the cold winter of 1914-15. The CWMF's first war artist, Richard Jack, followed Kennington's lead in his treatment of some of the participants in *The Second Battle of Ypres*. Edgar Bundy made individuals of the officers he included in his *Landing of the First Canadian Division at Saint-Nazaire, 1915* (Fig. 22). And Inglis Sheldon-Williams used his on-the-spot sketches of Major-General Currie and his staff as they crossed the Rhine at Bonn in December 1918 to give his monumental work, *Canadians Arriving on the Rhine*, something of a focus on personality and character. But Kennington continued to show, in such paintings as *The Conquerors* (Fig. 23), that he was the artist most concerned with capturing the quality of the individual soldier's experience. Even his on-the-spot pastel sketches were less a record of the war's participants than a glimpse into the soldier's private life. *Mustard Gas* (Fig. 24), for example, shows the quiet agony of a blinded soldier, while *Interior of a Nissen Hut* portrays his strewn-about belongings. Few artists, indeed, were as moved to illuminate the 'fine qualities & varied character & appearance' of the men as was Kennington. Augustus John and Alfred Bastien were better draughts-men, and in his early war work Nevinson was more dramatic, but their drawings of Canadian soldiers are impersonal figure studies by comparison. Kennington's 'passionate admiration for the men whom he drew' permitted him to look beyond their khaki uniforms in a way most of his colleagues found impossible to emulate.[44]

While Kennington made it his business to 'pursue heroes,' Jackson insisted 'we have no heroes.' Sitting on the line as a private in the spring of 1916, he did not 'feel heroic in the least.' 'We don't know nothing,' he wrote to J.E.H. MacDonald, 'except what we see in the newspapers, and we know that's not true.' Later, as an artist for the CWMF, he rendered the soldiers as tiny identical figures dwarfed by camouflage screens and rubble. In *Screened Road 'A'* (Fig. 25) he denies the soldier any individuality, just as he robs the land of its familiar associations. Nash does the same in *Void*, an extraordinary work in which a lonely mechanical figure scurrying across a duck-board is dominated by a vast landscape of broken trees, ladders, guns, and mounds of earth. In Wyndham Lewis' *A Canadian Gun Pit* (Fig. 26) the soldiers appear 'in the light of insects, working in unison'; the big gun battery tanks take 'on the aspect of a gigantic ant-hill, with a personnel as busy and as effective as ants, no more but no less significant.'[45]

The soldier not only lost his individuality in the canvases of Jackson, Nash, and Wyndham Lewis (the French artist Fernand Léger and the German Max Unold saw him in the same light) but also in the sculptured works of the Serbian artist Ivan Meštrović. In *The Canadian Phalanx* a series of iden-tically carved infantrymen march across a marble frieze. Had the work been done a few years later, it might have been seen as a prime example of socialist realism, for it shares that genre's concern with the collective strength of the ordinary man working in unison with his fellows. Its inspiration is, in fact, the flat patterning of the photograph and the successive frames of the cin-ematographic film.

The purpose in all of this activity was not to negate absolutely the reality of the individual. Even as Cyril Barraud's *The Stretcher-bearer Party* (Fig. 27) and David Bomberg's *Sappers at Work: A Canadian Tunnelling Company* (Fig. 28) show the soldiers' faces turned away from the viewer, the articles of clothing each of them wore are given a clearly definable character. But no matter how rendered, no soldier or group was depicted as having any decisive influence on the course of the war. Only in the commissioned portraits of Victoria Cross winners, of statesmen, and of generals – paintings that con-formed to traditional portrait conventions – did treatment of the individual give any suggestion that the soldier was capable of confronting the forces regulating the war.

The sense that the circumstances of modern warfare underscored the incapacity of the individual to affect his fate was powerfully reinforced by the imagery of the gun. At once capable of being seen as a bringer of death and as an instrument of deliverance, it was used both to underline the individual's vulnerability to forces beyond his control and to indicate on what he must now depend if he were to have any hope at all of asserting himself. Here, certainly, was technology at its most impressive. Fernand Léger was 'dazzled by the breadth of a 75-millimetre gun' and by the 'magic of light on white metal.' Modernist sculptor Henri Gaudier-Brzeska was no less fascinated by a Mauser rifle he took from the enemy: 'Its heavy unwieldy shape swamped me with a powerful IMAGE of brutality.' Wyndham Lewis found the huge German siege gun 'a stimulus of visions of power.'[46] Not surprisingly, these instruments came to figure prominently in the work of some of the war artists. Commissioned to portray some aspect of the Allied victory at Bonn, Rothenstein requested that a howitzer be placed on the banks of the Rhine so he could put it in his picture: *The Watch on the Rhine (The Last Phase)* (Fig. 29) thus shows a soldier dwarfed by an enormous gun, to the depiction of which Rothenstein has given more care and emphasis than he has to the man guarding it.

While artists such as Rothenstein paid some attention to these great instruments of destruction, their number was not, in the end, large. Surprisingly few weapons were painted. There were, for example, no major paintings of tanks made by CWMF artists, even though the first photographs of that new device had drawn large crowds at the CWRO exhibitions in 1916. Several reasons for this state of affairs may be found. The rendering of military equipment had to be done accurately. This meant either working from photographs or making arrangements to observe the equipment in use. Since most artists preferred to work in the field, this kind of activity seemed sterile and unappealing. Guns were, moreover, viewed as unaesthetic, especially by the more traditional artists, and as providing in their angular, hard regularity little scope for the imagination.

Equally unpopular as a subject, so far as many of the artists were concerned, was the actual fighting. Like Canadian war novelists of the same period, they rarely dealt with the experience of combat itself. Jackson had 'no interest in painting the horrors of war'; Kennington did not feel 'capable'; Rothenstein preferred 'noble ruins' to 'strife among men'; and Shannon took the view that films were the last word on the subject. Even the practitioners of modernism, not withstanding their claim that there was 'no beauty except in strife, no masterpiece without aggressiveness,' painted few pictures of combat. The painting of battles, most artists believed, had been a part of traditional war art. If battles were to be recorded now, that could, as Brown and Walker claimed, best be done by the sketch-artist, the photographer, or the cinematographer. One anonymous writer even went so far as to suggest that 'the attempt to paint battle scenes should be given up because what results from it is false and misleading.'[47]

Battle paintings were, none the less, to be an important part of the CWMF's collection. Nine of the forty large panels were given over to commemorating Canada's victory at Ypres, Courcelette, and Vimy Ridge. Among the many artists who took on these commissions, only Louis Weirter had actually witnessed the event he was asked to portray. On-the-spot sketches of engagements later found their way into the collection, but they were generally of little interest because they were almost always the work of amateurs such as Arthur Nantel and William Topham, men who took their inspiration from the sketch-artist. With no guide to help him other than the photograph and the moving picture, and handicapped by often conflicting oral and written accounts, the artist frequently had to rely on his war-zone experience, and above all upon his imagination. The canvases produced are, as a result, filled with heroic gestures, sentiment, and inaccuracies – the very things that had given traditional battle paintings a bad reputation. Richard Jack's *The Second Battle of Ypres*, freighted with the conventions of the past, sets the tone for this kind of work. Weirter, too, incorporates virtually every traditional convention in his *The Battle for Courcelette* (Fig. 30), ranging from puffs of smoke and a panoramic view through to a hazy atmosphere and activity that bears no discernible relationship to the main subject of the piece.

Only one large commemorative battle picture manages to combine historical accuracy with a modernist approach: this is *The First German Gas Attack at Ypres* (Fig. 31) by William Roberts, a former gunner in the Royal Field Artillery. Part of the picture's success lies in Roberts' having chosen to deal with a single incident: the Canadians' first experience of gas on 22 April 1915 during the Battle of Gravenstafel Ridge, at the specific moment when chlorine gas forced the Turcos and Zouaves to retreat from their front-line position through the Canadian support trench. Confusion clearly reigns as the twisted faces and writhing bodies of the 45th Algerian Division meet the surprised soldiers of the First Canadian Brigade. A less imaginative artist might have shown the Canadians gallantly moving forward through the yellow-green gas to fill the front-line gap. Roberts, however, chose to depict the moment before the Canadians moved ahead. One Canadian soldier is actually shown fleeing alongside the Algerian troops. Another is reaching for ammunition. An officer is directing the Algerians away from the aiming pole so that the gun battery can move into action. The self-possessed and wholly remarkable discipline of the Canadian troops is placed in telling juxtaposition to the break-up of the Algerian Division. Like no other painting in the CWMF collection, *The First German Gas Attack at Ypres* conveys the confusion and the horror of modern war.

While artists reconstructing aerial warfare were not as fully burdened by the conventions of the past, they had difficulties of their own, among the most awkward of which was the matter of depicting events taking place in the air. The lack of horizon, the relative motion of clouds and aircraft, of aircraft and earth, the relative size of objects on the ground as compared to those in the air, all had to be worked out from the open cockpit of a plane. Nor did artists find it any easier to portray an aircraft from a position on the ground. The plane could too easily end by resembling an insect or a bird, as in Nevinson's treatment of Billy Bishop's encounter with three German flyers in his *War in the Air*. Yet the effort could yield exciting results. In one of his works Nevinson does convey the sense of what it must have been like to bank at four thousand feet while looking over the shoulder of the pilot to the fields below. His lithograph, *In the Air* (Fig. 32), in fact marks something of a turning point in the development of technique appropriate to this kind of subject. John Turnbull's *Dogfight* (Fig. 33) also manages to suggest much of the confusion created by seven aircraft locked in aerial combat apparently unregulated by the normal forces governing man's movement.

The painting of men in action was not, it should be noted, the monopoly of those doing large commemorative works. Alfred Munnings, for example, painted *Charge of Flowerdew's Squadron* (Fig. 34) while accompanying General Seely's cavalry. Alfred Bastien, for his part, depicted soldiers during a night raid while he was attached to the 22nd Battalion of the CEF in 1918. In the work of both artists, indeed, one sees with particular clarity what Paul Fussell called the 'gross dichotomy' of the Great War.[48] Horses charge towards the front line, men scramble over the parapet, and a sniper crawls into 'no man's land.' The action in all of these pictures is unresolved because only its early stages are depicted. Munnings, for example, gives his viewers the commencement of Flowerdew's charge but leaves them ignorant of what happens when their lances meet the enemy's machine-guns and 70 per cent of them are lost. But for all the drama, excitement, and action contained in these pictures, it none the less remains true that the full sweep of battle is most commonly seen in the convention-ridden canvases referred to above.

With few exceptions, among them H.J. Mowatt's *Trench Fight* (Fig. 35) and Jack's *The Second Battle of Ypres*, Canadian soldiers are not shown in hand-to-hand combat – nor, save in rare cases, do their corpses appear on canvas. When artists portrayed the taking of enemy territory, however, they showed no end of fascination with the detail of battle: pillboxes, trenches, and German dead loom large. And when enemy troops surrendered or were taken prisoner, there was no hesitation in painting them in that sad state – as one observer put it, 'like a lost dog.'[49] Less sympathetic though equally detailed representations of German or Austrian soldiers are given in such pictures as Nevinson's *Coffin Looted by Germans* and Kennington's *A German*

Cage for Captured British. On the whole, however, not much attention was paid to the rendering of the enemy. Along with guns and battle, treatment of him occupies a clearly subordinate position to the painting of war-ravaged landscapes, devastated buildings, soldierly sacrifices, and the ordinary Canadian soldier. Shattered trees and torn earth join broken crosses and ruined cathedrals in comprising the nightmare world into which these paintings show men to have been thrust, a world at odds with both nature and civilization, devoid of all that was good and normal.

The home front artist, removed from the slaughter of battle, surrounded by the Red Cross volunteer, the Victory Bond agent, and the recruiting officer, dealt with a different, quieter kind of heroism than his counterparts overseas. Those at home, wrote A.B. Cooper in the *Windsor Magazine*, 'rally to the flag at the call of patriotism; [they display] the noble generosity of rich and poor alike ...' Particularly evident, he thought, was 'the splendid patience, the pathetic devotion, the utter self-abnegation of women.' All of this testified to 'the raising of the standards of duty; the deepening and broadening of national consciousness ... [caused] by the war.'[50]

For Eric Brown it was important to show that loyalty, patriotism, sacrifice, and the dignity of labour could be found in war work at home as well as in the trenches. Florence Wyle and Frances Loring were certainly much concerned to demonstrate the nobility of Canadian women through their sculptures of munitions workers: Wyle in one lithe figure, the *Munitions Worker* (Fig. 36), Loring of several women in her *Noon Hour in a Munitions Plant* (Fig. 37).

In gesture and in pose Loring's women could be Hellenic warriors skirting a Greek vase; meant to underscore the fact that Canadian females had taken up a new role, her work portrays them more heroically and with greater dignity than ever before in Canadian art.

While Loring and Wyle gave their sculptures an heroic grandeur, most home front artists were unreflective observers trying, frequently with little success, to adapt their style to what they, Cooper's comments notwithstanding, persisted in seeing as an uninspiring subject. Few possessed the enthusiasm evinced by Lawren Harris when suggesting home front subjects to Eric Brown in 1918. Most, with no direct experience of what they were asked to paint, felt out of touch with their subjects, for unlike many frontline artists who had experienced the war they had not worked in the fields or the factories, in the canteens or camps, that formed the subject of their pictures. (The one artist, Albert Robinson, who had spent three years working in a munitions factory was sent, oddly, to paint the Collingwood shipyard.) They did not, however, have to work under adverse conditions. Theirs was simply the problem of making a dull subject into an interesting one. But while they did not have to grapple with how to paint shipyards and factories – these were hardly new subjects – they did have to think of these subjects in relation to the war.

Evident in all home front paintings is a considerable measure of tension between worker and product, machine and operator. Mabel May's women in *Women Making Shells* (Fig. 38) are not posed, nor are they clad in flowing garments. Set amidst the smoke, pullies, and driving belts of the factory, they become no more and no less important than the machines they operate. Toronto etcher Frederick Jopling identified the worker and the machine even more closely, for his *Forging the 9-Inch Shell* (Fig. 39) portrays men silhouetted against the gaping flames and brilliant light of the blast furnace in a way that empties them of all humanity.

The work of British Neo-Realist Charles Ginner demonstrates with special clarity the fact that not every artist found the factory 'romantic in its mingling of grimness and mystery.'[51] In *The Filling Factory* (Fig. 40), Ginner depicts women with identical faces moving calmly and single-mindedly in a bright, spacious, high-ceilinged hall; neither yellow-faced and blistered from filling the shells with mustard gas nor apparently fatigued from long hours of work, their presence among Spartan surroundings and tiny metal boxes bearing the letters 'TNT' none the less indicates that they are working under challenging and difficult circumstances.

Artists painting shipyards were also concerned with the relationship between the worker and what he did. Edward Wadsworth's *Dazzle-Ships in Drydock at Liverpool* (Fig. 41) shows the Vorticist camouflaged ship lunging above the workers as if it dominates them completely. Robert Gagen's *Shipbuilding in Ashbridges Bay, Toronto* (Fig. 42), on the other hand, pushes the ship and drydock into the background, thereby inviting the viewer to focus on the activity and clothing of the workers.

Pictures of the home front did not always strike so serious a note. Arthur Crisp's *British and Canadian Recruiting on Boston Common* gives the subject it deals with a picnic-like atmosphere complete with bandstand, flags, pipers, speeches, and marching. Nor did behind-the-line artists always paint with clear-eyed accuracy. Gerald Moira's *No. 3 Canadian Stationary Hospital at Doullens* (Fig. 43) eschews a sense of death and disinfectant, giving its viewers the idea that the kind of institution it is dealing with is characterized by clean and airy surroundings, with the patients strangely serene, calm, and untroubled.

Most of these painters away from the front felt obliged, however, to record what they saw in rather different ways. C.W. Jefferys' *Polish Army Bathing at Niagara Camp* thus offers its viewers what Paul Fussell has described as a 'contrast between beautiful frail flesh and the alien metal that awaits to violate it.'[52] Even Arthur Lismer, accustomed to relying on his imagination

and on the inspiration of the northern Ontario landscape, felt the necessity
to use a kind of literal detail in rendering what was in front of him. Intending
to give free rein to his imagination while painting the *S.S. Olympic* entering
Halifax harbour after the armistice, he saw the ship come in 'on a grey day,
with a pretty even and dull light.' Though it was not, he continued, 'a day
one would choose for the fine scene,' there were thousands witnessing the
event. Because of this, and because he was making a record, he felt he could
do little else than record it accurately.[53]

After having fulfilled his commission with the CWMF in France, A.Y.
Jackson joined Lismer in Halifax. He soon discovered that his imagination
had less scope in the harbour than on the battlefield. 'My work,' he recalled
in reference to his Halifax pictures, was 'record work of a rather definite
character which imposed limitations on it.' J.W. Beatty felt the same: when
asked to paint the barracks at a Canadian training camp in England, he
claimed that the row upon row of tar-roofed huts were 'impossible from an
artistic point of view.'[54] David Milne, confronting the same kind of subject
in his *Location Sketch of Kinmel Park Camp from the Hills above Dyserth* (Fig.
44), dealt with it by paying an almost excessive degree of attention to detail;
squaring off his paper, he annotated the drawing with place names as though
following a military guide to field sketching.

Harold Gilman was perhaps less constrained by his subject matter than
any of the others. Sent by the CWMF's London office to paint the aftermath
of the December 1917 disaster that had turned Halifax's harbour and part
of the city into rubble, he produced *Halifax Harbour at Sunset, 1918* (Fig.
45), a picture in which hardly any descriptive details are to be seen at all.
The painting is more a study of defused light and space than of a harbour
crippled by an explosion and dominated by ships of war. The only hint of
war is a few distant camouflaged ships; of the explosion that had rocked the
city barely six months earlier, there is, quite simply, nothing.

Several home-front subjects, of course, went unpainted altogether. No
war artist painted the profiteers who so embarrassed the Canadian government, the internment camps that housed hundreds of German Canadians
and other enemy aliens, or the rioters in Quebec City who opposed conscription in March and April 1918. Nor were unofficial pictures, like Nevinson's *War Profiteers* or George Grosz's *Die Goldgräber*, produced in Canada.[55]
No artist working in Canada made any statement against the war. Those,
like Lawren Harris, who were unsupportive of it, simply refused to become
involved in the CWMF and continued to paint the landscape of northern
Ontario. For the most part, paintings produced at home – Stanley Turner's
A War Record (Fig. 46) is a good example – encouraged a positive view of
the war effort and those caught up in it. Turner certainly did not hide the
fact that the cost of victory was high – the loss of a leg for one man, the

acquisition of crutches for another; but the bright colours evident in the picture and the smiling faces of the veterans and their admirers on Toronto's Davisville Avenue make it clear that this is to be viewed as a happy scene, a gathering of men who think their sacrifice has been worthwhile.

Home front paintings added powerfully to the iconography of the war. Shipyards, munition factories, and hospitals were all used to demonstrate just how far the great struggle had reached into the lives of ordinary men and women, even those far from the actual fighting. When all was said and done, however, it was the pictures from the field of battle that remained the focus of the CWMF's work. As Eric Brown, despite his support for home front pictures, put it, paintings of activity away from the scene of the fighting remained merely 'a preface ... to the sterner epic which was being written within sound of the guns.'[56] It was, accordingly, with the stuff of that sterner epic itself that the artists were expected to be most fully concerned.

5   'Not only history, but art'

In March 1918 Lord Beaverbrook observed that the art commissioned by the Canadian War Memorials Fund ought to be seen as having a dual relevance: it 'partakes,' he wrote Sir Robert Borden, 'of the nature of publicity in so far as the pictures will be immediately exhibited and of record in so far as they are intended to be the perpetual possession of the Canadian nation.'[1] At the war's end, even after ill health and nervous exhaustion had forced him to give up his position as minister of information, he strove to insure that the collection would fulfil its potential in both these respects.

Many artists had finished their commissions by the autumn of 1918. Pictures were stored on the premises of the Royal Academy of Art; at Beaverbrook's English country house, Cherkley Court; at the Leicester Galleries; at the Colnaghi and Obach Galleries; and in the artists' studios. Some artists were still at work: George Clausen, William Rothenstein, and Eric Kennington were waiting to go to France; and there was talk of sending A.Y. Jackson and C.W. Simpson to Vladivostok with the 4000-strong Canadian contingent of the Allied forces fighting the Bolsheviks. By December there were, none the less, nearly four hundred paintings, sculptures, etchings, and lithographs completed – more than enough work to stage a major exhibition. These, for the most part, were as yet unseen by the public. A small number of paintings had been reproduced in *Canada in Khaki* as well as in the September 1918 issue of *Colour Magazine*. But few works had been exhibited. The Fund's committee was saving them for a London exhibition in January and February of 1919; the Royal Academy had agreed to lend its galleries at Burlington House (even to open them on Sunday afternoons) for a fee of £800.[2]

The timing of the Canadian War Memorials Exhibition could not have been better. A few months earlier the Canadians had led the hundred-day advance into Mons in Belgium, thereby confirming the reputation they had won at Ypres and Vimy Ridge. The exhibition would do more than pay public tribute to their bravery, however; it would also take the edge off a measure of discontent caused by some quite specific misfortunes. Following the armistice on 11 November, when the fighting had finally ceased, there had been minor mutinies on the Continent and in Britain at Bramshott, Kinmel Park, and Witley Camps by Canadian troops who were both demoralized by the influenza epidemic and anxious to be on their way home now the war was over. The exhibition might boost the spirits of these homesick soldiers by emphasizing what they had helped to achieve in the war. The display of Canada's wartime accomplishments would also help justify the right to sign the peace treaty that Sir Robert Borden had just secured for the Dominion.

Such an exhibition would also be more comprehensive than any thus far shown. Certainly the effort of the Australians had not even come close: in an exhibition of war pictures at Australia House in September 1918 and three months later in a group exhibition at Burlington House, Australia's most prominent artists had not participated, and those who did produced work of little style or interest. Other exhibitions dealing with the war, such as Britain's Sea Power Exhibition at the Grosvenor Galleries, offered even less of a challenge. The CWMF's one serious rival was the British Pictorial Propaganda Committee. A large portion of its collection was, however, touring the United States. It was therefore easy for Paul Konody to claim in his 'Art and Artists' column in the *Observer* that the CWMF's exhibition would be 'the most important artistic event that has happened in England for many a year.'[3]

Writing in a special issue of *Colour Magazine* devoted to the Canadian art program, Konody assured the British public that the exhibition would give it 'an opportunity of seeing what modern art can achieve, when properly encouraged and supported.' As the date for the opening drew closer, the expectation that, as a *Times* reporter put it, the show would be 'one of the most glorious chapters of Dominion history' grew markedly.[4] On 2 January the *Daily Express* added to the excitement by asking whether people had any idea of what it had really been like when the Germans made their first gas attack and the gunners, struggling to keep their machines firing, found themselves being choked by the poisoned air they were inhaling at every gasp. The *Canadian Daily Record* sought to sustain this kind of interest the following day by drawing attention to the 'terrible realism' of Derwent Wood's sculpture of the crucified Canadian.

It was, then, amid no small amount of advance publicity that the Canadian War Memorials Exhibition opened at Burlington House on Saturday, 4 January 1919. When Sir Edward Kemp had introduced Sir Robert Borden, the prime minister told the crowd that 'the dawn of a New Year, a year of victory and peace' had come, and it was fitting 'that Art, the handmaiden of civilization, should be called upon to interpret the meaning of the war as it was and as it would be understood.' Lord Beaverbrook, sharing the platform with Lord Rothermere, Sir George and Lady Perley, and Sir George Foster, the Canadian minister of trade, earned praise for his 'wonderful foresight,' his 'administrative genius,' his 'tremendous energy.' The artists were then recognized for having made 'the task a labour of love.' Everyone cheered. And at that point Beaverbrook rose. He paid 'high tribute to Lord Rothermere and others associated with him,' who had helped to organize an exhibition which, in his mind, 'symbolised and illustrated the meaning of war and the cause for which the Empire [had] fought.'[5]

Paul Konody was present, but despite his role in bringing the exhibition about he was absent from the platform; the members of the press, more interested in other guests at the event to which it seemed 'all London had come,' did not seek him out. Lord Halsbury, the 'doyen of public men' and 'a keenly interested student of the pictures,' was more the sort of person they found interesting, as was the actress Miss Ellen Terry – though reference to her was accompanied by the rather waspish observation that she was less concerned with the exhibition than with the 'little group of admirers who accompanied her on a tour of the pictures.'[6]

The major attractions of the exhibition were found in the central gallery, where the opening ceremonies had taken place. Dominating everything was Augustus John's ten-by-forty-foot charcoal cartoon drawing *The Canadians Opposite Lens* (Fig 47). Described by one journalist as a 'panorama of the life under the hammer of Thor,' this stupendous work brought together crowds of refugees, detachments of soldiers, multitudes of horses, trucks, casualties, camouflaged guns, observation balloons, a ruined château, and Vimy Ridge itself in a grand tableau that one observer called the 'epitome of modern war.'[7] In the same room were to be seen Richard Jack's far less commanding *The Second Battle of Ypres* (Fig. 1), Laura Knight's *Physical Training at Witley Camp*, Charles Shannon's portrait *H.R.H. Princess Patricia of Connaught*, Charles Ginner's *The Filling Factory* (Fig. 40), two seascapes by Julius Olsson and Norman Wilkinson, and the bronze sculpture *Canada's Golgotha* (Fig. 20) by Derwent Wood. The CWMF officials had thus demonstrated in one gallery the breadth of the entire collection; they had also, inadvertently, shown the extent to which British artists had dominated the scheme, for not one Canadian artist had his work exhibited in this focal gallery.

Along with canvases, watercolours, and sculptures went dry-points, etchings, and lithographs. One room was given over to the moderns such as Wyndham Lewis and William Roberts, another to Alfred Munnings' sketches of the Canadian cavalry. Visitors might also look at E.A. Rickards' architectural drawings of the proposed Ottawa building (Fig. 48) that would provide the collection with an even more monumental setting than that offered by the rooms at Burlington House. A catalogue, complete with excerpts from *Canada in Flanders*, citations of Victoria Cross winners, and material descriptive of the paintings and other work, guided visitors through the complicated and extensive whole.

For those who wanted a memento of the exhibition, there were limited editions of etchings and dry-points by Cyril Barraud, Gerard de Witt, Caroline Armington, and Gyrth Russell. F. Lessore's model of *Nursing the Wounded* was available in plaster or bronze. Ten colour prints, reproducing the paintings of Wilkinson, Olsson, James Kerr-Lawson, David Cameron, Edgar Bundy, John Byam Lister Shaw, C.R.W. Nevinson, Gerald Moira, and Richard Jack, could also be purchased. The most impressive of the souvenirs, however, was *Art and War: Canadian War Memorials*: 'The gift-book *de lux* of the season' brought together an essay by Paul Konody on the history of war memorials from antiquity to the present with forty-eight lavish colour illustrations of paintings from the collection.[8]

The sensational pre-exhibition publicity provided by the presses of Beaverbrook, Rothermere, and Northcliffe, the monumental canvases themselves, and the attractive souvenirs combined to make the exhibition an overwhelming success 'both from the spectacular and financial standpoints.' That success had of course largely depended, as with Lloyd George's 1918 general election campaign, on catering to the post-war mood of the public. Returned soldiers anxious to show their family and friends where they had been, the curiosity of the non-military public eager to see what censorship had long denied them from seeing, both played an important part in drawing audiences. But there was more to the success of the exhibition than these things. As the American art critic Duncan Phillips said of the Allied War Salon held a month earlier in New York, such exhibitions served 'to remind us of the crimes committed against our common humanity by the pack of beasts in the forms of men who we have now driven into their den ...'[9]

Paintings of ravaged villages and towns and of death and torture reinforced the press's demands that the government – or someone – 'make Germany pay'; they also helped to document the suffering and sacrifice that had been experienced by everyone over the last four years. One had only to see the captions describing the 'Huns' Holocaust at Cambrai,' which accompanied the CWRO photographs displayed at the Grafton Galleries, or to hear picture dealers talk of soldiers eagerly buying prints of devastated Ypres, or to read of Vera Brittain's disgust that all London should remain joyous and unaffected while photographs 'of the Canadian soldiers' wartime agony' hung 'accusingly on the walls' of the Grafton Galleries, to sense something of the horrified interest with which the exhibition of these pictures and photographs was greeted.[10]

The most popular painting and most sought-after reproduction in the exhibition was John Byam Lister Shaw's romantic and sentimental *The Flag* (Fig. 21). Konody, in fact, had at first thought the show should be built around this kind of work. He had rejected David Bomberg's Vorticist-inspired canvas altogether and had carefully explained in the catalogue why other work of the same style had been included in the exhibition. Yet the modernist canvases in the exhibition did not go unnoticed. Though their approach might have seemed bizarre to some observers, their themes of sacrifice and destruction were of general interest. Furthermore, to criticize or even to have ignored them would have been unpatriotic. It was true, too, that modernist painters, like their more conventional counterparts, had experienced war, and this added to the credibility of their work, earning it, rather to Konody's surprise, an audience even 'among simple soldiers who had witnessed the horror of the battlefield.' In these circumstances, as a critic wrote in review of an exhibition of Wyndham Lewis' work appearing concurrently at London's Goupil Gallery, 'the public, presuming to criticize a war picture without having experienced war, is merely impertinent.' Some critics did, of course, continue to dismiss modernist works, linking them with the destructive forces that had brought about the war: those associated with German *Kultur*. Even an artist, writing from 'Painter's Grove, Chelsea,' under the pseudonym 'Amber Brown,' joined the attack on the modernists.[11]

More typical was the reaction of Canada's prime minister, who felt that some of the pictures were 'so modern and advanced that one could neither understand nor appreciate them.' And Muirhead Bone, who was open to new trends in painting but partial to the British art scheme, pronounced the collection 'not very impressive.' In the end, however, the fact that the collection was not going to stay in Britain spared it some of the more abusive criticism that would greet the modernist component in the British Pictorial Propaganda Committee's exhibition when it was shown to the public several months later. 'Canada,' as one reporter observed, was a new country, 'and has an undoubted right to encourage even the most disconcerting forms of the New Art.'[12]

All in all, then, the exhibition was to be seen as a success. The Canadian government, declared the *New Statesman* on 8 February, was to be 'congratulated on its enterprise, and the committee on its liberality and choice of artists.' Most commentators in fact paid tribute to the government of Canada rather than to the enterprise of Rothermere and Beaverbrook, a circumstance that does much to explain the prominent role assigned to the state in this undertaking and why it would be cited for so long as a precedent for public patronage of the arts.

If the institutional apparatus underpinning the project got recognition, so too did the artists themselves. 'The Canadian artists who were sent over to us,' Konody recalled, 'were a great surprise.' Though outnumbered by the

British and not so well known, they were not overshadowed. Jackson was better represented, at least in quantity, than any other painter. Varley, seen by the critics as 'the most distinguished and forceful of the Canadian official artists,' contributed the one canvas *For What?* (Fig. 19) that attracted attention by virtue of its having asked for what purpose the supreme sacrifice had been made. Both these painters not only acquired something of a following, if short-lived, in Britain but also saw their status at home enhanced. The presence of such a distinguished body of Canadian painting in the exhibition as a whole was in fact 'a justification for those who had had faith in the future of Canadian Art.'[13]

Much in the CWMF exhibition at Burlington House appealed, like the wartime music-hall and film entertainment, to what British historian Arthur Marwick has called the public's 'unhealthy emotions.' *Canada's Golgotha*, the bronze sculpture by Derwent Wood depicting a crucified Canadian soldier surrounded by a group of jeering Germans, managed to do this in a way unmatched by any other work in the exhibition. Even before the sculpture was shown, newspapers predicted it would be 'the ghastliest thing in these rooms of courage, agony, and death'; it would leave 'to future generations a damning indictment of the nation whose soldiers crucified a Canadian soldier and mocked his long-drawn-out agonies.' Photographs of the bronze (made available by the CWRO) appeared in newspapers from the *Illustrated London News* to the *Denver Post*. *Canada's Golgotha* quickly became, as London's *Daily Mail* put it, 'Canada's sternest memorial to her sons' sufferings in the war.'[14] It also reinforced Northcliffe's vigorous attacks on Germany, launched at the delegates assembled in Paris for the Peace Conference.

Atrocity stories had abounded during the war and contributed as much as anything else to the hatred of the enemy. While 'the incidence of atrocity against civilians in occupied territory was almost nil,' stories such as that of the German corpse factory, which allegedly processed battlefield corpses for industrial lubricants, were concocted by a censored press that lacked hard news. Many soldiers were sceptical about these tales, accustomed as they were to 'the gap between newspaper reports and the actuality of events which they had experienced.'[15] But civilians were inclined to believe anything they thought would bring them nearer to the reality of the front and help to explain their sense of loss and suffering. The appetite for atrocity stories was, as a result, very nearly insatiable. French newspapers ran weekly columns under the heading 'Les atrocités allemandes.' Russia had a museum devoted to atrocities as early as 1916. A year earlier Lord Bryce's *Report of the Committee on Alleged German Outrages* 'judiciously confirmed' (or so it appeared) rumours of the enemy's having killed non-combatants, having abused women and children, and having used civilians as screens for military operations. On the other side of the line, the German counterpart to the Bryce Report, known as the White Book, accused the Belgians of 'throwing boiling tar, maiming the wounded ... assassinating the officers,' and crucifying *German* soldiers.[16]

The story of the crucified Canadian soldier was first reported in the *Times* on 10 May 1915. The ghastly event itself had allegedly occurred on 22 April, the day of the first gas attack on the Canadians during the Second Battle of Ypres. The Germans, feeling 'particularly vindictive' towards the Canadians because they had come over to help Britain, had singled out one of their number for a particularly gruesome form of punishment.[17]

Various reports by soldiers who had seen, or more often who had known someone who had seen, the incident appeared in the press following the first mention of it. It was also incorporated into war memoirs such as Harold Peat's *Private Peat* and became a central element in war films, of which William Fox's *The Prussian Cur* forms the best example. Thus absorbed into the Allied consciousness, it joined with other tales of horror to make everyone fear and hate the Germans all the more. Vera Brittain recalled being repeatedly told of how the Germans 'had crucified Canadians, cut off the hands of babies, and subjected pure and stainless females to unmentionable "atrocities." I didn't think I had really believed all those stories, but I wasn't quite sure.' And even if, as Siegfried Sassoon also remembered, one did not wholly believe these rumours of atrocities, 'it would have been unpatriotic to have said so publicly.'[18]

When he first came across reports of the crucified Canadian, Canada's press censor Ernest Chambers thought the incident had been invented 'in certain sections of the State of New York' by the Americans for recruiting purposes. But when accounts of it multiplied, including a letter from Rudyard Kipling claiming that it actually happened, he began seeking eyewitness reports. As he told the director of special intelligence at the War Office in the course of asking him for assistance, a 'thoroughly authenticated statement of one or more of such incidents would be extremely useful, for enemy sympathizers are pointing to these crucifixion stories as proof of lying statements as to German brutalities made by the Allies, and they are defying loyal people to prove that any such incidents actually occurred.' Even the Americans became anxious to verify the allegation. Some newspapers in the United States claimed that the Canadian was actually an American volunteer, and there was concern in some American quarters that this fact was being insufficiently exploited. Senator Miles Poindexter, for example, thought the American Committee on Public Information could use the allegation to generate much more propaganda than it actually had.[19]

So far as the sculpture itself was concerned, it appears to have been executed on the basis of information 'obtained by [Wood] from various sources' – most probably hearsay and the press. Unlike many atrocity stories, the incident had not been publicly repudiated as journalistic fabrication. No official statement regarding it had been made by any government. It had not been labelled false; neither had it been pronounced true. Everyone, including the CWRO officials who asked Major-General Sir Arthur Currie whether the incident was 'founded in facts,' thus seemed puzzled by the numerous reports protesting its authenticity.[20] These doubts were, however, overtaken by events, for once the sculpture was exhibited in January 1919 under the aegis of the Canadian government, the whole incident seemed to have acquired official approval.

This certainly was the view of the matter the German government took. One month after the opening of the CWMF exhibition, Under Secretary of State for Foreign Affairs Freiherr Langwerth von Simmern criticized the showing of the sculpture on behalf of his government. Complaining that photographs of Wood's piece were being reproduced in newspapers and that the sculpture itself was to be placed with other exhibits in a special building in Ottawa, von Simmern pointed out that the terms of the catalogue entry were 'couched in such a way as if the work represented a proved fact.' Reports of the incident had never been accompanied by details indicating 'place, time, or any other circumstances,' information which might have enabled the Germans to conduct a proper investigation. And now, exhibited during the early weeks of the Paris Peace Conference, the sculpture would do nothing to help restore Germany's image in the face of her adversaries. 'It is urgently necessary to turn from a propaganda of calumny,' von Simmern asserted, 'and in future to propagate all those things which will enable the nations to unite in work for social, cultural and ethical advancement.'[21]

The message was simple. Wood's sculpture was a tool of war, the war was now over, and the unverifiable accusations made by the bronze must stop.

The Canadians did not reply to the German complaint immediately. Sir Edward Kemp, still head of OMFC, took several days to decide what to do. First he asked Arthur Currie for his opinion of what von Simmern had said. Then he informed Major-General S.C. Mewburn, head of militia and defence in Ottawa, that he was 'anxious [to] obtain all possible evidence' and instructed him to secure sworn statements from those soldiers who had told the press they had witnessed the atrocity. He also wrote to Arthur Meighen, the minister of the interior, for the prime minister had written him that Meighen had seen a letter 'from a very reliable soldier in a Manitoba Regiment, in which this soldier declared that the incident had actually occurred.' Both military officials, however, remained sceptical. Currie, who had investigated the incident on several occasions, had already told Borden that he did not believe there was 'any truth whatever in any story setting forth that a Canadian was crucified by the Germans.' Mewburn had 'never come across any positive evidence that such a crucifixion took place' either. Meighen, it turned out, could not trace the requested letter. But Kemp persisted, taking the matter up with Beaverbrook who was confident that 'the necessary evidence would shortly be forthcoming.' By this time, however, Kemp himself was less confident. As he told Borden, 'At this date, it would be a difficult matter to run to earth eye-witnesses of any incident which happened at such a time and place four years ago.'[22]

On 1 April, to Kemp's surprise, it appeared that two such witnesses had in fact been run to earth. One was a British soldier, Bandsman Leonard Vivan of the 3rd Middlesex Regiment whose father 'was employed in a position of importance in London'; the other, William H. Metcalfe, a Canadian corporal of the 16th Battalion, wore the Victoria Cross.[23] Unlike the many 'eyewitness' reports that contradicted each other, these two seemed perfectly consistent. The men, unacquainted with each other, reported that the incident had occurred on or within a few days of 23 April 1915. Both described the soldier pinned to a barn door, his hands pierced with bayonets, his head hanging forward on his chest. Neither had stopped to investigate; both had moved on elsewhere. Here, however, the similarity of their stories ended. Vivan claimed he had witnessed the incident while returning from the village of St Julien; Metcalfe while proceeding along the Ste Jeanne Road. Not only were these locations some two miles apart, but no German troops had penetrated to the Ste Jeanne Road during the course of the fighting. Kemp failed to notice, or chose to overlook, this inconsistency. To him these pieces of testimony, one from a gentleman, the other from a Victoria Cross recipient, were adequate proof that the event had taken place.

In Kemp's view the proof had arrived at just the right time. On 28 March he had received a *note verbale* from the German Foreign Office. Originally sent to the Swiss government at Berne, it had been forwarded by the Swiss to the secretary of state for foreign affairs, Earl Curzon of Kedleston, who had then passed it on to Lord Milner, the colonial secretary. Milner then sent it to the governor general of Canada, the Duke of Devonshire, from whom Kemp had got it. The note requested proof of the 'serious accusations ... levelled against the German Army and spread broadcast through the world without any attempt being made to furnish proof of the facts, or to give the German Government an opportunity by communication of actual details to repudiate the libel.'[24]

Kemp was now able to make a full reply. Writing to the under secretary of state for the Colonial Office four days later, he first of all attempted to distance the Canadian government from any official connection with the idea that the atrocity had taken place. The sculpture, he noted, had been executed by Wood 'entirely on his own initiative and without any suggestion, so far as is known, from a Canadian source.' The CWMF was only 'a voluntary organization supported by private subscription and to which we from time to time allotted the proceeds of the sale and exhibition of certain Canadian official photographs and paintings.' But even if the government had never taken a position on the issue, there was ample reason, in light of the testimony of the two soldiers, to believe it had actually happened. These were, after all, 'sworn statements by soldiers of the best character serving both with the Canadian and Imperial Forces who were unknown to one another.' In any case, investigations were still being carried out.[25]

Kemp's letter went from the Colonial Office to the Foreign Office where it formed the basis of Lord Curzon's communication of 16 April to the Swiss foreign minister, M. Carlin.[26] By the time the Swiss had forwarded Curzon's reply to the Germans and it finally arrived in Berlin the CWMF exhibition at Burlington House was over. *Canada's Golgotha* was crated, along with the other works in the show, and shipped off to New York with the rest of the collection that was to be exhibited at the Anderson Galleries in June.

This by no means ended the incident. The Canadians continued their efforts to find testimony relating to it. They dispatched an officer, Captain F. Richardson, from Ottawa to France in order 'to establish the authenticity of the alleged outrage.' News of the German complaint reached the press and was discussed in the Canadian House of Commons. Kemp assured the House that he had given instructions 'that every effort should be made to ascertain if what we have represented could be substantiated.' Citing the testimonials of Vivan and Metcalfe, he concluded: 'I do not think there can be any doubt that Germans were guilty of this atrocity.'[27]

The Germans, for their part, were not satisfied with Curzon's reply to their communiqué. On 28 May came a second *note verbale*, and on 24 July a third. Both asked again that evidence giving proof of the incident be produced by the British government. The Canadians received the second note from the Colonial Office on 15 August, the third on the 20th. By that time additional testimonials, secured through Captain Richardson, had come to General Mewburn in Ottawa. None coincided with the others. Yet Kemp, who examined them, remained adamant in his belief that the atrocity had taken place: the fact that the reports lacked consistency only meant 'that more than one instance of the crucifixion of prisoners by the Germans occurred.'[28] Yet, when pressed by Milner to respond to the second German note, it was to the now familiar testimonials of Vivan and Metcalfe that Kemp turned, forwarding them to the Colonial Office on 21 August, from where they were then sent to the Foreign Office.

The Foreign Office was pleased with the testimonials. Its officials drafted a reply for the Swiss minister in the early autumn of 1919 incorporating the statements of Vivan and Metcalfe, though omitting their names. Weeks passed as the draft reply sat awaiting ratification by the War Office, the Foreign Office, the Colonial Office, and the OMFC. By November it had still not been authorized. Since nothing further had been heard from either the Swiss or the Germans the Foreign Office decided 'not to pursue the matter further unless it is re-opened by the German government.'[29]

The Canadians, who had no knowledge that British authorities had decided to let the matter lie, continued to gather 'eyewitness' reports over the autumn of 1919. Though most were 'hearsay,' doing 'little or nothing to strengthen the case already presented,' one, submitted by Major G.C. Carvell, formerly of the Princess Patricia's Canadian Light Infantry and now with the Canadian Trading Company in Harbin, China, forced a new view of the incident.[30]

According to Carvell, a Canadian soldier had been hung by wires from the loft of a barn during the Second Battle of Ypres. Those responsible were not German soldiers but Belgian farmers. Indeed, the character of the whole incident was quite different than had been reported. 'The "crucifixion," ' Carvell asserted, 'was not one IN FACT. [The soldier] had been tied up by wire attached to his wrists and feet, while a strand, which held his head in position against the wall, accounted for his semi-strangulation.' The atrocity, Carvell continued, could not have been committed by the Germans because the incident had occurred 'on an afternoon in April 1915' when the Germans were 'not less than 11,000 yards distant.' Like the other 'eyewitnesses' Carvell had not stayed, but he had 'placed the householders, men and women, under arrest, established a guard from the soldier details ... and galloped off.'[31]

In the meantime a fourth German note, again asking for evidence, arrived at the Foreign Office. The issue having been revived, the Foreign Office sent the reply incorporating the testimonies of Vivan and Metcalfe drafted the previous October. In light of the Carvell testimony, however, the Canadian government was now less than sure it had a case. On 4 February Eugene Fiset, deputy minister for militia and defence, told the Colonial Office that because Major-General Currie had found 'insufficient evidence to support the charge' and since further inquiries in Canada had yielded nothing, it had been decided that the allegations regarding the incident should be specified as 'not proven.'[32]

Kemp, however, could not agree with this decision. As he later told officials at the Department of Militia and Defence, in a communiqué that would be passed on to Milner early in 1920: 'In view of the declaration of Corporal Metcalfe ... Vivan ... and ... the fact that the contents of Declarations have actually been communicated by the British Government to the

Government of Germany, it is not considered fitting that the authorities administering the Canadian Military Forces should now declare the occurrence of the alleged incident "not proven." '

But the Germans, who had received the testimonies of the two 'eyewitnesses' in mid-January 1920, could prove that their troops were nowhere near either of the locations where the atrocity had allegedly taken place. Not surprisingly, the claim that the sculpture represented an actual event was never made again. And when the Canadian War Memorials Exhibition opened in New York in June, *Canada's Golgotha* was not on display; according to one report, however, it was there and could be viewed 'by special request.'[33]

Despite the conviction of Geoffrey Butler, Britain's Ministry of Information representative in New York, that Beaverbrook preferred the press, film, and photography to ' "cultural" propaganda,' Beaverbrook did not miss the opportunity to show the CWMF work in New York. It had done well in London, the Fund needed money, and New York was almost on the way home.

Harold Watkins, now promoted to major and in charge of the CWRO, remained with a small staff at the London office to oversee the exhibition and the sale of photographs still touring England. Captain Percy Godenrath, formerly in charge of the CWRO's exhibitions in London, accompanied the sixty wooden crates containing the CWMF's paintings and sculptures on the *S.S. Ixion* to New York. Once there he supervised the installation of the exhibition and arranged for advertising. He was also under orders to sell the CWMF's etchings and reproductions, to collect entrance fees, and to 'make every effort to obtain assistance, advertising, etc. free of charge, and ... make all exhibitions as great a financial success as possible keeping expenses down to an absolute minimum.'[34]

Paul Konody went to New York too. Bearing the title of art director, he was put on an annual salary of £1,000 (plus expenses) and charged, along with Godenrath, with organizing and advertising the exhibition. Shortly after arriving in New York he sent a promotional letter to organizations and newspapers praising the CWMF collection as 'the most complete artistic record of any country's share in the great war, and the most significant manifestation of artistic activity during this period.' He reinforced his prediction of success in New York by recalling the 'enormous stir' the exhibition had caused in London, where 'for two months the galleries were thronged [with visitors] from morning to night.' He wrote other articles extolling the collection's broad scope, the catholicity of taste it represented, the historical interest of its paintings, its reliance on on-the-spot activity by artist-soldiers, and the building in Ottawa that would house it, making that city 'a place of pilgrimage for art students and art lovers.' He also explained why an exhibition celebrating Canada's achievement in the war was being shown in New York: 'It has now been brought to New York as a tribute to the 10,000 or more brave American boys who enlisted in the Canadian forces. The memorial serves as much to honor their heroism and devotion as that of the Canadians who laid down their lives in the cause of freedom and justice.'[35]

This, indeed, became a commonly repeated theme. Lieutenant-Colonel R.F. Parkinson, by now honorary commanding officer of the CWRO in Canada, rehearsed it at a Canadian Club luncheon by praising 'the gallant 10,000 Americans' in Canadian ranks as 'vanguards of your citizen army.' In a sense the New York exhibition was an exercise in cultural diplomacy, a kind of gift offered to the Americans in an effort to build upon the wave of Canadian-American goodwill that had emerged over two years, thus reinforcing the bonds created by a co-operative war effort in which 'the resources, the money, the manufacturing and transport facilities, and, to some extent, the manpower of the continent were as one for war purposes.'[36]

The opening day of the exhibition 'was not the kind of day for an art gallery, or anywhere else except the sea.' Yet despite the mid-June heat, 'prominent society folk and many Canadian, British and American officials' gathered at the Anderson Galleries at 3 o'clock to witness a small group of men, Lieutenant-Colonel Parkinson and Arthur Knowlson, president of the Canadian Club, among them, declare the exhibition open.[37]

There was some doubt as to whether the fact that American boys had enlisted in the CEF before the United States had declared war in April 1917 would be enough to arouse American interest. There were no paintings dealing specifically with American volunteers and none of the artists were American. The Canadian exhibition, moreover, was being held in 'the last days of the dying season.' The American public none the less came to the Anderson Galleries in large numbers. The press, well briefed by Konody, wrote about the works with enthusiasm. 'This remarkable show,' went one review in the *New York Herald*, 'ought to appeal to every citizen on this side of the line for the simple reason that it is as much in honor of the United States ... While our land was restive under the delay that followed the sinking of the Lusitania thousands of boys from all over the Union swarmed to Toronto and Ottawa with but one thought, to "get in" and strike a blow at the unspeakable enemy.' Another reviewer saw the exhibition as 'an expression of the democratic, self-consciousness of a nation which, though daughter in her mother's house, is mistress in her own; though with a difference in ceremonial form, stands for the same sort of North American freedom that we enjoy.'[38]

While the exhibition was an overwhelming success from a political point of view, there was little discussion of the work itself. Konody, attempting to direct the critics' attention to the more innovative canvases, published an article in the New York *Sun* on 22 June focusing on the work of Nevinson, Nash, Wyndham Lewis, and Roberts. Photography's capacity to render exact images, he wrote, had made these artists strive 'for personal expression'; they aimed 'no longer at accumulating a quantity of accurate little facts, but at the rhythmic organization of a big truth.'

Konody hardly had to explain modern art to the American public. New York might not have been the centre of the Dadaist, the Suprematist, or any other avant-garde movement that had emerged during the war, but its public had been alive to new trends in painting ever since the famous Armory Show in 1913. Having viewed works far more advanced than those of Nash and Nevinson, it was not likely to find their paintings disturbing. Even where it did find the exhibition's modernist works not quite to its taste, it accepted them anyway, for, as the *Evening Post* of 3 July put it, 'the men who painted them are soldiers and, logically or illogically, ought to know how war looks.'

When the cwmf pictures were first shown in London critics had wondered what future generations of Canadians would make of them. Before the exhibition even arrived in Toronto, some of the Canadians who had seen it in New York were comparing it with the British Pictorial Propaganda Committee's exhibition then touring the United States. In their view the British pictures were not so grand either in scale or in subject and 'lacked the concentrated unity of purpose and idea that inspired these first-hand [Canadian] records.' Eric Brown, who attended the New York opening, was more sparing in his praise. 'Some of the pictures are fine,' he conceded, 'some very indifferent,' but – here his antipathy to large works manifested itself clearly – 'most of the big ones are much too big.'[39] It was only when the exhibition finally arrived in Toronto, opening at the Canadian National Exhibition in August 1919, that Canadians at large got an opportunity to judge the pictures and sculptures for themselves.

They found it, on the whole, an extraordinary event. 'Apart from the war itself,' Sir Edmund Walker enthused, it was 'one of the greatest events in Canadian history.' It certainly covered a good deal of ground. Besides the cwmf's collection of paintings and sculptures, there were Arthur Doughty's war trophies, the cwro's photographs, and, displayed at various points around the exhibition buildings, 'big guns, aeroplanes and other large relics.' There was also live entertainment. The British Grenadier Guards Band played during the first two weeks. Colonels Barker and Bishop, 'the world's greatest aces,' flew 'surrendered German Fokkers and types of British, French and Italian machines' over the grounds.[40] And for the first three days of the exhibition the Prince of Wales was in attendance.

In order to accommodate the cwmf's 447 works the Canadian National Exhibition's Fine Arts Gallery was extended by over one hundred feet. The pictures and sculptures themselves were set up in much the same way as they had been in London and New York. Konody secured pre-exhibition publicity space in the press to advertise the show. 'Pictures will be seen at which I should not be surprised if some people howl,' he wrote in what was becoming a familiar attempt to arouse interest in the controversial modernist work that formed part of the show. In this he was not without success. Critic Barker Fairley expressed the view that 'a wide popularity will not be expected for such pictures as *Void* [Fig. 6] by Paul Nash.' The *Globe* labelled some of the pictures 'Cubist monstrosities' and hoped that 'Canada would not have to provide a permanent home for such rubbish.' A few commentators defended the 'sane specimens of modern art.' Arthur Lismer, for example, saw the controversy as a healthy sign: these specimens of modern art were arousing 'the sentimentally inclined to voice their protest.' Most, however, accepted the work without comment, taking the view that, as one observer put it, 'The war memorials are not only national records, they are family records for most of us; and as such they will have a sure interest handed down from generation to generation.'[41]

Opinion of the exhibition as a whole ran the gamut from A.Y. Jackson's dismissal of much of it as 'a lot of stuff which sprawls over too much canvas ... and [was] of unhistoric importance' to the critic M.O. Hammond's complaint that more Canadian artists had not been commissioned to paint the larger pictures. There was, however, a general feeling that what work Canadian artists had done was praiseworthy indeed, and everyone was pleased that 'native artists should have contributed so much to the worth of the enterprise.' But, as in London, it was sentiment rather than nationalism that was most in evidence, for the work that gave visitors the 'most lasting impression,' according to the *Toronto World*, was Byam Shaw's *The Flag*.[42]

The Toronto exhibition was 'a great success, much greater than either ... [Beaverbrook and Konody] or the Exhibition authorities expected.' The galleries were 'crowded continuously with returned soliders who spent hours living again through the scenes depicted and describing them to their friends.'[43] At the end of two weeks, 107,865 Canadians had passed through the turnstiles, paying $25,945.05 for the privilege.

Lieutenant-Colonel Parkinson had intended to put the collection in storage after the Toronto showing, but 'at the last moment, for propaganda work [among the French Canadians], it was deemed desirable to go into Montreal.' Sponsorship by that city's Art Association was, accordingly, arranged, and the exhibition was opened by the Prince of Wales in October 1919. Montrealers were invited to 'Come and live 2 hours with the Canadians behind the lines, in the lines, and before the lines – review the war's tremendous moments – see a great conflict as it has never been granted home folks to see it heretofore.' Konody – by now playing a familiar role indeed – sought to stimulate interest by drawing attention to the ' "advanced" ' pictures of Roberts, Wyndham Lewis, and Paul Nash. Yet once again the favourite painting in the exhibition was Byam Shaw's *The Flag*. As the *Montreal Star*'s critic wrote, it captured 'the sacrificial spirit in which the sons of the Empire laid down the greatest gift they had to give that freedom might triumph.'[44]

While the exhibition was permitted to perform 'a valuable national service' by virtue of its propagandizing among the French Canadians of Montreal, it was not moved to another city.[45] Despite requests, such cities as Winnipeg and St Louis were denied the right to see the pictures and sculptures on the grounds that they had been improperly crated since leaving Britain and were in poor repair. When the Montreal show was over the exhibition was therefore packed up and sent off to Ottawa for storage.

The peripatetic show that had been seen in London, New York, Toronto, and Montreal represented, it should be noted, only part of the CWMF's collection: that concerned with the front and accumulated by Beaverbrook, Rothermere, and Konody. Another portion, dealing with the home front and completed by the forty-three artists commissioned by Walker and Brown, had also found an audience, though not in as many cities. It was, in fact, on display in the Art Gallery of Toronto at Grange Park where it could be seen even before the Montreal exhibition had terminated. Brown and Walker had already compared the work assembled in London with their own 180 pictures, sculptures, and prints. Now it was the critics turn. 'It may be said,' wrote one reviewer, 'that the work of the Canadian painters measures up to the average standard set by the British artists whose pictures were shown here six weeks ago'; the Canadian artists were, he continued, 'seen at their very best in their War Memorial paintings.' Another writer was surprised to find that the work was 'not only history, but art.' The pictures of shipbuilding, land workers, and flying camps, among other home front themes, attested to 'Canada's advancement in art during the war.' The collection's only shortcoming, noted a writer for the *Canadian Courier*, was the omission of western Canada 'except for one picture of lumbering operations in British Columbia, done, presumably from photographs.'[46]

Artists had their views too. Jackson thought 'the discipline the artists subjected themselves to in painting things of little aesthetic interest has done them a lot of good.' The work of Robinson, Johnston, Lismer, Loring, Wyle, and Jefferys had, he felt, proved this. The organizers were also pleased. Eric Brown told an audience at the Art Gallery of Toronto that 'the whole exhibition' had given those who had put it together 'the liveliest satisfaction,' and went on to pay particular attention to the forty aircraft camp pictures by Frank Johnston which dominated it. Manly MacDonald's oil sketches of girls working on the land were, he thought, 'the happiest and most joyous' pictures in the exhibition because they were the 'furthest removed from the grimness of war.' The sculptures of Frances Loring and Florence Wyle embodied Canada's 'determination to win the war.' Canada's home front pictures were, in short, a pleasure to see. Devoid of the horrible wastage of life in the trenches, they showed what constructive energy could do. What was even more noteworthy, they demonstrated beyond a doubt that 'native art in Canada' was 'equal to any demand that can be made upon it.'[47]

No matter where it took place, then, display of the work done under the auspices of the CWMF attracted widespread attention and had important results. It had set off London's first major post-war exhibition and heightened British appreciation of Canada's substantial contribution to the war effort. It had made Americans conscious of their northern neighbour and, by reminding them that ten thousand of their own men had fought before April 1917, extended their sense of their own involvement; it had contributed to the emerging belief that Canadians and Americans were capable of a special kind of co-operation thanks to the character they each possessed as North American societies. It had shown Canadians themselves how extraordinarily effective their war effort had been. Finally, it made plain that Canada had a group of artists doing work that could stand comparison with that being produced by their counterparts in any other nation. Their accomplishment was to be noted not only because of its quantity – the CWMF was consistently praised for having given Canada a record of its involvement in the war that was more complete than that of any other country – but also because of its quality. The country's cultural development – or at least that part of it represented by painting and sculpture – was, it seemed clear, keeping pace with all that had happened in the social, economic, military, and political spheres of its existence. In that department of national life, no less than in the others, the coming of war had forced the pace.

6 Lest we forget

By the end of 1919 Lord Beaverbrook had accomplished a major goal: work done for the Canadian War Memorials Fund had been widely exhibited. Completing the collection, housing it, and handing it over to the Canadian people were objectives yet to be gained, though movements in that direction were in evidence by the summer of 1919, when Major J. Harold Watkins travelled to Ottawa to oversee the transfer of the CWRO to Canada and to ensure that Lieutenant-Colonel R.F. Parkinson, its commanding officer, was well established there. Watkins, along with Konody, in North America since the CWMF exhibition in New York and still very much part of any arrangements being made, was anxious to meet both Sir Edmund Walker and Eric Brown. It was, in the end, Konody who met Walker, in August, earning from him the characteristic remark that he was 'a foreigner and apparently enamoured by all new forms of art.' A month later both he and Watkins talked to Eric Brown. The National Gallery, it was decided, would take care of the pictures until some action regarding their ownership and permanent exhibition could be taken. Brown constructed a fireproof room in the basement of the Victoria Memorial Museum, and when the exhibition ended in Montreal the works were stored there.

Parkinson's presence in Ottawa gave Brown and Walker a representative of the London-based CWRO close to hand. It was he who handed $12,000 of the Toronto and Montreal exhibition profits over to them in October (this covered their request to Beaverbrook for $11,263.23). But though he administered the Fund's finances in Canada, he did not control its budget as a whole. Cheques were issued and money transferred only on the instruction or with the approval of Beaverbrook. Indeed it was Beaverbrook who announced in August 1919 that the 'main work of the Committee is now accomplished and as the result of nearly three years of activity, it finds itself left with a deficit. Whether it is to continue its labours or bring them to a final close depends on future developments.'[1]

But there were no 'future developments,' not, at least, of the sort that would help the Fund's financial position. Despite its profits from photography exhibitions, publications, and print sales, it had a deficit of £8,521. This meant, as Beaverbrook announced late in October, that 'the Committee of the CWMF must bring to an end its labours so far as the purchase and gathering together of pictures is concerned.' Sir Edward Kemp's refusal to give the Fund its promised share of the £10,000 profits from the War Office's Cinematographic Committee – Beaverbrook himself had established this organization in 1916 – was a major cause of the problem. 'Unless,' complained Beaverbrook, 'the Government of Canada decides to give to the CWMF the money realized from the sale of films ... Lord Rothermere and myself will have to meet these commitments ... out of our own pockets.'[2]

By December 1919 the CWMF was 'running very short of funds.' There were 's.o.s calls from London' but Parkinson did nothing about transferring money in the Fund's various Canadian accounts to England because he believed that 'with the financial backing they have over there they can worry along some way or other.' The situation was now serious enough, however, to make reductions in the scale of the Fund's operation necessary. Further acquisitions and commissions, such as portraits of Victoria Cross winners, were curtailed. F.H. Varley, now back in Canada and eager to begin a 14-foot mural that promised 'to hold its own' with anything in Britain, was told not to proceed with the work. Plans to send Jackson and Simpson to Siberia were cancelled. No arrangements were made to acquire the working-drawings of major pictures in the collection. Bomberg, in fact, got permission to dispose of his sketch for *Sappers at Work: A Canadian Tunnelling Company* (Fig. 28), while John was permitted to sell the cartoon for the prodigious mural that was 'to rank with the mightiest achievements of European Art' (the asking price for the cartoon was £2,000).[3] And though Canada was well-represented at the Paris Peace Conference, no attempt was made to commemorate the occasion on canvas.

The Fund's resources were further strained when Sir Edmund Walker learned that Varley and Beatty had 'come back [from France] poorer than they went'; Beatty, Walker claimed, was short $320, while Varley was 'out of pocket' $715 for studio rent. There were complaints from other Canadian artists. Sculptors Loring and Wyle, who had borrowed money in order to meet foundry expenses, were anxiously awaiting payment. Frank Johnston had given up his job as a commercial artist to work full-time for the Fund; feeling that 'the transition back will require a certain amount of patience and capital before I get running right again,' he asked Eric Brown for a month's salary.[4]

By April 1920 the Fund was in 'desperate straits.' Only a month earlier Parkinson had been asked by the London office 'to remit immediately the money balances in the various accounts of the Canadian War Memorials

Fund.' The March financial statement, drawn up by the Fund's auditors in London, showed that the deficit had risen to £9,500. Beaverbrook and Rothermere guaranteed the bank a total of £5,000 and they also considered 'disposing of some of the pictures to cover the deficit.'[5] This time Parkinson did what had been requested of him: he transferred what remained of the Canadian account, roughly $6,000, to London. Canadian officials were now, however, without money.

It was in these circumstances that Konody, having returned to Britain at the end of 1919, found himself on the *Empress of France* in the spring of 1920. In the hope of replenishing the Fund's coffers, he was bringing the last group of CWMF pictures from London to Canada for exhibition. These works, along with the Canadian home front paintings and sculptures shown at the Art Gallery of Toronto the previous autumn, went on display at the 1920 Canadian National Exhibition. The show's theme was 'the final triumph of allied and more particularly Canadian arms,' for which the tone was set by Rothenstein's *The Watch on the Rhine (The Last Phase)* (Fig. 29) and George Clausen's *Returning to the Reconquered Land* (Fig. 49). The modernist exceptions were Bomberg's toned-down *Sappers at Work: A Canadian Tunnelling Company*, John Turnbull's *Air-Fight*, and 'the most "modern" picture in the exhibition,' Paul Nash's *Night Bombardment* (Fig. 50);[6] though the number of these works shown was fewer than in any previous CWMF exhibition, they set off a barrage of criticism.

'Low mutterings of surprise were heard last year when the first portion of the Canadian War Memorials paintings came to the Exhibition,' noted a reporter in the *Mail and Empire* on 4 September, but 'these murmurings have taken more definite shape this year, and many unflattering opinions may be heard daily concerning the second series of war paintings.' The *Star Weekly* reporter was among the first to complain: the modernist pictures were 'going to puzzle sorely several hundred thousand Canadians in the next two weeks.' Hector Charlesworth, the most reactionary art critic in Canada, was not surprised that 'the strange surge of emotion that assailed many of us on encountering the first series a year ago should be no less insistent this year.'[7]

Some part of the disinclination to take the paintings seriously was no doubt due to the fact that the war was clearly over. By 1920 patriotic sentiment had diminished. 'The superficial wartime unity of the country,' as two historians of the period have noted, had begun to crack 'under the pressure of a host of ethnic, regional, and class discontents.' As always, however, it was the modernist works that caused a particular problem, and Konody, indefatigable as always, continued to come to their defence: 'The test of a good painting is to look at it upside down. Its aesthetic appeal should not suffer by this reversion. The recognition of the representational element is only a minor attraction.' But this time his efforts did nothing to assuage the critics' dislike of modernist work or the public's suspicion that the pictures had been deliberately selected to make Canadians feel how far behind they were in their 'knowledge of art.'[8]

In Montreal the exhibition at the Art Association on Sherbrooke Street aroused little interest of any kind. It was poorly attended and collections at the gate amounted to only $100 a day. When it closed, Konody, Godenrath, and the other CWMF employees were abruptly dismissed. Deloitte, Plender, Griffiths and Company, the Fund's auditors since its inception, became the CWMF's secretaries. The pictures themselves were sent to the National Gallery in Ottawa; almost 900 CWMF works now crowded the small storage space in the basement of the Victoria Memorial Museum.

Despite the attention given to the exhibition in Toronto, the Fund's bank account was not replenished. Several artists, both in Canada and in Britain, remained to be paid. Impatient and needing money, some of them threatened to sue, while others went so far as to suggest that they would destroy work that had been commissioned and completed but not collected and paid for.[9]

With the last consignment of pictures now in Ottawa a new set of difficulties arose. Some of them were damaged. The condition of the historical paintings by Romney, Reynolds, Phillips, Lawrence, and West was, as Brown told Walker, 'very serious.' The state of West's *The Death of Wolfe* was particularly poor: tacks had been driven near the edge of the picture and it was badly 'scraped and scratched in many places.' Brown did not think, however, that anybody in Canada should have to assume responsibility for restoration work since ownership of the paintings was still technically on the other side of the Atlantic. Upon his urging, Rothermere and Beaverbrook agreed in April 1920 to pay $500 towards restoring the historical works, but the amount proved to be insufficient, especially when the last consignment of pictures to arrive at the gallery turned out to contain some damaged work too. With no funds for restoration, and no means of obtaining any in the absence of clear title to the works, Brown asked Walker whether authority over the collection might be established. This prompted F.B. McCurdy, the minister of public works, to present the matter of ownership to Arthur Meighen, now the prime minister. Within two weeks Meighen brought the 'very bad condition' of the pictures and the question of their ownership to the attention of Beaverbrook: 'They came into being through the efforts of a committee established by the Canadian Government, but they have not been formally handed over by the Canadian War Memorials Committee.'[10]

Long wanting praise and already angry for not getting it, Beaverbrook and Rothermere were outraged by the prime minister's ignorance of their involvement in the Fund. To correct this misapprehension Beaverbrook replied immediately, giving a full account of his, Rothermere's, and Lima's part in the creation, execution, and financing of the scheme. Then, in his capacity as committee member, he relinquished all responsibility for the collection. Rothermere, who was to visit Canada the following summer to take up the matter of a building, was, Beaverbrook informed Meighen, now not going to do so. The destiny of the CWMF collection was completely in the Canadian government's hands.

Meighen's letter to Beaverbrook, which according to its recipient resembled 'the reprimand to a subordinate of an angry Prime Minister,' came when he and Rothermere were settling the CWMF's financial accounts. Beaverbrook was in favour 'of paying off now.' But Rothermere, who was even more upset by Meighen's letter, wanted to wait until 'a message of thanks to you and me' had been extracted from the prime minister. 'With the passage of time much work that one does is forgotten,' Rothermere told Beaverbrook, 'and I do not think in this particular case the work you and I have done should pass into the limbo of forgotten things.' Rothermere nevertheless matched Beaverbrook's payment of £2,000. The remaining debts of the CWMF were thus paid out of the organizers' 'own pockets.'[11]

Meighen's apology finally arrived on 19 January. His letter of 25 November had, he told Beaverbrook, been written by the Department of Public Works and 'was signed by me along with the usual stack of correspondence and in the rush of business' he had endorsed the letter without reading it. He did not, however, attempt to amend his oversight by offering praise for what he had been told by Sir George Perley of Beaverbrook's and Rothermere's participation in the CWMF, nor did he seem concerned that Rothermere had cancelled his Canadian trip to arrange for the housing of the collection. Nor did he thank Beaverbrook for having, in his letter of 14 December, officially handed over the collection to the Canadian government. All of this left Rothermere still very much annoyed; as he told Beaverbrook, the prime minister 'still seems oblivious of the fact that I am contributing quite a considerable sum of money in addition to all my previous endeavours to provide Canada with the most striking war memorial that any nation owns today.'[12]

What Beaverbrook and Rothermere wanted, it seems transparently clear, was public recognition of the fact that they had not only inspired and guided Canada's war art scheme but had paid for a good deal of it too. Each of them certainly tried in his own way to bring the nature of his contribution to the attention of the public. At his own expense, Rothermere produced a modest publication, *Canadian War Memorials*, which set out the Fund's purposes: to compile historical and artistic records, to represent various tendencies in art, and to provide an impressive monumental setting in order 'to avoid the wearisome monotony of the ordinary picture gallery with its long unbroken rows of architecturally unrelated exhibits.' It listed the forty major canvases that were to dominate the building and illustrated the plans

E.A. Rickards had designed in 1918. Published on 'very lasting paper,' the book was to be 'duly deposited in the public libraries of Ottawa and in the building where the pictures are exhibited.'[13]

For his part, Beaverbrook compiled a lengthy report, which, like Rothermere's booklet, gave the history and objectives of the CWMF. He cited the organizers' monetary contributions and stressed the Fund's accomplishments. Set against this stirring story was Meighen's unappreciative letter of 25 November.[14]

The result of this activity was minimal. Only one copy of Rothermere's publication found its way into a public institution in Ottawa. Beaverbrook's report, long under preparation, did not arrive in Canada until May 1922. By that time the country had a new prime minister, W.L. Mackenzie King. And he waited six years before publicly thanking Beaverbrook for his CWMF and CWRO work.[15]

Running parallel with Beaverbrook's and Rothermere's concern with handing over the collection to the Canadian people was their wish to see it properly housed. As Konody had written a year earlier, 'The Committee of the Canadian War Memorials would have deemed their gift incomplete without at least [providing] a carefully worked out scheme for the kind of building required.'[16] The British architect E.A. Rickards had been invited to submit designs for such a building in 1918. He was a good choice. His status as a lieutenant in the British army allowed the Fund to acquire his services for nothing. His talent for combining architecture with sculpture had already been realized in such buildings as the Central Hall, Westminster, Colnaghi and Obach's prestigious Bond Street gallery, and the Bristol Memorial to King Edward VII. Rickards began work on the CWMF building in September 1918. Four months later the designs were finished.

Beaverbrook described the proposed building – it was modelled on the Panthéon in Paris – as 'a domed building in a plain, monumental style, symmetrical in its conception, so as to present the same aspect from all points of the compass.' It was to consist of nine major parts: the rotunda under the dome; four main galleries with short cross-arms forming the pattern of the crusader or Jerusalem cross; and four large oval galleries between the arms of the cross. The sunken floor beneath the rotunda would contain a fountain, and from there short staircases would lead to all the main galleries. A terraced garden would surround the entire building.[17]

Beaverbrook and the CWMF committee found Rickards' plans 'excellent.' Here was a building to complement the pictures and sculptures they had been gathering over the last year and a half. It would be both a memorial and a gallery: a 'mecca' for art lovers and a 'shrine' to those who had fallen in the war. The estimated cost was $1,250,000. Beaverbrook offered, in

December 1918, to donate $25,000 if Rothermere would do the same.[18] The remainder of the funds would be raised through CWMF exhibitions and CWRO publications. Ottawa, the city of the federal government, would provide a suitable site free of charge.

Realizing that the Canadians themselves would appreciate being consulted on the building's design, Beaverbrook asked Sir Edmund Walker in January 1919 if the government's architect, Frank Darling, could travel to Britain to advise Rickards on the proposed plans. Walker responded by cable. 'Heartily agree with proposal,' he told Beaverbrook, 'Great hope of solution of complete building programme for war records through such collaboration. Believe free site available.' Walker, however, was not entirely satisfied with Rickards' plans because they did not include exhibition space for war trophies and photographs – a possibility at which he had hinted in his cable and one with which, as adviser to the Commission on War Records and Trophies, he was very much concerned.[19] Beaverbrook, for his part, was not happy sharing his art collection with trophies and photographs in a space of only 3484 square feet. Both men stood their ground: Walker for a building to house war records, art works, and trophies; Beaverbrook for a building, following Rickards' plans, that would contain only the CWMF collection. Further complications were created by the fact that Rickards, now ill, never travelled to Canada as had at one stage been intended, while Darling did not in the end go to Britain. And when Walker left in March 1919 on a four-month trip to Japan, the project to construct a separate building for CWMF works came to a complete halt.

Brown's and Walker's own scheme for housing the CWMF works did not fare any better. Their idea, it will be recalled, had been to use the need to get a home for those works to promote construction of a new National Gallery, part of which would be set aside for the CWMF. Patriotic sentiment would then be played upon, but the result would be a building devoted, in the main, to the works of countries other than Canada. Towards the end of 1919, however, the Department of Public Works assigned the National Gallery to its old premises: the east wing of the Victoria Memorial Museum at the foot of Metcalfe Street. Brown's and Walker's hope for a building of their own had been ignored. But far from admitting defeat, they began to move almost immediately in another direction; its character was made plain in the National Gallery's annual report of 1920-1, where they asked that 'the Canadian War Memorials' Committee ... be properly appreciated and their work carried to completion by the creation of an appropriate building where the works may be kept on continuous exhibition.'[20]

Support for a Canadian-organized building fund for galleries that would be devoted exclusively to CWMF art was sought through the medium of two exhibitions of war pictures, one in 1923, the other in 1924, both taking place in the Victoria Memorial Museum under the auspices of the National Gallery. These were intended to impress upon the government 'and the people of Ottawa the fact that sooner or later the pictures and other war relics must be suitably housed.' 'The future of the Canadian War Memorials,' Brown wrote in the preface of the 1923 catalogue, 'is a question demanding both earnest and early consideration. The National Gallery is greatly overcrowded in every department and from no point of view are its present premises adapted to the proper and safe presentation of valuable works of art, nor do they permit growth and proper educational classification. It possesses no storage space that will allow any of the largest of the War Memorials to be stretched or attended to. The needs, therefore, of a new National Gallery Building and of adequate provision for the War Memorials become inseparable from each other.'[21]

In time, the Art Gallery of Toronto, which Walker had played no small part in founding, joined the National Gallery in attempting to raise support for a CWMF building. The catalogue for its 1926 exhibition of 261 works from the war art collection pointed out in no uncertain terms that it was 'by means of such exhibitions as the present one' that 'it is hoped to demonstrate to the country at large and to the Government in particular, what a truly magnificent painted record of its participation in the war Canada possesses, and the duty and value of treating it as a great historical monument to those who gave their lives or their energies to the defense of the right.' A statement, prepared by Sir Edward Kemp and read at the exhibition's opening ceremonies, expressed the hope that 'the present display will help to draw public attention to the importance of these paintings, and ... that at no very distant date there will be a memorial building erected for the purpose of properly housing them and that they will not be stored very much longer in seclusion.'[22]

The National Gallery itself made yet another attempt to interest the public and the government in the war art collection by holding, in 1934, an exhibition in conjunction with the Dominion Convention of the Canadian Legion of the British Empire Service League. Percy Godenrath produced a lavishly illustrated catalogue, *Lest We Forget*, and once again a plea for a building was made.[23] The exhibition caused others, including the Canadian Legion, to lobby for a building too.

While there was still some tendency to question the commemorative value of such modernist works as Nash's *Void* (Fig. 6), the exhibitions of 1923, 1924, 1926, and 1934 did receive hearty support. They were festive occasions with military bands playing the old tunes and veterans wearing their worn uniforms. Most who attended saw the exhibitions as a testimony to the fact that the collection had been 'unceremoniously buried alive' and was now 'regarded as dead.' The *Ottawa Journal* suggested in 1929 that a committee be established to locate the records and paintings, to make recommendations regarding their temporary care, and to make suggestions for a suitable building in which to house them permanently. Other newspapers simply asked: 'What has become of the collection?'[24]

The exhibitions and the support given them by the press and retired servicemen did nothing, however, to arouse the government's interest. When asked by Sir George Perley in the House about the matter in April 1928, Mackenzie King said simply that 'up to the present time we have felt that there were other demands more imperative than the demand for a building for the purpose of housing these particular works of art.' He did offer to provide the land if some 'public-spirited citizens' would donate the money for a building, but that was as far as he was prepared to go.[25]

Beaverbrook and Rothermere, for all their disenchantment with the Canadian government, were the persons most likely to fulfil the role of 'public-spirited citizens' as King envisioned it. There was, in fact, some hope that they would do it in the spring of 1923 when Beaverbrook assured Walker that 'Rothermere and I will stand the racket to the end, which, we hope, may not be far distant.' But a year later Brown reported from London to his assistant Harry McCurry that 'Beaverbrook, at present takes no interest and couldn't or wouldn't see me.' This was not surprising. Neither man had yet been thanked to his satisfaction for his contribution to the Fund. By 1924, moreover, they were more out of than in the political arena. After the death of his friend Bonar Law, Beaverbrook remained 'on the outside of political life' until 1940. Rothermere spent most of his time in the south of France. And Paul Konody had no interest in continuing 'to work and waste my time on completing the collection, considering that my 3 years of strenuous and absolutely gratuitous effort have brought me no sort of acknowledgement.'[26]

By 1924 the impulse that had got the CWMF under way eight years before had played itself out. King's plea to 'public-spirited citizens' four years later fell on deaf ears. Public money could not be allocated to a gallery in depressed times; even if the money were found, the building of a gallery would arouse the public's ire. Borden had shown enthusiasm for displaying the collection by stating publicly that 'it would be necessary that the great collection of pictures should be properly housed.' But that was only months after the armistice. By the end of the 1920s a wave of pacifism, which resulted in anti-war novels such as Charles Yale Harrison's *Generals Die in Bed*, prompted many to question Canada's involvement in the Great War. Anti-war sentiment, indeed, helped to undermine the very goal that Beaverbrook, Rothermere, and Konody had set out to reach: 'to provide a memorial to sacrifice and heroism so that future generations might not forget.'[27]

That Canada's war paintings were failing to fulfil this purpose was made particularly clear by the public's reaction to the Imperial Order Daughters of the Empire's efforts to circulate reproductions from the CWMF collection. In keeping with the order's program of supplying Canadian schools with reproductions of historical interest, eighteen pictures – mostly of Canada's participation in France and Flanders – were chosen by a committee of IODE members and Paul Konody. It was hoped the reproductions would serve to remind Canada's school children of 'the glory and valor of the Canadian men,' of 'the magnitude of the sacrifices of the sons and daughters of the Empire,' and of 'the terrible wastage of war.'[28] By the mid-twenties they had been distributed to school boards throughout the country.

Lucy Woodsworth, the wife of the social reformer and founder of Canada's socialist party, J.S. Woodsworth, was the first to protest. Writing in the *Railroad Employees' Monthly* of the gift of some six thousand prints to Ontario schools, she condemned the reproductions for glorifying war: 'They make for hostility instead of understanding among the various groups in Canada, they perpetuate distrust and hatred toward the people of other nations, and they associate patriotism and militarism and slaughter.' The Vancouver Parent-Teachers' Association refused the IODE's gift, passing 'by a large majority the resolution that no pictures tending to glorify war or to perpetuate feelings of prejudice and hatred towards the people of other countries shall be hung in the schools.' 'The teaching in schools,' the resolution continued, 'shall be of such a nature as to propagate peace.' The reception was the same in Winnipeg. And in 1926, when the reproductions were placed in the assembly hall of Central High School in Calgary, 'the objection taken was that these pictures glorified war and the heroism of war, throwing that part of history into undeserved relief.'[29]

The CWMF paintings might well demonstrate 'the glory and valor of the Canadian men' as well as 'the terrible wastage of war.' Yet the pictures chosen from the CWMF for reproduction dealt with artillery in action, men climbing over the parapet into battle, troops arriving in France, ships patrolling Canadian shores, and aircraft engaged in combat. The few paintings in the collection that did show the 'wastage of war' and questioned the purpose for which it had been fought – Varley's *For What?* (Fig. 19), Nash's *Void*, Roberts' *The First German Gas Attack at Ypres* (Fig. 31) – were not among those selected by the IODE committee and Konody.

Besides being improperly housed and in some instances kept from display in reproduction, the CWMF collection was in danger of being dispersed. Shortly after the government officially acquired it, eight large panels were moved to the Senate chamber where they hang to this day. In July 1925 an order-in-council transferred the historical pictures by West, Romney, Reynolds, and Lawrence to the Public Archives of Canada. A year later the deputy minister of public works proposed that a portion of the collection hang 'in the rooms and corridors of the House of Commons.' But the National Gallery's trustees stood firm: 'Only if these works are kept in a single building, specially designed for the housing of art objects, and under constant skilled technical care' could they be 'kept from rapid deterioration and preserved for posterity.'[30]

Other changes took place. In July 1930 H.W. Brown, acting deputy minister of militia and defence, asked Eric Brown to withdraw *Canada's Golgotha* (Fig. 20) from the collection: 'In view of the feelings aroused by the publicity given to the alleged incident and kept alive by persons whose motives may be open to question, it is suggested that the bronze group should be packed up and placed in permanent storage, so that the Government may be protected against the embarrassment of its being exhibited or photographed at any further time as the portrayal of an event.'[31] The trustees agreed. Two days later *Canada's Golgotha* and the photographs reproducing it were confined to permanent storage where they remain.

While the CWMF collection was being broken up and *Canada's Golgotha* hidden away, war monuments and trophies were being erected across the country. Every city and most towns had at least one 'Lest We Forget' monument; every service club a trophy of war. The new Parliament Buildings had a Peace Tower with a carillon and a Memorial Chamber with books of remembrance. These works – cenotaphs, memorial sculptures, war trophies – like Wood's controversial bronze and Byam Shaw's *The Flag* (Fig. 21), embodied an idea rather than the artistic expression of an event. Unlike most of the works in the CWMF, they could possess any meaning the viewer wished to give them: sacrifice, waste, sorrow, pride, even redemption.

Even more work of this kind had been in evidence following the Boer War when the Advisory Arts Council had allocated large sums for a monument but had refused to acquire paintings of the war. Once again, it seemed that the conventional war monument was taking precedence over the commemorative picture. The works exhibited in 1919 and 1920 by the CWMF had done their job, but that job now seemed to have been little more than serving as a bridge between Arthur Doughty's Dominion War Exhibition train, which exhibited relics of the war throughout Canada and the United States from 1917, and the erection, early in the 1920s, of the first cenotaphs. While Beaverbrook had had the energy and the genius to make a war record for Canada, he could do nothing to sustain the post-war mood that had made the exhibitions at Burlington House, the Anderson Galleries, and the Canadian National Exhibition a success. As he lamented to Augustus John years later, he had been 'quite willing to build a Gallery in Ottawa but the Canadians did not have a suitable site and also there seemed little enthusiasm for the project.'[32] The truth of the matter was that war trophies, the town memorial, and Cook's tours to the remains of Ypres and to Vimy Ridge took precedence over paintings and sculptures as a means of commemorating Canada's achievement in the war.

Beaverbrook and Rothermere may have been disgruntled by the Canadian government's lack of appreciation for their efforts after the CWMF collection was officially handed over to the Canadian people in December 1920, but the artists who had contributed to the collection could hardly complain. Arthur Lismer had earned enough money by working for the CWMF to draw a cheque for $2,500 which he used to purchase a house in Toronto. After recovering their foundry expenses, sculptors Frances Loring and Florence Wyle bought an old wooden framed church in Toronto's Moore Park and converted it into a studio-home. And A.Y. Jackson was not to earn as much money again until after the Second World War.

Even if some CWMF artists did not have more money by the war's end, their wartime experience put them in a good position to bid for war memorial commissions. Loring produced sculptures for Galt, Ontario, for a church in St Stephen, New Brunswick, and for Osgoode Hall in Toronto (the commissions not only brought her a financial return but gave her the opportunity of experimenting 'in monumental concepts').[33] Frank Brangwyn painted a commemorative mural for the cupola hall of the Manitoba Legislative Building in Winnipeg. Unharmed by the publicity surrounding *Canada's Golgotha*, Derwent Wood, along with Augustus John and William Orpen, was sent by the British Pictorial Propaganda Committee to model busts of the dignitaries at the Paris Peace Conference. When Wood returned to London another commission awaited him: a monumental sculpture in memory of machine-gunners for Hyde Park Corner. Painter Eric Kennington turned to the three dimensional by accepting a commission to carve a memorial in Portland stone for Battersea Park; the piece would commemorate all ranks of the 24th Division.

Alfred Munnings did not receive a memorial commission but his CWMF portrait of General Seely mounted on his horse Warrior 'helped to fix [him] in the public mind as an exceptionally skillful painter of formal equestrian subjects.'[34] Others won recognition for their war work too. Orpen was elected to the Royal Academy of Art and was also knighted for giving his entire war output to the Imperial War Museum. William Rothenstein became head of the Royal College of Art, Augustus John an associate member of the Royal Academy, and Richard Jack a full academician. When Jack travelled to Canada in 1921 he was commissioned to paint Sir Edward Kemp's portrait. Before leaving Europe, F.H. Varley painted Lord Beaverbrook's daughter.

Other artists were patronized by the Fund's organizers. Pictures by John, Beatty, Wyndham Lewis, Orpen, Paul Nash, and many others who had worked for the Fund, found their way into Lord Beaverbrook's private collection. Paul Konody never gave David Milne the exhibition the artist had wanted, but he did continue to support the modernists he had hired, even allowing the Vorticist William Roberts to paint his portrait in 1920. He also wrote a superb article on Nevinson in 1931 and a year later, with Sidney Dark, a monograph on Orpen.[35] And, just months before his death in 1933, he helped David Bomberg – the artist he had made repaint *Sappers at Work: A Canadian Tunnelling Company* – to exhibit in the Soviet Union.

Those who had been involved in the CWMF as administrators or organizers also did well. After the war J. Harold Watkins went to work for the prestigious *Colour Magazine* and maintained a special interest in at least one artist who had worked for the Canadians, Gerald Moira. Percy Godenrath, who had handled the CWMF's fine art publications, became a dealer and importer of prints in Ottawa. In 1921 he purchased what remained of the CWMF's collection of etchings, dry-points, lithographs, and reproductions. The work, which formed the basis of his stock, further publicized Canadian and British artists who had been associated with the Canadian war art program. Bertram Lima, who had sat on the CWMF's committee, died in February 1919 only months after receiving the order of Officer of the British Empire for rendering 'valuable aid to the Propaganda of Canada during the war.' Sir Edmund Walker, who along with Eric Brown had favoured English, European, and particularly Japanese woodcuts before the war, now added to his status as a figure in the Canadian art world by purchasing more contemporary Canadian pictures for his private collection. Having become increasingly more popular among Canadian artists as time passed, his death in 1924 was viewed as 'a calamity'; everyone agreed, as Arthur Lismer said, that they would 'miss a great soul.'[36]

Most artists did not wait for a war memorial commission, election to an art institution, or the patronage of the Fund's organizers, but reaped some benefit from their association with the CWMF through the publication and exhibition of their war work. William Wood lent several eastern Mediterranean watercolours to illustrate A.J. Mann's *The Salonika Front*. Inglis Sheldon-Williams provided illustrations to accompany his brother Ralf's text for *The Canadian Front in France and Flanders*.[37] Edward Wadsworth added the woodcut *In Dry Dock, 1918* to several prints of blast furnaces, minesweepers, and other industrial subjects and exhibited them at London's Adelphi Gallery in 1919. In the same year, Gyrth Russell gathered up his war work, travelled to Halifax, and held an exhibition there. Augustus John cashed in on his war and peace portraits at London's Alpine Club Gallery in the spring of 1920. Wyndham Lewis, who had refrained, along with John and Russell, from exhibiting until after the war, staged an impressive exhibition called Guns at the Goupil Gallery in London with the aim of giving 'a personal and immediate expression of a tragic event.'[38]

Despite Wyndham Lewis' belief that the real story of the war could only be written long after hostilities had ceased and his conviction that a serious interpretation of it had still to be done, CWMF artists displayed, as the foregoing suggests, a continuing interest in the war, one which led them to produce a host of new works. Paul Nash created a number of linocuts, including a few abstract interpretations of the front, to accompany Richard Aldington's privately printed 1919 publication of anti-war poems, *Images of War*. Stanley Spencer spent more than a decade working on a series of frescoes for the Burghclere Chapel in Berkshire which portrayed soldiers digging, map reading, erecting tents, building dams, folding blankets – indeed doing everything except fighting; he omitted the less pleasant aspects of the war because he wanted to redeem himself 'from all that I have been made to suffer.' Orpen's post-war painting, *To the Unknown British Soldier in France*, was less a memorial or record than a statement against the war. Commissioned by the British Pictorial Propaganda Committee to set forty eminent faces amidst the grandiose surroundings of Versailles, Orpen came up with a coffin flanked by two half-crazed, loin-clothed soldiers. The work was exhibited to a startled audience at the Royal Academy's spring exhibition in 1919. Orpen eventually painted out the sentries, and typical British 'Tommies' took their place. Nevinson, who felt his war pictures had been 'the last word on the "horror of war" for the generation to come,' dealt with the same theme fifteen years later; *The Unending Cult of Human Sacrifice*, exhibited at the Leicester Galleries in 1934, combined a mélange of Great War symbols – guns, a madonna, the crucifixion, aircraft, and marching knights.[39]

For other artists it was not the iconography of war that remained to haunt their canvases but its chaotic atmosphere. A.Y. Jackson 'wasn't satisfied to paint anything that was serene' when he returned to Canada from France; he wanted 'to paint storms and ... things that had been smashed up.' Paul Nash felt the same: his post-war watercolours were fraught with violent weather. F.H. Varley simply wanted a chance to go back again so that he might capture what he had missed. 'The feeling of spring is having a restless effect on me,' he told Eric Brown in 1920, 'I find myself day after day over in France again longing to tackle so many of the problems again, with a keener vision – but my wife tells me I can't expect them to put on another war – no!!'[40] After completing his war memorial commission for Battersea Park, Kennington dropped the war theme altogether. He soon began to hanker after excitement, however, and seeking more action in 1922 accompanied one of the Great War's heroes, T.E. Lawrence, to the Near East. For five months he sketched Lawrence's bedouin soldiers, and in 1926 these drawings appeared in *Seven Pillars of Wisdom*.

Few artists had not been 'jolted' by the Great War. Paul Nash claimed that his war experience had developed the technical side of his art: he refined his sense of colour, uncertain before the war; his work acquired 'a greater sense of rhythm'; and in making 'the rapidest sketches in dangerous positions' he gained a freer handling. Orpen 'abandoned certain impedimenta of traditional oil painting' after the war and, as one critic observed, 'he flirts delightfully with Post-Impressionism.' Charles Sims, a painter of landscape before the war, now 'turned away from the visible world to the heavenly imagination of his "sacraments." ' F.H. Varley became more concerned with landscape and the human beings inhabiting it: his figures no longer cowered under clouds of yellow-green gas or wallowed in the mud, but clung like 'little bits of mind' to the craggy surfaces of British Columbia's coastal mountain range.[41]

The most significant consequence of the war for Britain's modernist painters was one that conservative critics had predicted: a 'Return to Order.' Before the war Vorticists Wyndham Lewis, Bomberg, Roberts, and others had expelled both nature and man from their work; during it their canvases became dominated by these very subjects. It was no different for the Futurist Nevinson: his style became more realistic and his subject matter encompassed a wider range of themes. This was, according to one critic, 'a confession of Futurism's failure.' The trend towards realism convinced many critics that the war had restored 'to sanity many of the most promising of the younger artists.' The impetus for this post-war 'union between art and life' lay, many felt, in the two dominant pictorial themes of the Great War: the figure and the land.[42]

While theoreticians attributed the 'new spirit' in art to the subject matter of war, artists such as Nevinson saw things differently: 'Having lived among scrap heaps, having seen miles of destruction day after day, month after month, year after year, they are longing for a complete change. We artists are sick of destruction in art. We want construction.' Bomberg was less dramatic: he claimed that in dropping abstractionism from his art he 'could more surely develop on the lines of Cézanne's rediscoveries that the world was round and there was an out through the sunlight.' Among the staunchest of Britain's abstractionists in 1914, Bomberg now refused an offer to join Piet Mondrian's Dutch-based Non-Objective De Stijl Group; he travelled instead to Palestine where he painted rather placid landscapes. Wyndham Lewis returned to realism because after the war he 'found an altered world: and I had changed too, very much. The geometrics which had interested me so exclusively before, I now felt were bleak and empty. They wanted *filling*.'[43]

By putting artists into uniform, and by radically altering the infrastructure of the art market, the war had disrupted the newly formed modernist movements in Britain and elsewhere. The hiring of artists to paint the war, and the placing of them in the chaotic, machine-dominated landscape of the front, caused both modernist and traditionalist artists to realize the limitations of their styles. Some modernists returned, after the war, to representational art; those who had never strayed away from it remained convinced of traditional painting's merits. Considering the always tentative character of innovative art movements and modernism's particular penchant for stylistic change, one might argue that Nevinson, Roberts, Wyndham Lewis, and other modernists would have moved beyond their early experiments whether the war had taken place or not. The Great War might not, then, have been entirely responsible for the demise of Vorticism and other avant-garde movements, but only for nudging them in that direction.

So far as Canadian painting was concerned, modernism had not asserted itself before the war, and even six years after the armistice A.Y. Jackson could tell the Empire Club that the 'modern painter in Canada is not much concerned with abstract problems in art. His immediate work is to interpret his background and he is too interested in doing this to ape every movement that rises abroad.' It was in interpreting that background – primarily the northern Ontario wilderness – that the war had its greatest impact on painting in Canada. The misty atmosphere of Flanders offered a dramatic contrast to the unclouded air of the northland. 'The clearest sky is misty in comparison,' wrote Varley from France, 'the sun-sets, when we have them, are smoky and dreary.' The low-keyed colours of no man's land and the trenches – muddy brown, yellow ochre, and cool grey – came to permeate the postwar canvases of Varley, Jackson, and others who had lived and painted at the front. Exposure to modernist British styles through the CWMF exhibitions of 1919 and 1920 also had its effect on those Canadian artists who had not participated in the Fund. Lawren Harris found Paul Nash's pictures 'terribly penetrating and big'; under the influence of Nash, he placed a row of dead defoliated trees across the foreground of a distant barren landscape and painted what was to become an icon of Canadian art, *Above Lake Superior* (Fig. 51). Jackson's *First Snow* was equally derivative in form and composition of Nash's work. While detailed study is necessary to document the extent to which Nash and others influenced these artists, it seems clear that exposure to modernist British trends in painting did help to 'stamp under' the decorative Art Nouveau motifs that dominated the paintings of those Canadians who had worked as commercial artists before the war.[44]

The colour and the atmosphere of the front, along with the exemplary interpretation of the war by modernist British artists, helped to strengthen a landscape aesthetic that had begun to take shape before the war in the work of the emerging Group of Seven. Appreciation for the Canadian wilderness that had its roots in cottaging, in the woodcraft movement, and in the creating of national parks, had been expressed long before the war in the wildlife stories of Ernest Thompson Seton and in the work of the Confederation Poets. Now, with the founding in 1920 of the Group of Seven, the wilderness ethos was fully realized in Canadian painting. What was more, the stark, bleak, muddy-coloured landscape of the front, as experienced by those who had been there or as seen through the works of those artists who had been to the front, had given Jackson, Varley, Lismer, Johnston, Frank Carmichael, J.E.H. MacDonald, and Lawren Harris a new appreciation for the irregular and barren wilderness of northern Ontario. After the war Jackson and his fellow artists deliberately sought to paint 'swampy, rocky, wolf-ridden, burnt and scuttled country with rivers and lakes scattered all through it.' The Group of Seven's concern to demonstrate, as Lismer called it, the 'spirit' of painting in Canada, was thus associated with a sense that this could best be done by employing methods and techniques they and their colleagues had either seen used or themselves employed to paint the war-torn landscape of the Old World.[45]

As well as being influenced by modernist trends, nationalist tendencies, and in some cases by exposure to the unique landscape of the front, Canadian artists were given more attention by the country's art officials, art patrons, and writers. Ottawa's National Gallery, thanks in part to the recognition the artists had won for themselves during the war, was particularly responsive to Canada's post-war nationalist mood. Canadians had done well on the battlefield and the artists had shown themselves, through successful CWMF exhibitions in London and New York as well as at home, to be capable of providing a memorial second to none. As chairman of the National Gallery's board, Sir Edmund Walker instigated a program to recognize and to encourage Canadian artists by direct purchase and circulation of their work throughout the country.[46] As the gallery's director, Eric Brown gave Canadian artists, most notably those members of the Group of Seven, more attention by exhibiting their work abroad – particularly in the United States and Britain – and by speaking of it in public lectures. Patrons J.S. McLean, Vincent Massey, Mr and Mrs C.S. Band, among others, followed suit by purchasing Canadian works, while critics Robert Ayre, Graham McInnes, Donald Buchanan, and Barker Fairley wrote about them.

Without the Canadian War Memorials Fund there can be little doubt that Canada's critics, patrons, and gallery officials would have been slower to recognize and to promote Canadian art. Without the CWMF it is likely that Canada's artists would not have been exposed so early to modernist trends in painting, and certain that many would not have experienced the conditions, visual and otherwise, of painting at the front. Nor would so many artists have had the opportunity of exhibiting their work in New York and London. The CWMF thus gave Canada more than a memorial of its participation in the war: Canadian art and Canadian artists were given an important place within the cultural framework of post-war Canada.

Epilogue

The Canadian War Memorials Fund was a tribute to the energy, ability, and enthusiasm of Lord Beaverbrook and a small group of collaborators. Virtually without official encouragement, and with little public money, they created an organization that sent scores of artists, including some of Britain's and Canada's most distinguished, to work at the task of memoralizing Canada's participation in the Great War. Like many wartime organizations faced with mobilization of unprecedented dimensions, the one they created grew quickly and without bureaucratic planning. Almost completely self-financed, and with its own selection procedures, the Beaverbrook organization assembled an impressive collection of artistic portrayals of the war. It was, that is to say, a concern with recording and memorializing that great event that motivated the CWMF and its artists: the artists were given no particular instructions, and until the war's conclusion their work was not used for propaganda purposes. What they produced was catholic in scope; the traditional and conservative vied with the modernist and avant-garde.

These characteristics owed much to the Fund's autonomy and to the astuteness of Paul Konody, a man of broad sympathies who had no particular ties with the Academy, with schools, with art movements in general, or, indeed, with Canada.

The CWMF began its work in Britain and its headquarters remained there. Aside from Beaverbrook, none of its central figures had any Canadian affiliation. In a war in which Canada was fighting side by side with her imperial motherland, it did not seem strange that this should be so, nor that the first artist chosen by Beaverbrook and Konody should have been British. With the first signs of Canadian sensitivity to the virtual exclusion of Canadian artists, Beaverbrook not only enlisted several Canadians serving in Britain and France but also co-opted into his scheme people active in the Canadian art world – Walker and Brown were of course the best known. While British artists always outnumbered Canadian, the balance was quickly brought to justifiable proportions.

The organization of the CWMF was *sui generis*. It existed as an interesting example of the kind of personal and *ad hoc* organization that could be assembled by a hard-driving entrepreneur of means and connections in the early days of an unprecedented situation.

The collection, uneven in quality and diverse in style and approach, marked in many ways the transition between conservatism and modernism. In others, it demonstrated the fact that a clear break with the old style of battle-painting, confined to specialized artists who adhered to a strict iconography, had occurred. Much of it was very good, both as painting and as new symbolic iconography. Yet the collection itself could not sustain the interest either of the Canadian public or of government officials. To post-war Canadians, increasingly under the influence of isolationist and even pacifist sentiments, it represented a war best forgotten. It was not by means of these pictures, drawings, prints, and sculptures that they wished to be reminded of the sacrifice. The town memorial and city cenotaph, found everywhere from Halifax to Victoria, were an indigenously generated memorial somehow more satisfactory as reminders of what the war had meant than pictorial reconstructions of the Second Battle of Ypres or of a munitions plant. Even the government took this view, insisting that the most fitting memorial to the war and what it represented would be a gigantic 'Peace Tower' on Parliament Hill in Ottawa.

Not until war broke out again did a set of circumstances come into being which, it seemed, might make possible a more enthusiastic appreciation of the CWMF's collection than any it had received over the previous twenty years. Harry McCurry, who had become the National Gallery's director upon the death of Eric Brown in 1939, moved soon after the war began to construct an exhibition hall on the ground floor of the Victoria Memorial Museum. There, from 1940 until the war's end, a portion of the CWMF collection was always on display. In addition to these works, over one hundred etchings, lithographs, and dry-points were brought into service by being exhibited through 1940 and 1941 in a large number of communities across Canada.

While the collection itself was receiving renewed attention, the organization that had once stood behind it was serving as a model for the establishment of new war art schemes in Britain and in Canada. The British War Artists' Advisory Committee came into existence under Sir Kenneth Clark in October 1939; creation of the Canadian War Artists' Committee, with Harry McCurry as chairman, followed three years later.[1]

Nor had the CWMF been forgotten by the Germans. The bronze sculpture depicting the alleged crucifixion of a Canadian soldier by Derwent Wood became one of the Nazi's foremost examples of how fallacious Allied propaganda had been during the First World War.[2]

With the end of the Second War, enthusiasm for war art once again diminished. The paintings gathered by the Canadian War Artists' Committee joined those of the CWMF in the National Gallery's basement. Both collections remained uncatalogued and – apart from a rotating exhibition on the gallery's sixth floor – in storage. Even so important an art historian as Lord Clark of London's National Gallery found it difficult to view them: while visiting Ottawa in the 1950s, he asked to see both collections; the storeroom where the paintings and sculptures were kept was 'very reluctantly unlocked' and 'the dusty pictures were hauled out of their racks.' This situation was improved somewhat in 1960 when the collections were given a curator, Stuart Smith, but it was not until the appointment of Major R.F. Wodehouse to this post in 1962 that they received a published catalogue. But then, in 1971, the National Gallery gave most of the works to the Canadian War Museum, where they still languish largely unviewed.[3]

If, finally, the fate of the CWMF collection is a sad one, the impact the making of that collection had on the country's cultural life remains substantial. In keeping artists employed; in helping to introduce them to new styles, techniques, and methods; in playing a part in the creation of a patronage network; and in contributing to the emergence of a national movement in painting, putting these works together in fact did much to influence the contours of the country's artistic life in the early decades of the twentieth century. In this sense the project's significance lies not so much in what finally happened to the work it inspired as in the process by which that work was created and brought together. It is to the creative act itself, rather than the fate of the particular works resulting from it, that one must look if one wishes to understand the real meaning of the events that have been chronicled here.

Notes

Abbreviations used for papers frequently cited are as follows:

BKP   Lord Beaverbrook Papers, House of Lords, London
BP   Sir Robert Borden Papers, PAC
CWM   Canadian War Museum, Ottawa
DND   Department of National Defence, Army Historical Section, PAC
DP   Sir Arthur Doughty Papers, PAC
IWM   Imperial War Museum, London
KP   Sir Albert Edward Kemp Papers, PAC
NGC   National Gallery of Canada, Ottawa
PAC   Public Archives of Canada, Ottawa
WP   Sir Edmund Walker Papers, Thomas Fisher Rare Book Library, University of Toronto

Chapter 1: Artists and the war

1   Borden Papers, Thomas Fisher Rare Book Library, University of Toronto, MS 184, Box 5, Borden to Mrs Borden, 5 Jan. 1919. The total number of artists associated to the Canadian War Memorials Fund by the scheme's termination in 1921 was 116: 1 Dane, 3 Belgians, 2 Australians, 1 Serbian, 66 Britons, and 43 Canadians. For an annotated list of the artists employed by the CWMF, see R.F. Wodehouse, *Check List of the War Collections* (Ottawa 1968).

2   John quoted in William Lipke, *David Bomberg: A Critical Study of His Life and Work* (London 1967) 45; Roberts, *Memories of the War to End War, 1914–1918* (London 1974) 1; Wyndham Lewis to Kate Lechmere, summer 1915, in W.K. Rose, ed., *The Letters of Wyndham Lewis* (London 1963) 69; Fitzwilliam Museum, Cameron to S.C. Cockerell, 19 Oct. 1915; Archives, Tate Gallery, David Brown, 'Duncan Grant to 1920' 8; John Woodeson, *Mark Gertler* (London 1972) 182; NGC, Jackson to Dr James MacCallum, 23 April 1915; McCord Museum, Clarence Gagnon Papers, Box 1, Brymner to Gagnon, 31 Dec. 1917

3   David French, 'Spy Fever in Britain, 1900–1915,' *Historical Journal*, Cambridge, XXI, 2 (1978) 365; Donald W. Buchanan, *James Wilson Morrice* (Toronto 1936)

124; Munnings, *An Artist's Life* (London 1950) 296; NGC, Lismer to Eric Brown, 12 Jan. 1918

4   'War's Failure to Inspire the Modern Artist,' *Current Opinion,* New York, LIX (Aug. 1915) 123; Haward, *The Effect of War upon Art and Literature* (lecture delivered to the University of Manchester, 28 Feb. 1916) 13, 16; 'Art and War,' *American Magazine of Art,* New York, IX, 8 (June 1918) 303-4

5   See, for example, *Blast,* London, 1914 and 1915; Wyndham Lewis, *Plan of Campaign*, Allied Artists' Exhibition, London, June 1914, and 'The Cubist Room,' *The Egoist*, London, I, 1 (1 Jan. 1914) 9; John Cournos, 'The Death of Futurism,' *ibid.*, IV, 1 (1 Jan. 1917) 6-7

6   Paul Konody, 'The Futurist Paintings at Exhibition Defended,' *Globe*, Toronto, 2 Sept. 1920; see also Barker Fairley, 'Canada's War Pictures,' *Canadian Magazine*, Toronto, LIV, 1 (Nov. 1919) 5

7   Richard Aldington, 'Notes on the Present Situation,' *The Egoist* I, 1 (1 Sept. 1914) 326; Public Archives of Ontario, M.O Hammond Papers, Diaries, 22 March [1917]

8   IWM, John Papers, Campbell Dodgson to C.F.G. Masterman, 1 Sept. 1917; Aldington, *ibid.*; 'Malstick,' London Correspondent, *Arts Journal*, London, XXXII (March 1915) 115

9   *Times*, London, 27 April 1915; Kerr, 'The Etcher's Point of View,' *Canadian Magazine*, Toronto (Dec. 1916) 158

10   Nevinson in Richard Cork, *Vorticism and Abstract Art in the First Machine Age: Synthesis and Decline* (Berkeley 1976) II, 483; PAC, J.E.H. MacDonald Papers, Jackson to MacDonald, 31 May [1916]; Lewis in *Blast*, London, War Number (July 1915) 11

11   Gertler to March, 19 Oct. 1915, cited in Woodeson, *Mark Gertler*, 181-2; Cohen cited in Archives, Tate Gallery, Alice Mayes, 'The Young Bomberg, 1914-1925,' 11 (this manuscript must be used with extreme care; much of the material is improbable and unverifiable)

12   Marguerite Steen, *William Nicholson* (London 1943) 124

13   Public Archives of Ontario, Ontario Society of Artists, Minutes, 1 Dec. 1914 (after 1916 the Canadian government provided pensions for dependants and widows); Lamb, 'Canadian Artists and the War,' *The Studio*, London, LXV (Sept. 1915) 260

14   *Drawings from the Imperial War Museum and the National Maritime Museum*, exhibition catalogue prepared by the Imperial War Museum (London, 1 July 1966) np

15   McMichael Canadian Collection, J.E.H. MacDonald to editor, *Star*, 17 March 1916; *Canadian Courier*, Toronto (Feb. 1916) 13

16   C.R.W. Nevinson, *Paint and Prejudice* (London 1937) 70-1. In 1908 the Artists' Rifles became part of the National Territorial Army as the 28th Battalion of the County of London.

17   Jackson, 'Reminiscences of Army Life, 1914-1918,' *Canadian Art*, Ottawa, XI, 1 (Autumn 1953) 6; MacDonald Papers, Jackson to MacDonald, 5 Oct. 1914; CWM, R.F. Wodehouse, 'Notes on a Conversation with Douglas Duncan,'

13 Dec. 1962. Duncan said that Milne joined because he was unhappy about the American attitude to the war. On the other hand, Rosemarie Tovell declared that 'it was likely that both the threat of being drafted and the critical state of the war changed Milne from observer to participant.' *Reflections in a Quiet Pool* (Ottawa 1980) 46

18   Mina C. and H. Arthur Klein, *Käthe Kollwitz: Life in Art* (New York 1975) 65

19   Among the exhibitions Meštrović organized was the *Exhibition of Serbo-Croation Artists: Meštrović – Rački – Rosandic,* at the Grafton Galleries, Dec. 1917.

20   'A Notable Series of Mural Paintings,' *Magazine of Art*, New York, x (Oct. 1919) 475-8; Estelle M. Kerr, 'Those War-Time Jig-Saw Toys,' *Canadian Magazine*, Toronto (Dec. 1915) 97-8; WP, Box 23, MacDonald to Eric Brown, 4 Dec. 1918. Augustus John's poster is in the possession of the Canadian War Museum.

21   Wilkinson, *A Brush with Life* (London 1969) 79; Olga Somech Phillips, *Solomon J. Solomon* (London 1933) 116-17 – see also Solomon's *Strategic Camouflage* (London 1920); Lewis Weirter, *A Few Hints on Military Sketching with the Whirter Retractor* (Aldershot 1915) – 'Whirter' was no doubt an anglicization of the German 'Weirter'

22   Colin S. Macdonald, *A Dictionary of Canadian Artists* (Ottawa 1967) I, 34

23   'An Art Exhibition behind the "Big Push," ' *Artists' Rifles Journal*, London, I, 3 (Nov. 1916) 52; thirty soldier-artists of the Artists' Rifles had already exhibited in Jan. and Feb. 1916 at the Leicester Galleries

24   NGC, Fosbery to Eric Brown, nd; Klaus Lankheit, *Franz Marc, Sein Leben und seine Kunst* (Köln 1976) 150; University of London, Thomas Sturge Moore Papers, P. Wyndham Lewis to Moore, 23 May 1917, nos 76-7, Wyndham Lewis to 'Mother' [1916], no 80, in Rose, *Letters of Wyndham Lewis*, 86; PAC, David Milne Papers, Milne to James A. Clarke, 16 Oct. [1918]; IWM, Sound Archives, tape interview with John Nash

25   Archives, Tate Gallery, Nevinson Clipping Book, no 7311-12, Frank Rutter, 'War Pictures and Photographs,' *Sunday Times*, London, 5 Aug. 1917; Jackson, 'Reminiscences of Army Life,' 91

26   Roberts, *Memories of the War to End War*, 23; IWM, Konody Papers, Gill to Konody, 22 May 1918; Michael Holroyd, *Augustus John: A Biography* (London 1976) 543; on Kennington, IWM, John Papers, Dodgson to Masterman, 2 April 1917; Bodleian Library, Nevinson Papers, Diaries, 15 Nov., 12 Dec. [1916], 8 May [1917], 8 April [1918]; Jackson, *ibid.*, 7

27   Janet Dunbar, *Laura Knight* (London 1975) 95; Milne Papers, Milne to Clarke, 23 Jan. [1919]

28   CWM, Wodehouse File, Eric Brown, 'Canada's Own War Memorials' Exhibition in Toronto,' 28 Oct. 1919, p 6; NGC, Gagen to Brown, 19 Sept. 1918; Rothenstein, *Augustus John* (London 1944) 15

29   NGC, Lismer to Brown, 22 Jan., Harris to Brown, 29 Oct. 1918

30   NGC, Crisp to Brown, 12 Sept. 1918; on Lavery, IWM, Konody Papers, C.R. Chisman to J. Harold Watkins, 17 Dec. 1918; Munnings, *An Artist's Life*, 318

31   Orpen to Ross, 7 Feb. 1918, in Margery Ross, ed., *Robert Ross, Friend of Friends:*

Letters to Robert Ross, Art Critic and Writer (London 1952) 326; on Palmer and Gagen, WP, Box 34 1, Walker to Brown, 24 Sept. 1918, NGC, Walker to Brown, 18 Oct. 1918; IWM, Nevinson Papers, Nevinson to Masterman, 10 March 1918

32   NGC, Beaverbrook to Walker, 14 Dec. 1917

Chapter 2: Canada's impresario of art

1   DP, Diary, vol. 8, 19 March 1916, 3 May [1916]; Beckles Willson, *From Quebec to Piccadilly* (London 1929) 210-11; BP, no 3249, Doughty to Borden, 11 May 1916

2   DP, *ibid.*, 3 May

3   A.J.P. Taylor, *Beaverbrook* (London 1972) 87; Order-in-Council no 32300, 6 Jan. 1915

4   BP, vol. 64, Report on the Joint Establishment of the Canadian War Records submitted by Sir Max Aitken the Officer in Charge to Rt. Hon. Sir Robert Borden, 19 May 1916, p 14

5   BP, vol. 170, Canadian War Records Office Report submitted by the Officer in Charge to the Right Hon. Sir Robert L. Borden, 11 Jan. 1917, p 1; no 21445, Aitken to Borden [cable], 1 Jan. 1916

6   Beckles Willson, *From Quebec to Piccadilly*, 201; BP, *ibid.*, Report, p 7, vol. 64, Report, 19 May 1916, p 13; BKP, Aitken to Hughes, 14 Feb. 1916

7   BP, *ibid.*, vol. 64, p 12. Aitken borrowed most of the illustrations from *Punch* and *Sphere*. He did, however, commission R.F. Matthews and Norman Wilkinson to produce paintings, and also considered purchasing the sketch-artist W.B. Wollen's reconstruction, *The Canadians at Ypres, 23 April 1915*.

8   DP, vol. 10, Doughty to Col. White, 12 Aug. 1916

9   DP, Diary, vol. 8, 3 May [1916]; BP, vol. 64, Report, 19 May 1916, p 12, no 39563, Aitken to Borden, 30 Oct. 1916, vol. 170, Report, 11 Jan. 1917, p 1, vol. 64, Report, pp 6, 10

10   DND, Overseas Military Forces of Canada, RG 9, vol. 4746, anon., 'Canadian War Records Office Report,' typescript, nd. Lord Northcliffe conceived his program for propaganda in enemy countries as early as Aug. 1916. British Library, Northcliffe Papers, MS 131/9

11   *Can. H. of C. Debates*, Official Report, 10 April 1916, p 2692; see also 3 Feb. 1916, p 534. Aitken drew neither pay nor personal expenses and his Lombard Street office was given rent-free to the CWRO; CWRO employees received a salary according to their rank. Beaverbrook, *Men and Power* (London 1956) 271

12   Aitken in BP, vol. 64, Report, 19 May 1916, p 12; Northcliffe in John Charteris, *At G.H.Q.* [8 April 1917], (London 1931) 211 (see also Beaverbrook, *ibid.*, 268); BKP, Buchan to Sir Reginald Brade, 4 Aug. 1917; IWM, Picture Division, Clipping File, *Manchester Guardian*, 23 Dec. 1919

13   A collection of photographs taken by John Horace Brown, who fought with the 2nd Battalion until June 1916, show that some Canadians did continue to take photographs. Andrew Roger, 'Horace Brown – Soldier-Photographer,' *The Archivist*, Ottawa, X, 1 (Jan. – Feb. 1983) 9-12

14   Robert Craig Brown, *Robert Laird Borden: A Biography, 1914-1937* (Toronto 1980) II, 26

15   C. Lewis Hind, quoted in 'War's Failure to Inspire the Modern Artist,' *Current Opinion*, New York, no 59 (Aug. 1915) 123

16   DND, RG 24, vol. 449, Eugene Fiset, deputy minister, Militia and Defence, to Thomas Mulvey, under secretary of state for Canada, 14 Jan. 1915; Lilly Koltun, 'Seeing Is Believing? – A Critique of Archival Visual Sources for Material Culture Research,' *National Museum of Man, Material History*, Ottawa, Bulletin 8, Special Issue (1979) 64

17   Peter Robertson, 'Canadian Photojournalism during the First World War,' *History of Photography*, London, II, 1 (Jan. 1978) 43; *Canadian War Pictorial* (London, nd) 1 [p 8]

18   Crawford, *The Great War Fourth Year: C.R.W. Nevinson* (London 1918) 8; C.H. Collins Baker, 'War Paintings,' *Saturday Review*, New York (7 Oct. 1916) 342 ·

19   Holliday, 'Posing the War for the Painter,' *Bookman*, New York, no 47 (July 1918) 516; Heinrich Kley, 'The Krupp Devils,' illustrated in *Current Opinion*, New York, no 59 (Aug. 1915), 123; 'Germany's War Pictures,' *Literary Digest*, New York, no 52 (1916) 68; *Ein Krieg wird ausgestellt* (Frankfurt-on-the-Main 1976) 69; *Times*, London, 30 April 1915; Paintings from French artists George Scott, F. Flameng, and George Bund date, however, from 1914 (see works in Les Invalides, Paris); *Anzac Book* (London 1915)

20   M.L. Saunders, 'Official British Propaganda in Allied and Neutral Countries during the First World War with Special Reference to Organisations and Methods,' unpublished M.Phil. thesis, University of London, 1972, p 106; IWM, Bone Papers, E.A. Gowers to Bone, 12 July 1916

21   DND, RG 24, vol. 1749, 'Canadian War Records Office Official Report,' 31 Aug. 1919: app. 1, 'Canadian War Memorials Report of Executive Committee,' p 1

22   BKP, Aitken to Hughes [cable], 17 Oct. 1916 (Aitken probably made his request to Hughes, referred to in this cable, in Aug.); DND, Overseas Military Forces of Canada, RG 9, vol. 4746, Minutes of the Conference held 22 Sept. 1916

23   G.W.L. Nicholson, *Canadian Expeditionary Force, 1914-1919* (Ottawa 1962) 212

24   Charteris, *At G.H.Q.* [30 Oct. 1916] 176; BKP, Aitken to Hughes, 27 Oct. 1916; John Terraine, *Douglas Haig: The Educated Soldier* (London 1963) 101

25   BP, no 57759, Aitken to F.B. McCurdy, 4 Nov. 1916

26   Paul Ferris, *The House of Northcliffe* (London 1971) 212; Reginald Pound and Geoffrey Harmsworth, *Northcliffe* (London 1959) 146

27   The War Charities Act was established in Sept. 1916; every organization collecting funds for charitable purposes was required to register.

28   BKP, Aitken to Northcliffe, 4 Oct. 1916; BP, vol. 170, Report, 11 Jan. 1917, p 5; PAC, Secretary of State, RG6, E, vol. 564, Ernest Chambers to Aitken, 4 Nov. 1916; *Telegram*, Toronto, 12 Jan. 1917

29   KP, vol. 133, Beaverbrook to Kemp, 17 April 1918

30   Records Office, London Guildhall, Application for Registration in the matter of the War Charities Act, 1916, 7 Nov. 1916; Registrations Granted by the County

Purposes Committee of the Corporation of the City of London, 1920, p 4

31   The Secretary [Paul Konody], 'The Canadian War Memorials Fund: Its History and Objectives,' *Canada in Khaki* (London 1918), II, 26

32   Robertson, 'Canadian Photojournalism,' 41; BKP, Beaverbrook to Kemp, 6 Sept. 1917

33   Archives, Tate Gallery, Nevinson Clipping Book, no 7311-2, Frank Rutter, 'War Pictures and Photographs,' *Sunday Times*, London, 5 Aug. 1917; BKP, Beaverbrook to Lima, 29 Aug. 1917

34   BKP, Beaverbrook to Borden, 8 Aug. 1917; Beaverbrook, *Men and Power*, 43

35   'The Great War: Britain's Efforts and Ideals depicted by British Artists,' *The Studio*, London, LXXI (Aug. 1917) 103. Dodd and McBey were, like Bone, given commissions as lieutenant and paid an annual salary on the condition that all their work be deposited in the Imperial War Museum; the other four obtained neither commissions nor a salary, but rations and transportation for the privilege of working at the front.

36   NGC, Fosbery to Eric Brown, nd [Oct. 1917], enclosed: Fosbery to Perley, nd, handwritten copy [June 1917]

37   WP, Box 22, Beaverbrook to Walker [cable], 26 July, Box 34, Walker to Beaverbrook [cable], 30 July 1917

38   WP, Box 34. Borden was prompted to ask the Advisory Arts Council for assistance after being approached by the English author F. Moir Bussy, who suggested that R. Caton Woodville be commissioned 'to paint a great national picture for your chief Art Gallery of some wonderful exploit of the Canadian Contingent at the front.' Box 22, Bussy to Borden, 30 June 1916

39   BP, no 121588-9, Brown to Borden, 11 July 1917. Brown and Walker asked the painter Charles W. Jefferys to suggest artists and salaries: he recommended F.H. Varley, Wyly Grier, and J.W. Beatty, and felt that $3,000 a year would see an artist through 'with an untroubled mind.' NGC, Jefferys to Brown, 5 Aug. 1917

40   H. Mortimer Lamb, 'Studio-Talk,' *The Studio*, London, LXII (Sept. 1914) 313, LXI (Feb. 1914) 81; Eric Brown, 'Studio-Talk,' *ibid.*, LXIV (April 1915) 211

41   DND, Overseas Military Forces of Canada, Minister's Record, RG9, vol. 2, Perley to Beaverbrook, 8 Aug. 1917

42   Bennett to Thomas Bodkin, no 52, 4 April 1918, in James Hepburn, ed., *Letters of Arnold Bennett, 1916–1931* (London 1970), III, 54; *Velasquez: His Life and Work* (London 1903), *Filippino Lippi* (London 1905), *The Brothers Van Eyck* (London 1907), *The Art of Walter Crane* (London 1902)

43   Wyndham Lewis, *Blasting and Bombardiering: Autobiography 1914–1926* (London 1937) 191

44   Nina Hamnet, *Laughing Torso* (London 1932) 226; BKP, Bennett to Beaverbrook, 12 June 1918; Munnings, *The Second Burst* (London 1951) 30

45   IWM, John Papers, John to Campbell Dodgson, 11 Sept. 1917; Archives, Tate Gallery, Nevinson Clipping Book, no 7311-2, *Nottingham Guardian*, 15 Oct. 1917

46   'The Canadian War Memorials Fund,' *Canada in Khaki*, London, 25, 27; Archives, Tate Gallery, Nevinson Clipping Book, no 7311-2, Konody,

'Futurism and the Friday Club,' *Observer*, London, 14 Feb. 1915; Konody, *Modern War: Paintings by C.R.W. Nevinson* (London 1917) 14

47   Konody, 'Art and Artists,' *Observer*, London, 8 March 1915, 26 Nov. 1916; *Globe*, Toronto, 2 Sept. 1920; 'Art and Artists,' *Observer*, 26 March 1916 (see also *Modern War, ibid.*, 20)

48   Konody, 'On War Memorials,' Art and War: Canadian War Memorials (London 1919) 15; WP, Box 22, Beaverbrook to Walker, 19 Oct. 1917; Konody, 'The Canadian War Memorials Fund,' *Canada in Khaki*, 25

49   Konody, 'The Canadian War Memorials,' *Colour Magazine*, London, IX, 2 (Sept. 1918) 26, 36; IWM, Konody Papers, Konody to J.S. Sargent, 5 Sept. 1917

50   Munnings, *Second Burst*, 30; Konody, 'The Canadian War Memorials Fund,' 26, 27. Augustus John got the largest size picture: 'a gigantic decoration some 30 ft. by 40 ft. in length'; most received a more modest 10 × 12 foot specification.

51   C.R.W. Nevinson, *Paint and Prejudice* (London 1937) 114; Michael Holroyd, *Augustus John: A Biography* (London 1976) 553

52   *Times*, 2 March 1918

53   Konody, 'The Canadian War Memorials Fund,' 26; NGC, Beaverbrook to Walker, 14 Dec. 1917

54   IWM, Orpen Papers, Orpen to John Buchan [Oct. 1917], copy; *ibid.*, McBey Papers, Masterman to Clement K. Shorter, 20 Dec. 1917

55   Marion Ryan, 'Art versus the Royal Academy,' *Weekly Despatch*, London, (6 Jan. 1918) 6

56   Janet Oppenheim Minihan, 'The Nationalization of Culture: The Development of State Subsidies of Art in Great Britain,' unpublished PhD thesis, Columbia University, 1975, p 254 (published in 1977, New York). Konody, 'The Canadian War Memorials,' 25

57   NGC, Beaverbrook to Walker, 14 Dec. 1917

Chapter 3: 'Up in arms'

1   WP, Box 27, Beaverbrook to Walker, 17 Sept. 1917; DP, vol. I, Walker to Doughty, 5 Sept. 1917; NGC, Brown to Walker, 2 Oct. 1917

2   WP, Box 22, Brown to Walker, 2 Nov. 1916, Oversize Box, Beaverbrook to Walker, 19 Oct. 1917

3   NGC, Walker to Brown, 14 Nov., to Beaverbrook, 11 Oct. 1917; WP, Diary, vol. II, 19 Dec. 1917, p 284

4   NGC, Beaverbrook to Walker, 14 Dec. 1917

5   NGC, Walker to Brown, 14 Nov. 1917; WP, Box 27, Walker to Beaverbrook, 29 Dec. 1917

6   WP, Box 34, Walker to Brown, 7 Nov., to Beaverbrook, 11 Oct. 1917

7   Brown, 'Canada and Her Art,' *Canadian National Problems, Annals of the American Academy of Politics and Social Sciences*, XLV (Jan. 1913) 176; NGC, Brown to Walker, 20 Nov. 1917 [copy]

8   WP, Box 27, Walker to Beaverbrook, 29 Dec. 1917

9   NGC, Jackson to Brown, 12 March 1913; Harris, 'The Federal Art Commission,' *Globe*, Toronto, 4 June 1914; Bridle, *Sons of Canada* (Toronto 1916) 182

10   See Canada, *Sessional Papers*, Reports on the National Gallery of Canada,
1913-16; Katherine E. Jordan, *Sir Edmund Walker: Print Collector* (Toronto:
Art Gallery of Ontario 1975); Barbara Ruth Marshall, 'Sir Edmund Walker,
Servant of Canada,' unpublished MA thesis, University of British Columbia,
1971, pp 18-20; Newton MacTavish, 'Sir Edmund Walker's Collection of Art,'
Canadian Magazine, Toronto, LII (1919) 833-9

11   WP, Box 30, Walker to Sidney Fisher, 3 Feb. 1909

12   It was decided that 'as the RCA is the body that officially represents the art of the
Dominion, the Council should undertake to visit its annual exhibitions officially.'
WP, Box 44, Advisory Arts Council Minutes, 3 June 1912

13   WP, Box 33, Walker to Brown, 22 Oct. 1915; Madge MacBeth, 'The National
Art Gallery,' *Maclean's*, Toronto (Sept. 1915) 21

14   WP, Box 34, Walker to Beaverbrook, 18 March 1918

15   PAC, Jefferys Papers, Clippings, *Star*, Toronto, nd [Nov. 1917]; NGC, File 1,
Gibbon to Brown, 24 Dec. 1917; WP, Box 21, Cooke to Walker, 2 April
1918, to Brown, 6 Dec. 1917 (Beaverbrook's defensive reply to Cooke stated:
'our first endeavour was to find out any Canadian artists serving with the
Canadian Forces' – *ibid.*, Beaverbrook to Cooke, 4 Jan. 1918); WP, Box 22,
Brown to Walker, 20 Nov. 1917. It is interesting to note that all photographers
employed by the CWRO were British; no complaints were lodged.

16   WP, Jefferys to Walker, 25 Nov. 1917; see also PAC, Royal Canadian Academy
of Art, Minutes, 14 Nov. 1917. Members of the committee: E. Maxwell, E.
Dyonnet, J.W. Beatty, Wyly Grier, and W. Brymner.

17   WP, Diary, vol. II, 19 Dec. 1917, pp 283-4. The names put forward were
Cullen, Simpson, Beatty, and Jefferys; Varley stepped in for Jefferys. NGC, Walker
to Beaverbrook, 29 Dec. 1917 [copy]. The salary, $2,500 a year, was the fee
Britain's first war artist, Muirhead Bone, received.

18   NGC, J. Gibbon to Brown, 24 Dec. 1917; Augustus Bridle, 'Canadian Artists to
the Front,' *Canadian Courier*, Toronto, XXIII, 10 (16 Feb. 1918) 7

19   NGC, Walker to Brown, 27 Dec. 1917

20   Public Archives of Ontario, Ontario Society of Artists, Beatty to Gagen, 8 July
1918; WP, Box 34, Walker to Hugh C. James, 9 Jan. 1918; NGC, Brown to
Walker, 23 Jan. 1918

21   *Great Britain, H. of C. Debates,* 11 March 1918, pp 73-8; Beaverbrook, *Men and
Power* (London 1956) 266: Guest to Lloyd George, 23 Jan. 1918

22   M.L. Saunders, 'Official British Propaganda in Allied and Neutral Countries
during the First World War with Special Reference to Organisations and
Methods,' unpublished M.Phil. thesis, London University, 1972, p 152

23   BP, no 57814, Beaverbrook to Borden, 21 May 1918, 'private.' This was not
the first time the CWMF had set a precedent: the Australians had modelled their
scheme after the CWMF in the summer of 1917.

24   IWM, Bone Papers, Bone to Art Committee, 29 Jan. 1919. The building was
never erected; the pictures were deposited in the Imperial War Museum.

25   BKP, Minutes, British War Memorials Committee, 29 May 1918. The Treasury
did not match Rothermere's and Beaverbrook's amount but came up with a
disappointing £11,000. There is no evidence to show that the British War

Memorial scheme was registered as a charity fund. Records Office, London Guildhall, 'Registrations Granted by the County Purposes Committee of the Corporation of the City of London.'

26   WP, Box 23, Beaverbrook to Walker, 15 April [cable], Box 34, Walker to Beaverbrook, 31 Jan. 1918. Lord Grosvenor, the Duke of Westminster's ancestor, purchased *The Death of Wolfe* from West after it was exhibited in the Royal Academy in 1771.

27   Stacey, 'Benjamin West and *The Death of Wolfe*,' *Bulletin*, National Gallery of Canada, IV Ottawa, 1 (1966) 4

28   Roy Strong, *And When Did You Last See Your Father?* (London 1978) 80. As pointed out by C.P. Stacey, West was not the first artist to introduce modern costume into historical painting, or even the first to portray the death of Wolfe. *Ibid.*, 1

29   WP, Box 34, Walker to Beaverbrook, 18 March 1918 [cable]; DND, RG 24, vol. 1749, 'Canadian War Records Office Official Report,' 31 Aug. 1919: app. 1, 'Canadian War Memorials Report of Executive Committee,' p 7

30   DND, OMFC, RG 9, vol. 2105, Canadian Secretary, Headquarters to the Secretary, OMFC, 27 Oct. 1918

31   KP, vol. 170, 'Canadian War Records Office, Official Report,' 27 March 1918, 'Statement of Canadian War Memorials Fund,' np; *Canadian Daily Record*, London, 5 March 1918. A third Canadian Exhibition of War Photographs was not held in London until Jan. 1919.

32   WP, Box 23, Beaverbrook to Brown, 6 May 1918 [copy]

33   See Imperial War Museum Catalogue of Pictures, no 2616; IWM, Lavery Papers, Lavery to Sir Alfred Mond, 14 Nov. 1919

34   *Ibid.*, Mond to Beaverbrook, 7 June 1918 (though Mond accepted the picture, it seems to have been eventually returned to the CWMF collection); NGC, CWMF, 'List of Pictures Commissioned for Purchase of Presented to the CWMF,' p 7. *A Howitzer in Action at Roisel* was purchased by the Canadians in 1918 and appears on the above list; it was later transferred to the IWM collection (see IWM Catalogue entry no 1197).

35   *Can. H. of C. Debates*, 20 March 1918, pp 50–1, 29 April 1918, pp 1195–6

36   WP, Box 23, Beaverbrook to Walker, 20 May 1918 [cable]

37   WP, Box 34, Walker to Beaverbrook, 18 March, 22 April 1918

38   WP, Box 34, Walker to Newton McTavish, 6 Jan. 1919. Walker received the following amounts from Beaverbrook: $2,500 in Jan., $5,000 on 21 May, and $10,000 on 4 July 1918.

39   The artists suggested by Grier and Jefferys included Franklin Brownell, Frederick Challener, Edmond Dyonnet, Fosbery, Robert Gagen, Wyly Grier, Jefferys, Arthur Lismer, J.E.H. MacDonald, and George Reid. The subjects ranged over portraits, shipping, Halifax harbour, munitions, and training camps. NGC, copy of a letter from Grier to Walker, 26 April 1918

40   NGC, Brown to Gagen, 4 Sept., to Loring, 10 Sept., to Crisp, 3 Sept. 1918

41   NGC, Brown to Walker, 17 Oct. 1918; WP, Box 34, Walker to Beaverbrook, 18 March 1918

42   NGC, Walker to Beaverbrook, 4 Oct. 1919

43   NGC, Brown to Harris, 31 Oct. 1918
44   NGC, Brown, 'Painting the War at Home,' typescript, nd, pp 1-2, 3-5, Brown to
       Walker, 14 Dec., 17 Oct., to Manly MacDonald, 4 Sept. 1918
45   PAC, Harry McCurry Papers, vol. 1, Brown, 'Art to Order,' typescript, nd –
       This later appeared as 'Canadian War Art to Order,' *Christian Science Monitor*,
       Boston, 4 Nov. 1918

Chapter 4: 'Work which cries to be done'

1   Rothenstein to Max Beerbohm, 29 March 1918, in Robert Speaight, *William
      Rothenstein: The Portrait of an Artist in His Time* (London 1962) 293; Rothenstein,
      Men and Memories, 1900-1922 (London 1932) II, 328
2   Public Archives of Ontario, Ontario Society of Artists, Beatty to Gagen, 8 July
      1918
3   Sheila Watson, 'Canada and Wyndham Lewis the Artist,' George Woodcock, ed.,
      Wyndham Lewis in Canada (Vancouver 1971) 62; PAC, J.E.H. MacDonald Papers,
      Jackson to MacDonald, 6 April [1918]; IWM, C.F.G. Masterman to John Buchan,
      18 May 1917, Nevinson to Thomas Derrick, 21 June 1917
4   Rothenstein to Alice Rothenstein, 22 March 1918, Speaight, *William Rothenstein*,
      295; IWM, Konody Papers, Kennington to Konody [Jan. 1919]; IWM, Sound
      Archives, tape interview with Carline
5   Jackson, 'Reminiscences of Army Life, 1914-1918,' *Canadian Art*, Ottawa, XI, 1
      (Autumn 1953) 9; Reginald Pound, *The Englishman: A Biography of Sir Alfred
      Munnings* (London 1962) 64 – see also General Jack Seely, *My Horse Warrior*
      (London 1934) 114-18; Nevinson, *Paint and Prejudice* (London 1937) 103
6   Konody Papers, Wyndham Lewis to Konody, 1 Jan. 1918; on Orpen, see Cecil
      Lewis, ed., *Self-Portrait* (London 1939) 278
7   Jackson, *Maritime Art*, Halifax, II, 3 (1942) 90
8   DND, OMFC, RG9, vol. 2105, Beaverbrook to R.F.M. Sims, 14 Aug. 1917
9   WP, Box 23, Brown to Walker, 15 Feb. 1919; Konody Papers, Beaverbrook to
      Moira, 3 Nov., Konody to Nevinson, 5 Sept. 1917; Roberts, *Memories of the
      War to End War, 1914-1918* (London 1974) 24; on Mann, BKP, Sam Hughes to
      Beaverbrook, 6 June 1918; anon., *David Bomberg*, Hull Ferens Art Gallery (Hull
      1967) 25; Wyndham Lewis to Herbert Read, 17 Dec. 1918, no 97, in W.K.
      Rose, ed., *The Letters of Wyndham Lewis* (London 1963) 101; Konody Papers,
      Roberts to Konody, 1 Jan. [1918]
10   NGC, Lismer to Brown, 25 Aug. 1918, Johnston to Brown, 22 Aug. 1918,
      Robinson to Brown, 3 April 1919; Sheridan, *To the Four Winds* (London 1957)
      80; Airy to Robert Ross, 8 June 1918, Margery Ross, ed., *Robert Ross, Friend
      of Friends* (London 1952) 329
11   Knight, *Oil Paint and Grease Paint* (London 1936) 213; Carlyle to Russell Carlyle,
      3 April 1918, Woodstock Public Library and Art Gallery, Woodstock, Ontario;
      WP, Box 23, Johnston to Walker, 15 Oct. 1918; NGC, Lismer to Brown, 12
      Oct. 1918

12   Munnings, *An Artist's Life* (London 1950) 305; Jackson, 'Reminiscences,' 9

13   IWM, McEvoy Papers, McEvoy to Commander Walcott, nd [Aug. 1918];
      Archives, Royal Academy of Art, George Clausen papers, Orpen to Clausen,
      4 May 1917; Konody Papers, Kennington to Konody, nd [Jan. 1919]; John,
      Chiaroscuro (London 1952) 127; Konody Papers, Rothenstein to Konody, nd
      [1918]

14   BKP, Robert Ross to Arnold Bennett, nd [1918]

15   Siegfried Sassoon, *Memoirs of an Infantry Officer* (London 1978, first published
      1930) 150

16   McMichael Canadian Collection, Varley to Lismer, 2 May 1919; Holliday,
      'Posing the War for the Painter,' *Bookman*, New York, XLVII (July 1918) 512 –
      see also Albert Eugene Gallatin, *Art and the Great War* (New York 1919) 22

17   Nash to Margaret Nash, 6 April 1917, in Nash, *Outline: An Autobiography and
      Other Writings* (London 1949) 195-6; Wyndham Lewis, 'The Men Who Will Paint
      Hell,' *Daily Express*, London, 10 Feb. 1919

18   Keene, *'Crumps': The Plain Story of a Canadian Who Went* (Boston 1917) 140;
      Harold Mears, 'Nature Study at the Front,' *Windsor Magazine*, London, XLV, 268
      (April 1917) 659; Nash to Margaret Nash, 7 March 1917, *Outline*, 187; Leed,
      No Man's Land (New York 1979). On p 14, Leed sees the combatant or group as
      undergoing 'rites of separation, which remove an individual or group of
      individuals from his or their accustomed place; liminal rites, which symbolically
      fix the character of the "passenger" as one who is between states, places or
      conditions.'

19   Jackson, 'Reminiscences,' 9

20   Compare Barraud's *The Horse Lines* with his *Evening on the Ypres, Poperinghe
      Road Near the Asylum.*

21   Rothenstein to Rabindramath Tagore, 10 June 1919, Mary M. Lago, ed.,
      Imperfect Encounter (Cambridge, Mass. 1972) 255; Jackson, 'The War Memorials:
      A Challenge,' *Lamps*, Toronto (Dec. 1919) 72; Moore, *Modern Painting* (London
      1898) 119; on Dobson, Stanley Casson, ed., *Artists at Work* (London 1933) 46;
      McMichael Canadian Collection, Varley to Arthur Lismer, 2 May 1919;
      Bennett, *Over There* (London 1915) 41

22   Herbert Read, ed., *Speculations: Essays on Humanism and the Philosophy of Art*
      (London 1924) 97

23   Laurence Binyon, 'Three Artists,' *New Statesman*, London (30 June 1917) 304

24   Nash to Gordon Bottomley, 16 July 1918, no 117, Claude Colleen Abbott and
      Anthony Bertram, eds., *Poet and Painter* (Oxford 1955) 99; Nash to Margaret
      Nash, 16 Nov. 1917, *Outline*, 211

25   Wyndham Lewis, *Rude Assignment* (London 1950) 128

26   Richard Cork, *Vorticism and Abstract Art in the First Machine Age: Synthesis and
      Decline* (Berkeley, 1976) II, 483

27   Gombrich, *Art and Illusion* (London 1962) 75; Taylor, 'War and Art,' *Colour
      Magazine*, London, I, 2 (Sept. 1914) 46; McMichael Canadian Collection, Varley
      to Lismer, 2 May 1919

28   Varley to Maude Varley, 27 Dec. 1918, cited in Ann Davis, 'An Apprehended Vision: The Group of Seven', unpublished Ph.D. thesis, York University, 1973. The sketch for *The Sunken Road* is in the permanent collection of the Art Gallery of Ontario.

29   Barker Fairley, 'F.H. Varley,' Robert L. McDougall, ed., *Our Living Tradition* (Toronto 1959) 162

30   Whitney Warren, 'The Destruction of the Monuments of France,' *The Architectural Review*, London, IV (April 1916) 54. It should be pointed out that the Germans made similar accusations against the Allies; see, for example, Joseph Sauer's *The Destruction of Churches and Art Monuments on the Western Front* (Freiburg 1917)

31   Clayton Hamilton, 'The Assassins of Art,' *Munsey's Magazine*, New York, LXV, 3 (Dec. 1918) 407; Library, Victoria and Albert Museum, Burlington Fine Arts, Minute Book, vol. 5, 1914-1930, 19 Oct. 1915; and anon., *Oh, Canada* (London 1916)

32   J. Lewis May, *Pictures of Ruined Belgium* (London 1917) 17; Fussell, *The Great War and Modern Memory* (London and New York 1975) 132; DND, RG 24, vol. 1749, 'Notes on Kerr-Lawson's *The Dead City*,' typescript; *Report of the Committee on Alleged German Outrages* (London 1915) 43

33   Warren, 'The Destruction of the Monuments,' 55; Ontario Society of Artists, Beatty to Gagen, 8 July 1918

34   Michael Holroyd, *Augustus John: A Biography* (London 1976) 554

35   Léon Maccas, *German Barbarism: A Neutral's Indictment* (London 1916) 179; Bennett, *Over There*, 88

36   Alan Wilkinson, *The Church of England and the First World War* (London 1978) 325

37   *Ibid.*, 161; Christopher Varley, *F.H. Varley: A Centennial Exhibition*, Edmonton Art Gallery (Edmonton 1981) 38. On civilian graveyards, see Varley's *Some Day the People Will Return.*

38   See Chapter 5, pp 81-7. The metaphorical crucifix was a common image in First World War paintings, sketches, and cartoons; see, for example, the etching *The Crucifixion of Belgium*, depicting a *putti* nailed to a cross. Edmund J. Sullivan, *The Kaiser's Garland* (London 1915)

39   Interview with the artist's youngest son, James Byam Shaw, London, March 1981

40   J.E. Crawford, *The Great War Fourth Year: C.R.W. Nevinson* (London 1918) 15; IWM, Nevinson Papers, Nevinson to Major Lee, 25 Nov. 1917. Nevinson was particularly sensitive as to how the British soldier should be depicted because his painting, *A Group of Soldiers*, met with the objection of the British censor Major Lee, who feared that if the atypical painting of British soldiers by Nevinson fell into enemy hands it might be used against the British. *Ibid.*, Lee to Masterman, 13 Dec. 1917

41   Arnold Bennett to J.W. Light, 17 June 1917, James Hepburn, ed., *Letters of Arnold Bennett, 1916-1931* (London 1970) III, 35; Robert Graves, *Goodbye to All That* (London 1977; first published 1929) 151; David Lloyd George, *War Memoirs* (London 1936) VI, 3367; George F.G. Stanley, *Canada's Soldiers* (Toronto 1960) 321

42   Dyson, *Australia at War* (London 1918) np; Konody, *Modern War: Paintings by
C.R.W. Nevinson* (London 1917) 13; Fussell, *Great War and Modern Memory*, 82;
McMichael Canadian Collection, Varley to Lismer, 2 May 1918; PAC,
MacDonald Papers, Jackson to MacDonald, 31 May [1916]

43   Will Foster, 'A Day with a Sketch-Book on the Front,' *Scribner's Magazine*, New
York, LXV (April 1919) 450

44   IWM, Kennington Papers, Kennington to Masterman, nd, to Alfred Yockney,
6 June 1918; CWM, Clipping File, *Christian Science Monitor*, Boston, 15 Nov.
1920; William Rothenstein, 'Eric Kennington,' *Apollo*, London, III (June 1926)
318. *The Conquerors* was reputedly first named, by Kennington, *The Victims*,
and was changed to *The Victors* and subsequently to *The Conquerors* on the request
of Colonel Peck of the 16th Battalion. Kennington exhibited the painting at the
Alpine Club in the autumn of 1920 as *The Victims*. According to the *Christian
Science Monitor, ibid.*, 'the title was changed by the Canadian Government ... this
is a pity for the picture is a statement by an artist ... and it is very easy to see
why he called it *The Victims.*'

45   Kennington Papers, Kennington to Masterman, nd; MacDonald Papers, Jackson
to MacDonald, 31 May [1916]; on Lewis, see Frank Rutter, *Some Contemporary
Paintings* (London 1922) 186

46   Cork, *Vorticism*, II, 549, I, 295; Gaudier-Brzeska, 'Vortex,' *Blast*, London, War
Number (July 1915) 34

47   Crawford Kilian, 'The Great War and the Canadian Novel, 1915-1926,'
unpublished MA thesis, Simon Fraser University, 1972, p 15. Cyril Barraud
filled over eight sketchbooks when accompanying his Winnipeg Regiment and
not one scene was devoted to the fighting (sketchbooks are in the possession
of John C. Crabb, Winnipeg); in Handley-Read's exhibition, *The British Firing
Line* (London 1917), the preface of the catalogue notes (p 2) that 'beyond the
glimpse that his loophole or periscope affords' he saw nothing of the fighting.
Jackson, 'Reminiscences,' 9; Kennington Papers, Kennington to Yockney, 6 June
1918; Rothenstein to Tagore, 10 June 1919, in Lago, *Imperfect Encounter*, 255;
'A Futurist's View on the War,' *Daily Express*, London, 25 Feb. 1915; 'The Lay
Figure: On Pictures Suggested by War,' *The Studio*, London, LXXI (June 1917) 40

48   Fussell, *Great War and Modern Memory*, 83

49   O. Elton, *C.E. Montague: A Memoir* (London 1929) 197. See F.H. Varley's
German Prisoners and Anna Airy's more subtle *Fruit, Flowers and Foliage* illustrated
in *The Studio*, LXIV (April 1915) 189-95

50   Cooper, 'War Themes in Modern Art,' *Windsor Magazine*, London, XLI
(Jan. 1915) 259

51   Murihead Bone, *Munitions Drawings* (London 1917), np

52   Fussell, *Great War and Modern Memory*, 299

53   NGC, Lismer to Brown, 25 March 1919

54   NGC, Jackson to Brown, 24 Feb. [1919]; Dorothy Hoover, *J.W. Beatty* (Toronto
1948) 30

55   Nevinson's *War Profiteers* was exhibited at Pictures of War, Leicester Galleries
(London), March 1918; see Grosz's work *Die Goldgräber* in *Das druckgraphische
Werk* (Munich 1979) 132

56   NGC, Brown, 'Painting the War at Home,' typescript, nd, p 2

Chapter 5: 'Not only history, but art'

1   KP, vol. 170, 'Canadian War Records Official Report,' 27 March 1918, p 6
2   Library, Royal Academy of Art, Minute Book, vol. 23, 19 Oct. 1917, p 485,
      1 Nov. 1917, p 487. It should be noted that Royal Academy approval was
      contingent upon Paul Konody 'not being prominently associated' with the
      exhibition (most likely because he had attacked the academy in the *Observer*); he
      did play a prominent role, though, as a concession to the academy, the CWMF
      committee omitted his name from the exhibition catalogue. *Ibid.*, vol. 24, 7 Jan.
      1919, p 51, 14 Jan. 1919, p 63
3   Frank Rutter, 'Australian War Artists,' *Sunday Times*, London, 1 Sept. 1918;
      'Art and Artists,' *Observer*, 15 Dec. 1918, 5 Jan. 1919
4   Konody, *Colour Magazine*, London, Special Canadian War Memorials Number,
      IX (Sept. 1918) 41; *Times*, London, 4 Jan. 1919
5   *Canadian Daily Record*, London, 8 Jan. 1919
6   *Daily Express*, London, 6 Jan. 1919
7   *Ibid.*, 4 Jan. 1919; *Colour Magazine*, IX (Sept. 1918) 28-9. The inspiration
      for John's cartoon sketch may have come from the *Panthéon de la Guerre*, a
      45 × 360-foot work incorporating every phrase of the war, painted by over fifty
      French artists. 'France's War Panorama to Be Brought to America,' *Current
      Opinion*, New York (Sept. 1922) 395-7
8   'Art and War Memorials,' *Canadian Bookman*, Toronto (Oct. 1919) 40; *Art and
      War* (London 1919)
9   DND, RG24, vol. 1749, 'Canadian War Records Office Official Report, 31 Aug.
      1919: app. 1, 'Canadian War Memorials Report of Executive Committee',
      p 7; *American Magazine of Art*, New York, x (Feb. 1919) 121
10   *Exhibition of Official Canadian War Photographs* (London 1919) 1, 2; Charles F.G.
      Masterman, *England after War* (London 1922) 9; Brittain, *Testament of Youth*
      (London 1933) 468
11   *The Canadian War Memorials Exhibition* (London 1919) – see, for example, the
      catalogue citation (p 7) accompanying David Bomberg's *Sappers at Work: A
      Canadian Tunnelling Company*; *Observer*, 12 Jan. 1919; 'About Wyndham Lewis,'
      Colour Magazine, x (March 1919) 26; *Observer*, 16 Feb. 1919
12   BP, MS 184, Diaries, 6 Jan. 1919; IWM, Bone Papers, Bone to Alfred Yockney,
      nd [Jan. 1919]; Archives, Tate Gallery, Nevinson Clipping File, 7311.3, *Star*,
      Toronto, 8 Jan. 1919
13   *Observer*, 19 Jan. 1919; on Varley, 'By "T" in the London Nation,' cited in
      Lamps, Toronto (Dec. 1919) 81; A.Y. Jackson, 'The War Memorials: A
      Challenge,' *ibid.*, 78
14   Marwick, 'British Life and Leisure and the First World War,' *History Today*,
      London, xv (June 1965) 416; *Daily Express*, 4 Jan. 1919; IWM, Canadian War
      Memorials Papers, *Daily Mail*, London, nd [Jan. 1919]

15   John Keegan and Joseph Darracott, *The Nature of War* (London 1981) 208; Alan
Wilkinson, *The Church of England and the First World War* (London 1978) 213

16   James Morgan Read, *Atrocity Propaganda* (New York 1941) 81. None of the
1200 people interviewed for the Bryce Report were put under oath and their
names were omitted from the report.

17   *Globe*, 12 May 1915

18   *Private Peat* (Indianapolis 1917) 154; *Literary Digest*, New York (13 Sept. 1918);
Brittain, *Testament of Youth*, 374; Wilkinson, *Church of England*, 213

19   PAC, Secretary of State, RG6, E, vol. 621, no 4, Chambers to District Intelligence
Officer, 8 Nov. 1917, Major F.E. Davis, assistant director of military intelligence, Ottawa, to Chambers, 21 March 1918 – see, for example, *ibid.*,
'Testimony from August Nelson,' claiming that he saw three Canadians being
crucified, nd; C. Hanbury-Williams of the censor's office stated that 'the
"reported" crucifixion of a Canadian sergeant was no "report", but a "fact" ' and
cited a letter from Kipling dated 28 June 1915 – *ibid.*, Hanbury-Williams to
Chambers, 25 March 1918; *ibid.*, Chambers to General George Cockerell,
director of special intelligence, War Office, 24 March 1918; DND, RG 24, vol.
817, *Gazette*, Montreal, 22 Oct. 1918

20   DND, *ibid.*, Colonel, Director Historical Section to H.V. Casey, 14 May 1923;
KP, vol. 133, Assistant Officer in Charge to Currie, 22 Oct. 1918 – there is
no evidence to indicate that Currie replied.

21   DND, *ibid.*, Wireless Press Ltd., Serial no 8194 to Kemp, 10 Feb. 1919

22   KP, vol. 133, Kemp to Currie, 17 Feb. Mewburn to Kemp, 30 March 1919;
DND, *ibid.*, Kemp to Mewburn [cablegram], 4 March, Kemp to Borden,
24 March 1919; PAC, Meighen Papers, no 3942, Kemp to Meighen, 19 Feb.
1919; BP, #55894, Currie to Borden, 15 March 1919

23   *Can. H. of C. Debates*, 27 May 1919, p 18; KP, vol. 167, sworn statements 'In
the Matter of Canada's "Golgotha" by Metcalfe and Vivan, both dated 1 April 1919

24   DND, RG 24, vol. 817, Milner to Governor General the Duke of Devonshire,
28 March 1919, no 4606/GG enclosing the Swiss Minister to Right Honourable
the Earl Curzon of Kedleston, 13 March 1919; *ibid.*, 111a/3114/17234,
translation of the *note verbale* of the German Foreign Office, 28 Feb. 1919

25   KP, vol. 167, Major E. Bristol, private secretary to Kemp, to the Under Secretary
of State, Colonial Office, 1 April 1919

26   Public Records Office, London, Foreign Office, News General 1919,
no 001483/N/50, Curzon to Carlin, 16 April 1919

27   *Gazette*, 7 May 1919; *Can. H. of C. Debates*, 27 May 1919, p 18

28   KP, vol. 167, no 111a/7376/46318, Auswärtiges Amt to Die Schweizerische
Gesandtschaft, 28 May 1919; *ibid.*, no 111a/12072/64295, *Verbalnote*,
Vertretung Deutscher Interessen to Die Schweizerische Gesandtschaft, 24 July
1919; *ibid.*, Kemp to Borden, 21 Aug. 1919. The testimonies can be found in
DND, RG 24, vol. 817, and KP, vols. 167 and 133.

29   Public Records Office, Foreign Office, News General 1919, no 004006/N/50,
Foreign Office to the Under Secretary of State, Colonial office, 19 Nov. 1919

30   DND, RG 24, vol. 817, Acting Deputy Minister, Militia and Defence, to the
Under Secretary of State, External Affairs, 9 Nov. 1919

31   *Ibid.*, Carvell to Chief of the General Staff, 20 Aug. 1919. In one incident of
animosity between Belgian farmers and the Allied forces, cited by the CEF's official
war historian G.W.L. Nicholson, it was claimed that around 25 April a Belgian
farmer had a 'tendency to drive his cattle in circles in front of the gun sites and
those of a neighbouring battery of French 75's.' The farmer, Nicholson said, was
arrested. *The Gunners of Canada* (Toronto 1967) I, 229

32   DND, *ibid.*, Berlin *note verbale* [translation], 26 Nov. 1919, Fiset to the Under
Secretary of State, Colonial Office, 4 Feb. 1920

33   KP, vol. 167, Secretary to Minister OMFC to Mewburn, 25 March 1920 (there is
no evidence such a statement was passed by Kemp to Milner); Werner Schaeffer,
Englische Lügen in Weltkrieg (Berlin 1941) 30 'Canadian War Memorial Show,
'*American Art News*, New York, XVII (14 June 1919) 1

34   BKP, Butler to Beaverbrook, 9 July [1918]; IWM, Konody Papers, Watkins to
Godenrath, 2 May 1919

35   NGC, Clipping File, 'Canadian War Memorials Exhibition, Anderson Galleries,'
no title, nd [June 1919]; *ibid.*, *Sun*, New York, 3 June 1919

36   *Ibid.*, *Sentinel Review*, Woodstock, 13 June 1919; Robert Craig Brown and
Ramsay Cook, *Canada, 1896–1921: A Nation Transformed* (Toronto 1974)
279-80

37   NGC, Brown to G.R. Grieg, 16 June 1919, *Sentinel Review*, 13 June 1919

38   *Sun*, 3 June 1919; The *British Government Exhibition of War Paintings and Drawings*,
the *Allied War Salon*, as well as exhibitions of French and British war lithographs,
preceded the Canadian exhibition. NGC, Clipping File, *New York Herald*, 18 June
1919, *Times*, Toronto, reprinted from New York correspondent 26 July 1919

39   *Mail and Empire*, 19 June 1919 (the comparison was unfair because, of the 247
works shown, 103 were by William Orpen); WP, Box 24, Brown to Walker,
21 July 1919

40   WP, Box 34, Walker to Mewburn, 8 Oct. 1919; NGC, Clipping File, *Countryman*,
London, 2 Aug. 1919

41   *Ibid.*, NGC, *Gazette*, 16 July, *Globe*, 1, 5, 12, 8 Sept. 1919; Fairley, 'Canada's
War Pictures,' *Canadian Magazine*, Toronto, LIV (Nov. 1919) 5

42   NGC, Jackson to Brown, 1 Sept., Clipping File, 23 Sept. 1919, *Toronto World*,
nd [Sept. 1919]; Fairley, *ibid.*, 11

43   NGC, Jackson to Brown, 1 Sept. [1919]; Archives, Tate Gallery, Nevinson
Clipping File, no 7311.3, no title, 25 Aug. 1919

44   WP, Box 24, Parkinson to Walker, 26 Nov. 1919; Library, Montreal Museum
of Fine Arts, Clipping Book, p 273, *Gazette*, 7 Nov. 1919; NGC, Clipping File,
Montreal Herald, 8 Nov., *Montreal Star*, 7 Nov. 1919

45   WP, *ibid.*, 26 Nov. 1919: see complementary articles in *Le Devoir*,
Montreal, 28 Nov. and 30 Oct. 1919

46   NGC, Clipping File, *Mail and Empire*, Toronto, 20 Oct. 1919; *Canadian Courier*,
Toronto, XXV (8 Nov. 1919) 12

47   NGC, Jackson to Brown, 30 Oct. [1919]; CWM, Wodehouse File, Brown,
'Canada's Own War Memorials' Exhibition in Toronto,' 28 Oct. 1919

Chapter 6: Lest we forget

1   WP, Journals, vol. II, 12 Aug. 1919, p 476; NGC, Walker to Beaverbrook, 4 Oct.
     1919; DND, RG 24, vol. 1749, 'Canadian War Records Office Official Report,'
     31 Aug. 1919: app. 1, 'Canadian War Memorials Report of the Executive
     Committee,' p 7

2   WP, Box 24, Beaverbrook to Walker, 30 Oct. 1919; DND, *ibid.*

3   NGC, Parkinson to Brown, 26 Dec. 1919 (the CWMF evidently got more than its
     25 per cent share of film profits, receiving £3,500); NGC, Varley to Brown,
     2 March 1920; WP, Box 35 1, Walker to Parkinson, 15 April 1920 – According
     to Christopher Varley, F.H. Varley's *Night before a Barrage* was to accompany
     Augustus John's *The Canadians Opposite Lens*; a rival of John's, Varley saw the
     commission as a 'chance to blow one of his mentors out of the water' – *F.H.
     Varley* (Edmonton 1981) 52; Konody, 'The Canadian War Memorials,' *Colour
     Magazine*, London, IX, 2 (Sept. 1918) 28 (the John cartoon was purchased in
     1951 by Vincent Massey, and presented to the National Gallery of Canada)

4   NGC, Walker to Watkins, 29 May 1920, Johnston to Brown, 21 Feb. 1919 (it
     is not known whether Brown paid Johnston the amount requested)

5   KP, vol. 133, Beaverbrook to Kemp, 30 April 1920; NGC, Parkinson to Walker,
     'Personal,' 15 March 1920; BKP, Beaverbrook to Rothermere, 8 March 1920
     ['cancelled' is inscribed across the letter]; while Beaverbrook and Rothermere did
     not, to my knowledge, dispose of any works, several shown in the CWMF London
     exhibition were not later acquired by the Fund: among them are Ethel Wright's
     The Late J.G. Pattison, V.C., Major F. Lessore's *Nursing the Wounded*, and John
     Lavery's *Embarkation of Canadian Troops for France*, retitled *Troops Embarking at
     Southampton for the Western Front* when acquired by the Imperial War Museum,
     London

6   NGC, CWMF Clipping File, *World*, Toronto, 14 Aug. 1920, *Star Weekly*, Toronto,
     28 Aug. 1920

7   *Ibid.*, *Star Weekly*, 28 Aug., *Saturday Night*, Toronto (18 Sept. 1920) 2

8   Robert Craig Brown and Ramsay Cook, *Canada, 1896–1921: A Nation
     Transformed* (Toronto 1974) 321; NGC, CWMF Clipping File, *Globe*, 2 Sept., *Mail
     and Empire,* 4 Sept. 1920

9   BKP, Moon, Gilks and Moon to Watkins, 23 June 1920; Library, Royal Academy
     of Art, Sir George Clausen, notebook, 27 Aug. 1920. Jackson's *Halifax Harbour*,
     commissioned by the CWMF in 1918, was exhibited by the Fund at the Art
     Gallery of Toronto in 1920; Jackson never received payment for the work and
     so when it became a 'nuisance in the studio' he 'shoved it in the furnace.' Jackson,
     A Painter's Country: The Autobiography of A.Y. Jackson (Toronto, Vancouver
     1958), 51

10   On West's painting, NGC, Brown to Walker, 14 Jan. 1920; PAC, Meighen Papers,
     no 30673, Meighen to Beaverbrook, 25 Nov. 1920

11   *Ibid.*, Perley to Meighen, 23 Dec. 1920; BKP, Beaverbrook to Rothermere,
     17 Dec., Rothermere to Beaverbrook, 21 and 23 Dec. 1920. The Canadian
     CWMF account was settled on 15 April 1921; the outstanding amount was
     $2,036.69. NGC, 'CWM Statement,' 15 April 1921

12   Meighen Papers, no 30688-9, Meighen to Beaverbrook, 19 Jan. 1921 (also see
      no 30693, draft by Perley, undated); BKP, Rothermere to Beaverbrook, 10 Feb.
      1921

13   BKP, *Canadian War Memorials*, nd [1921], anon., Rothermere to Beaverbrook,
      23 Dec. 1920

14   IWM, Konody Papers, no title [20 May 1922], inscribed 'Lord R's Draft'

15   *Can. H. of C. Debates*, vol. II, 16 April 1928, pp 2050, 2051. King's praise
      was, Beaverbrook told the prime minister, a 'source of great gratification to me
      more than repaying me for my labour.' PAC, King Papers, no 128165, 28 April
      1928. This copy of Rothermere's publication is in the Canadian War Museum.

16   Konody, 'On War Memorials,' *Art and War: Canadian War Memorials*
      (London 1919) 15-16

17   DND, as in note 1 above, p 6; CWM, Wodehouse Papers, R.F. Wodehouse,
      'Lord Beaverbrook's Plan for a Suitable Building to House the Canadian War
      Memorials,' later published in *Organization of Military Museums in Canada*,
      Ottawa, VII (1978-9) 1-8. The archives of the Royal Institute of British architects
      possesses a colour drawing of the building; Rickards may have been assisted by
      sculptor Derwent Wood. See Konody Papers, 'Suggestions for a War Memorial
      by F. Derwent Wood,' nd

18   Konody, 'On War Memorials,' 16; WP, Box 23, Beaverbrook to Walker, 9 Dec.
      1918. Rothermere agreed to make a donation, but neither he nor Beaverbrook
      donated any funds towards the construction of a building.

19   Walker's cable to Beaverbrook, 31 Jan. 1919, WP, Box 34, Walker to Wakin
      [*sic*], 19 Feb. 1919; Box 34 1, Walker to Mrs E.C. Walker, 12 Feb. 1919.
      Walker was appointed adviser of the Commission on War Records and Trophies
      along with Arthur Doughty and Brigadier-General E.A. Cruikshank in Dec.
      1918; as well as distributing war trophies and overseeing the erection of war
      monuments, the commission was empowered with providing a building to house
      the war records, photographs, and works of art.

20   NGC, Annual Report of the Board of Trustees, 1920-1 (Ottawa 1921); the
      trustees made similar requests every year until the mid-1930s.

21   NGC, Walker to Captain Balfour, secretary to the governor general, 7 Nov. 1922;
      Exhibition of Canadian War Memorials, National Gallery of Canada, 5 Jan. to 31
      March 1923, p 4

22   *The Canadian War Memorials*, Art Gallery of Toronto, Oct. 1926, p 4; NGC,
      Clipping File, *Telegram*, Toronto, 4 Oct. 1926

23   (Ottawa 1934)

24   NGC, Clipping File, *Saturday Night*, 9 Oct. 1926, *Ottawa Journal*, 14 Feb. 1929,
      Montreal Herald, 22 Dec. 1928

25   *Can. H. of C. Debates*, 16 April 1928, p 2050

26   NGC, Beaverbrook to Walker, 28 May 1923 [copy]; NGC, McCurry Papers,
      vol. 2, Brown to McCurry, 8 April 1924; A.J.P. Taylor, *Beaverbrook* (London
      1972) 211; WP, Box 24, Konody to Brown, 2 Sept. 1921. It should be
      pointed out that Konody was, in 1919, given a salary by the CWMF.

27   *Canadian Daily Record*, London, 8 Jan. 1919; *Generals Die in Bed* (London 1930);
      Konody, 'On War Memorials,' 15

28   NGC, Clipping File, *Globe*, Saint John, 9 Oct. 1919. Among the works chosen
for reproduction were Frederick Challener's *Canada's Grand Armada, 1914*, Edgar
Bundy's *Landing of the French Canadian Division at Saint-Nazaire, 1915*, Nevinson's
War in the Air, Alfred Bastien's *Over the Top*, Kenneth Forbes' *Canadian Artillery
in Action* and *The Defence of Sanctuary Wood*, James Kerr-Lawson's *The Cloth
Hall, Ypres* and Norman Wilkinson's *The Surrender*, Julius Olsson's *The Night
Patrol*, and Inglis Sheldon-Williams' *Canadians Arriving on the Rhine. Globe*,
Toronto, 19 Oct. 1926

29   NGC, Clipping File, *Globe*, Toronto, 9 Feb. 1924, *Albertan*, Calgary, 9 Oct. 1926

30   NGC, 'Resolution of the Board of Trustees of the National Gallery,' 20 Jan. 1926

31   NGC, H.W. Brown to Eric Brown, 13 May 1930. Harrison's *Generals Die in Bed*
recounts the incident on p 251.

32   Beaverbrook to John, 26 Aug. 1959, cited in Michael Holroyd, *Augustus John*
(London 1976) 556

33   Rebecca Sisler, *The Girls* (Toronto 1972) 29

34   Reginald Pound, *The Englishman* (London 1962) 65

35   See Roberts' painting *The Art Critic* in William Roberts' *Paintings, 1917-1958*
(London 1960); Konody, 'The Art of C.R.W. Nevinson,' *Art in Australia*, Sydney
(15 Feb. 1931) 18-23, with Dark, *Sir William Orpen* (London 1932)

36   J. Harold Watkins, *The Art of Gerald Moira* (London 1922); on Lima, BKP,
unidentifiable, 7 June 1918; NGC, Brown to Jackson, 7 Dec. 1920, Lismer to
Brown, 20 June 1924

37   Both published in London in 1920.

38   Michael Holroyd has written that John's portraits were merely 'exercises in the
higher journalism of art – pot-boiling commissions that gave little evidence of his
genius.' *Augustus John*, 561; Walter Michel and C.J. Fox, eds., *Wyndham Lewis
on Art: Collected Writings, 1913-1956* (New York 1969) 105

39   *Images of War* (London 1919); Archives, Tate Gallery, Spencer Papers, Notebook,
'Effect of War Treatment,' p 15; on Orpen, Nevinson to Ross, 11 June 1918,
in Margery Ross, ed., *Robert Ross, Friend of Friends* (London 1952) 331; *Unending
Cult* reproduced in *C.R.W. Nevinson: The Great War and After*, Maclean Gallery
(London 1980)

40   On Jackson, Ann Davis, 'An Apprehended Vision: The Philosophy of the Group
of Seven,' unpublished Ph.D. thesis, York University, 1973, p 347; NGC, Varley
to Brown, 21 March 1920

41   IWM, Nash Papers, Press Clippings, unidentified, 16 Feb. 1919; Robert Ross,
'William Orpen at the Front,' *Country Life*, London, XLIII (25 May 1918) 494;
Sims, *Picture Making, Technique and Inspiration* (London 1934) 119; Varley quoted
in Donald W. Buchanan, 'The Paintings and Drawings of F.H. Varley,' *Canadian
Art*, Ottawa, VII (Autumn 1949) 3

42   On Nevinson, John Cournos, 'The Death of Futurism,' *The Egoist*, London, IV
(Jan. 1917) 6; Sir William Orpen, ed., *The Outline of Art* (London 1924) II, 438;
John Rothenstein, *British Artists and the War* (London 1931) 20-1

43   Nevinson, 'Painting the War As a Soldier Sees It,' *New York Times* Magazine
(25 May 1919) 13; Richard Cork, *Vorticism and Abstract Art in the First Machine
Age* (Berkeley 1976) II, 519 (as Cork points out, in returning to Cézanne

Bomberg was not leaving abstractionism but returning to its origins); Percy Wyndham Lewis, *Rude Assignment* (London 1950) 129

44   NGC, Jackson, 'The Modern Canadian Artist's Point of View,' read before the Empire Club, 1925, p 1; Varley in Davis, 'An Apprehended Vision,' 249; McMichael Canadian Collection, Harris to J.E.H. MacDonald [Aug. 1918]; John A.B. McLeish, *September Gale* (Toronto 1955) 67–8

45   Jackson 'The Modern Canadian Artist's Point of View,' p 2; NGC, Lismer to Brown, 21 March 1920

46   'National Gallery Will Encourage Art,' *Globe*, Toronto, 28 May 1919

Epilogue

1   Kenneth Clark, *Another Part of the Wood* (London 1974) 77; Annual Report of the Board of Trustees of the National Gallery of Canada for the fiscal years 1939-40 and 1940-1; Joan Murray, *Canadian Artists of the Second World War*, Robert McLaughlin Gallery (Oshawa 1981)

2   Werner Schaeffer, *Englische Lügen in Weltkrieg* (Berlin 1941) 34–9

3   Clark, *Another Part of the Wood*, 77; *Check List of the War Collections* (Ottawa 1968). The National Gallery of Canada has retained works by David Milne, Paul Nash, Percy Wyndham Lewis, F.H. Varley, Charles Ginner, Edward Wadsworth, Robert Gagen, David Bomberg, William Roberts, Augustus John, and Harold Gilman.

Index